MW00396317

It's me, Billy

BearManor Media

2022

All rights reserved. No part of this publication may be reproduced, distributed, or transmitted in any form or by any means, including photocopying, recording or other electronic or mechanical methods, without prior written permission of the publisher, except in the case of brief quotations embodied in critical reviews and certain other non-commercial uses permitted by copyright law.

Any unauthorised duplication, copying, distribution, exhibition or any other use of any kind may result in civil liability and/or criminal prosecution.

COPYRIGHT © 2022 BY BEAR MANOR MEDIA

https://bearmanor-digital.myshopify.com

Notice of Copyright

This book is an independent editorial work and is not authorised by or affiliated with August Films, Film Funding Ltd. of Canada, the Canadian Film Development Corporation (CFDC), Famous Players, Film Funding Ltd. of Canada, Vision IV, Dimension Films, Miramax Films, Blumhouse Productions or any other entity related to the Black Christmas series. The photos contained within are copyright of their respective owners and appear here only to illustrate the points of the commentary and criticism within the text.

Edited By:

Léyla Richardson

Cover Art By:

Peter Harper @Forsaken_Art

Printed By:

Bear Manor Media

Printed in the United States of America

Available from https://usedtotech.com and other retail outlets

First Printing Edition, 2022

ISBN 978-1-62933-870-5

DEDICATION

This book is dedicated to the memory of Bob Clark, the visionary Director behind Black Christmas and his son, Ariel Hanrath-Clark.

(1939 – 2007)
(1984 – 2007)

It's me, Billy

BLACK CHRISTMAS REVISITED

Paul Downey

David Hastings

Table of Contents

A Note from the Authors

Paul Downey

THE wind was howling against my bedroom window, on the 24th December 1998 as I was channel hopping between our five terrestrial channels in search of something to watch. Christmas Eve always brings along festive favourites such as *Home Alone, Gremlins* and *National Lampoon's Christmas Vacation*, but on this night, I would be introduced to something completely different. It was around 9:30 pm and I switched over to Channel 4. It was at the point in a film where a group of teenage girls were receiving harassing phone calls. The noises that came down that phone didn't sound human, until the voice changed and said bluntly, "I'm going to kill you".

At that point, a chill ran down my spine. The delivery of this line with such chilling conviction was something I'd never heard before. Who was this person? Why did they want to kill that girl? I needed to watch the rest of the film to find out. We didn't have a TV guide (surprising, I know, around Christmas too), so I had to wait until the closing credits to find out the name of this chilling film; it was called *Black Christmas*.

Not since around the age of 7 years old had I been so affected by a film. This was the age when I accidentally saw a VHS recording of *Halloween*, and my obsession with horror began. For a couple of years afterwards, I always wondered about *Black Christmas*, as it felt like I'd never see it again. As if Channel 4 got their knuckles wrapped for putting on something so scary. Whilst in my third year of college three years later I was accumulating a decent amount of disposable income from a part-time job and started to build a collection of DVDs - mainly horror of course. I was also in the final year of A-Levels in Film and Media Studies, and thus was accumulating knowledge on film making and separating the great from the indifferent.

At the time, we had a store in my hometown called Music Mania, which did discount deals on DVD's, and it was here that I stumbled upon *Black Christmas* again. I couldn't believe my eyes and had to double-take before grabbing it off the shelf and rushing to the till to buy it before someone else did. I'm sure no one else in the store understood the joy I felt knowing I could finally watch this film that completely terrified me once again. It was this second watch and the many more after that really gave me the passion and appreciation for Bob Clark and this little Canadian horror film. Even more surprising was joining the dots to see that the same director also created *Porky's*, one of the classic raunchy comedies of the 1980s as well as Billy.

This book is a labour of love for both myself and co-author David Hastings, who also understands the importance of *Black Christmas* as one of the first slasher films, and one of the greatest horror films put to screen. We hope you find some stories you've never heard of before and gain a better understanding of a true horror classic.

Dave Hastings

I first encountered *Black Christmas* in the late nineties, first when Channel 4 screened it over the festive period and then again when it was subsequently released as a special edition DVD in 2003. Being a kid in the UK, and a horror fan at that had been tough since the 80s, with these sorts of films being hidden away on the shelves in video stores for our own wellbeing. Yet the controversial video nasties had long since cast a stigma over us fans and these films we so dearly loved.

At the end of the day, horror movies to me were escapism, just as much as Arnie was when bloodily blowing up the bad guys, so I was always frustrated by these double standards in regard to o-n screen violence. Instead, we horror fans and the films we wanted to see were seen as a difficult and freakish set of commodities. *Black Christmas*, with its extreme expletives and sinister vibe, was naturally one of these titles left in the shadows for years in the UK, with the odd few being lucky enough to track down a worn-out copy as part of a Sunday morning car boot sale.

Sadly, I wasn't one of those lucky ones. After years of searching for this fabled slasher film I'd heard so much about (primarily from John Carpenter and associations through my love of *Halloween*), I was over the moon when I finally got my chance to rewatch it. I remember sitting down in my bedroom, firing up the TV and getting ready to see again what I'd heard so much about, with my own eyes. And my goodness it was more than I could ever have imagined!

Right from the start, I was captivated once more, as we heard the joyful Christmas Carols in the distance, juxtaposed against the ominous eerie score and heavy breathing of someone who clearly doesn't fit into this facade of colourful lights, snow and genuine yuletide celebrations. The shocks and suspense just kept building too, with those horrendous and extreme phone calls, a tapestry of mythology building outside the main plot (the murder of the little girl in the park), all ratcheting up the tension towards a terrifying finale, with only the littlest of peeks at the antagonistic yet unseen - Billy, as his psychotic eye stared at us from behind a door, forever scorching itself into horror history!

Yet this was the film's beauty, and Bob Clarke's genius; an extraordinary cocktail of the most wonderful time of the year mixed with the most hideous of evil, amplified by an overall sense of deep, sinister foreboding. From the young ladies, who despite their flaws, still long for comfort and joy; to those infamous phone calls, which even today, are still as chilling as they would have been in 1974. And Billy, one of cinema's most infamous icons of horror, is equally on par with the likes of Michael Myers, Freddy, Pinhead and Jason.

Despite all of these wonderful attributes, the most disappointing aspect of *Black Christmas* is the lack of definitive material on the film, despite some well-intended and marvellous avenues, all with great merit. There has been a strong lack of attention and academic interest towards the film, as well as a lack of comprehensive insight into the making of the film; the stories from behind the scenes as well as understanding the lasting legacy the film has had on fans and other celebrated filmmakers, all of which have been afforded to other franchise counterparts. So, when Paul asked me to help him write this book, I jumped at the chance, because it deserves the attention just as much as Carpenter's *Halloween* has over the years, and all in one place for accessibility.

Clare in the attic window -

We have scoured and trawled as far and wide as we can to try and present as comprehensive a book as we can here. As definitive of a database, we can provide, based on our own resources as well as battling against the ravages of time. I hope you will enjoy what we have been able to put together here, as it was done with a great passion and love for the original material.

So, like me, late on every Christmas Eve as tradition dictates now, I hope you will sit back, pour a glass of blood-red coloured wine and indulge yourself, as we take a trip back to that infamous sorority house, its residents and an unseen killer within, all of whom made an indelible mark on the genre - one that only now in recent years, is being given the recognition it so dearly deserves.

The infamous wreath artwork for Black Christmas (1974)

Foreword

Dan Duffin - *Webmaster of Itsmebilly.com*

I was incredibly honoured when the Bloody Flicks team reached out to me around a year ago about the possibility of writing the foreword for this book. At that time, I wasn't sure what I would be able to say after so many years, but my friend and editor Paul Downey made a comment that left an impression on me - "You'll always be Mr. *Black Christmas* to us".

Wow, it has really been around 20 years since I first launched the *Itsmebilly. com* website. At that time, *Black Christmas* was a cult classic horror movie known by very few and even the most ardent of horror fans had somehow missed it. Over the next 10 years, the movie really gained recognition and I heard from many fans around the globe. The movie caught up a lot of ground on *Halloween* in those years. I managed to meet almost the entire cast and crew of both the 1974 and the 2006 movies. I spent part of my honeymoon in the 1974 *Black Christmas* House, and for a period of time, I looked after the 35mm prints in my office here in Toronto. I guess I was Mr *Black Christmas* after all.

The real Mr *Black Christmas* was of course Bob Clark. A creative genius and a true hero of mine. I introduced myself to him on many occasions, and he eventually knew me by name. It's so sad that we lost him the way we did, I cried when I heard the news. I think it's also important to remember Roy Moore here, the original writer under the title; *The Babysitter Murders*. I managed to get to know Roy's friends and family here in Canada. Lovely people who cherish his memory.

To me, *Black Christmas* exists on two levels. The 1974 dark movie that I adore and watch every Christmas, and the 2006 live-action version that I witnessed being created by Director Glen Morgan when I spent time on the set of the remake.

I'm proud to have taken some role in the resurrection of *Black Christmas*, and it's wonderful to see it being recognised in this fantastic book. The cast and crew of both the 1974 and 2006 movies have all been incredibly welcoming and open with their stories and experiences, and I think you will enjoy delving into this classic a little deeper in these pages. The past 2 decades with *Black Christmas* have been an interesting ride, and the movie seems to have a habit of pulling me back in from all angles even when I pay it no attention at all. I wonder why that is? And what will be next?

I long aspired to remake the movie myself, but I think with the 3rd remake, that time has now passed. I would never be happy with anything less than total control. But I will leave you with this. After calling my website *itsmebilly.com* for many years, and helping push the notion that the killer was in fact called Billy... I eventually developed a new theory on why he is not called Billy at all and exactly how I would reveal that... And like the 1974 classic, we will leave it at that...for now.

Toronto, Canada - 2020

Italian poster for Black Christmas (1974)

Chapter 1: Introduction

IT is hard to believe that at the time of writing this book, there has not already been a definitive account of *Black Christmas*. With the *Friday the 13th, Halloween* and *A Nightmare on Elm Street* franchises all taking the limelight, this classic has often been relegated to solely cult status. Back in 1974 long before Freddy, Michael Myers and Jason, there was another killer running amok and creating a bloody body count of teenagers; and no, we are not talking about Leatherface. The mysterious Billy is the essence of what makes *Black Christmas* such a special and terrifying experience; from his heavy breathing, harassing phone calls, to his brutal attacks, all whilst never seeing this perpetrator of the crimes.

This is one of the reasons the film remains such a bone-chilling experience today, as most horror villains are unmasked or revealed at some stage, but not with Billy. The most we get is a silhouette and one shot of an eye, clearly of a crazed individual in the final showdown with Olivia Hussey's Jess. Before his untimely demise Bob Clark did hint at a wider origin for Billy, which we will explore in these pages, but with the film comfortably part of horror history those answers will now never come. However, this book is intended to give you as comprehensive a history of *Black Christmas* as possible, with the exploration of themes running throughout the narrative such as urban legends, abortion and the idea of reading the film in a new academic way.

In 2006, *Black Christmas* was revived with Clark taking a backseat to a blood-soaked 80s-style slasher clone with an obsession for eye-gouging. Whilst this version was a critical and commercial failure, in 2019 it was revived again for a reboot (in name only), focusing on a group of sorority girls fighting back against their male oppressors. While these films will be covered (as well as much more), with interviews obtained for them, we have been primarily concerned with the 1974 original, obtaining a series of exclusive interviews with crew members involved, alongside some insights from Horror Historians such as Justin Kerswell (*The Teenage Slasher Movie Book*) as well as authors Adam Rockoff and Anthony Masi (former Editor of *Halloweenmovies.com*).

As previously alluded to, perhaps the most iconic visual from the film is Billy's eye staring at not only Jess but us; the captive audience, who have been along for the festive thrill ride so far. Additionally, the film itself has been seemingly developing a resurgence, with more modern horror fans rediscovering this classic of the genre, as well as embracing it so much so, that it has become part of their annual festive horrorthon, alongside the likes of *Gremlins*, numerous incarnations of the ghostly *Christmas Carol* and more recent festive classics such as *Krampus*.

However, while this is a welcoming addition by aficionados, *Black Christmas* never received a longer life through various sequels, which could have pitted Billy against more sorority houses on Christmas Eve, allowing him in the process to succumb to the laws of ever-diminishing returns (which is not a bad thing of course!). Hence, while not inspiring a part 2 or final chapter of his own, the image of Billy's eye has remained like our killer himself, an elusive cinematic experience.

Made on a modest budget of £620,000 (in today's world, $4.4 million), the film was released by Ambassador Film Distributors and made $2 million ($11.1 million in 2020 terms), on its initial Canadian release while overall, combined with international receipts, the film made a total of £4.4 million ($24.5 million, again in 2020 terms), despite some critics being scathing in their reviews such as A.H. Weiler in The New York Times, who observed a "murky script...dull direction [that was] hardly worth the efforts of all concerned", while finishing with "the question of why it was made".

However, others exclaimed the film *as* "a classy stylish horror picture" as well as praising the film for capturing a unique and "uninhibited campus milieu with accuracy and often raunchy hilarity" (Kevin Thomas, L.A.Times).

This insistence on vulgarity and taboo themes such as abortion seemingly prevented *Black Christmas* from interacting with more mainstream audiences, especially in a Conservative America under the leadership of Gerald Ford, where the moral compass swung in a completely different direction in terms of decent societal values. Though released, the film was

Silent Night Evil Night artwork

renamed initially *Silent Night, Evil Night*, as the studio were worried audiences would mistake Clark's film as part of the blaxploitation genre. Over in the UK, the BBFC made numerous major cuts to the film, removing the word 'cunt' as well as dumbing down the more sexual and obscure references made between characters, both protagonist and antagonist in nature.

Such treatment meant the film's overall power, themes and stylistic choices were either not promoted as much or watered down for years to come, hence impacting on its commercial viability. Despite these concessions, the film was a modest hit though and did reclaim its budget and beyond.

2 Girls Slain headline featured in St Petersburg Times

Moreover, the timing was not on the film's side either as its eventual scheduled Television premiere, unfortunately, coincided with the Chi Omega Sorority House double murder, wherein two students were violently murdered as well as others being brutally attacked by a killer who would become known to the world as Ted Bundy.

After being asked by the then Governor of Florida, Reuben Askew, NBC President Robert Mullholland pulled the film from their schedules in light of the recent troubling and traumatic events, further limiting the film's reach, but rightly so in the circumstances.

Despite the poor timings, as well as mixed reviews, *Black Christmas* is stylistically notable in the hands of Bob Clark, who utilised Steadicam technology to force us into the psychotic point of view of Billy, predating Carpenter's *Halloween* by four years, even going one step further by having the camera attached literally to Camera Operator Albert J. Dunk who scaled the building in order to simulate Billy's undetected entrance to the house's attic.

Such technological decisions as well as other techniques and pre-production choices had rarely been seen by the horror community, so it has been great to unearth some new fascinating insights into this realm of the *Black Christmas'* production. Such practical considerations as well as insistence on much more mature and taboo themes not often seen in generic slasher films has allowed the film to only now over the last two decades, the opportunity to truly find a more appreciative mainstream audience. Some, like ourselves, only discovered it by chance at the dawn of the DVD format (in the UK, the film was released under the now-defunct Tartan label), as well as it receiving its rare aforementioned terrestrial screening on Channel 4 in 1998, on Christmas Eve no less, at 12.10 am (ok, Christmas Day then technically!).

The channel was already well known for its controversial programming, commissioning such shows as *Queer as Folk* as well as screening *Eurotrash* in the 90s amongst other infamous shows, so the story of a sexually coarse worded psychopathic surrounded by themes of abortion, foul-mouthed sorority girls and anti-religious symbology accompanied by horrific and traumatic scenes of violence felt right at home on the channel.

Scream Factory's Blu Ray cover for *Black Christmas*

Over the last decade, the film has also been gathering even more renewed interest via multiple international releases via both DVD and Blu Ray. With the recent Shout Factory release presenting a brand new 2k scan of the original negative surrounded by a huge variety of special features, all of which had been reclaimed and packaged into this one attraction to provide the ultimate *Black Christmas* experience through home video.

Of course, this begs the question, if there are already so-called definitive editions and interviews out there, why read this book? Well, there is still a fascinating wealth of information out there on the film that has yet to be unearthed. We have gone to great lengths to secure new and revealing interviews with select cast and crew whose thoughts are still new to the public domain and have not yet been revealed in print.

Additionally, very little has been discussed about the film on an academic level, with just a host of reviews and summary revaluations being written for numerous websites, but which have not delved further into the narrative, themes as well as stylistic choices of the film as well as its cultural repercussions. After watching the film for the first-time decades ago, both of us have been frustrated by this lack of serious analysis on the film, while praising what little information and behind the scenes trivia was available by Dan Duffin.

We wanted to know more about this special film and what we have discovered over the years gone by, especially more so now the film is being rediscovered on new formats. We have been fortunate enough to interview both select cast and crew from the film, joining together both archive and brand-new commentary from the players involved, as well as those who have been inspired by its legacy and impact on cinema through their own mediums, such as remakes and even a recently released crowdfunded fan film sequel which is currently available on YouTube.

We hope you will join us on this very festive journey back to the infamous Canadian sorority house that started it all. Our many humble thanks to everyone who has helped us bring this book to life with their kindness and valuable insight, helping us uncover further secrets from the *Black Christmas* legacy. So, take the phone off the hook (you wouldn't want to be disturbed now, would you?), draw the curtains and switch on the Christmas tree lights. And don't worry about that piercing eye staring back at you from behind the nearest door, it's just Billy…

Chapter 2: *Black Christmas* (1974)

i) Origins of a *Black Christmas*

ON Wednesday, November 17th, 1943, a 14-year-old boy named George Webster employed his baseball bat to brutally bludgeon his mother to death, while subsequently then trying to kill other family members in the household. Such an event shocked the city of Westmount, which is situated not too far from Montreal. A location that up until then, was a place where neighbours were welcoming to one another.

However, this event cast a huge shadow on the city, and while newspapers such as the local Gazette ran with the story, giving it huge space in their publications, the actual details of what happened to George have been a lot harder to pinpoint.

Alongside this tragedy, the urban legends whispered as gospel around late-night campfires and slumber parties were becoming more and more popular, such as the babysitter being stalked by a killer, leaving the rural landscapes and becoming more ingrained back into cities and towns (ironically where they had come from in the first place). This led aspiring Screenwriters Roy Moore and Timothy Bond, two close friends, to plot a script that would essentially attempt to combine these two avenues into one chilling overall narrative.

Despite these urban legends typically being associated with fictional scary stories used to terrify our friends to drive fear of the boogeyman, lots were rooted in some tragic reality. The most infamous story believed to be the main source for the babysitter and the man upstairs legend comes from Columbia, Missouri and the still-unsolved murder of babysitter Janett Christman in March 1950.

According to reports, Janett had decided to babysit instead of going to a party with her friends, using her time to watch over a 3-year-old boy. However, a few hours later, the 13-year-old girl was found raped and strangled to death with what Police said was an iron cord. Horrifically, she had tried calling the police, screaming to them down the line to "come quick!", but Police were unable to trace the calls. While there isn't any evidence that the killer was calling Janett, the case today still remains unsolved, and the killer was never officially identified.

Originally titled as the rather chilling *Stop Me!*, further macabre inspiration for Moore and Bond had come after hearing of another story involving a serial killer who wrote a chilling message in lipstick on the wall of his second murder.

Stop Me! Roy Moore's original script

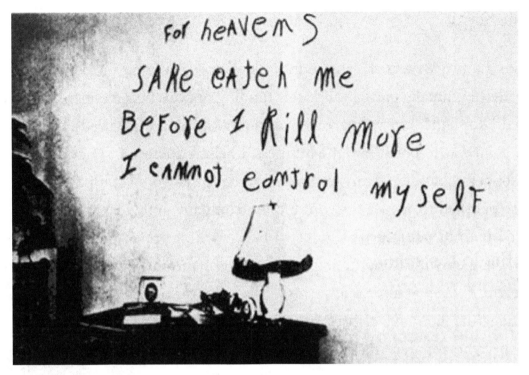

"For Heaven's sake, catch me before I kill more. I cannot control myself"

After this chilling communication, the offender became known as the Lipstick Killer and was ultimately apprehended and identified as William Heirens in June 1946, after a third murder in his spree months before in January where he had abducted six-year-old Suzanne Degnan and cut her to pieces.

While a dignified line was drawn between these and many more actual crimes, which had been spun and sensationalised into Urban Legends, the parallels are clearly there when you reflect on these reports and just how eerie the character of Billy is in the script. Like Webster, Billy brutally bludgeons those in the household. In the babysitter legend, the phone is used as an important plot device for both killer and sisters, either threateningly or trying to cry out for help, and like Heirens, Billy enters the homes undetected. There is definitely a great deal of these urban legends and more rooted in the genesis of *Black Christmas*.

Billy's silhouette seen behind the glass unicorn in Barb's room

ii) The Script

Despite the two writers sharing redraft duties to streamline the script more and more, they eventually parted ways after funding options became increasingly convoluted. "Roy and I were young, eager and ambitious, and we figured a horror movie was a good way to break into the business. I believe there was a news story at the time about a babysitter terrorising kids in his care, that got us started" recalls Bond.

The pair had formed a film production company and what would eventually become *Black Christmas*, was going to be their first project under their collaborative banner, with Bond taking up the directing duties, given his background in theatre. However, after many close calls with various investors, all of whom were dictating their own clauses into contracts that were nearly signed and closed off, it became apparent that too many financial burdens were in their way and would not be in place to fall back on, should the project fall behind or have issues arise. At the same time, and after meeting with a variety of investors and coming away with nothing, Moore and Bond decided to part ways too. "We were kind of at another's throats by now" comments Bond. However, the two decided that while Bond would keep the company, Moore would keep the script and credit.

Fangoria 'Im dreaming of *Black Christmas*' article

A while later, the script eventually made its way to Bob Clark, who began to also take some time to revise Moore and Bond's initial ideas. Speaking in Fangoria #159, Clark remembers how "the script was brought to me and with Roy Moore's blessing [however]; I made my own changes to it".

He also recalled how "if we had played it straight, without adding the lighter touches to give some humanity to the characters, it wouldn't have worked for me. It would have been too grim. Adding humour makes it more realistic".

Some examples of this humour Clark added was to characters such as Mrs Mac, who "was based on my dear Aunt Mabel. Except she used to hide wine bottles around the house, not whiskey", he mused. "The original script was more graphic, but Roy was very pleased to see it move towards the sort of subtle, more subliminal ideas suggested, more than graphic. That was probably the biggest shift".

Additionally, redrafting the script further allowed Clark to fully immerse himself into his role as director, in which Editor Stan Cole comments helped make post-production a lot easier in some ways; "Bob designed the movie with his shots, and I innately understood his intention laying out the drama and powerfulness of the scenes which I think I contributed too". While Clark was adding his own touches to the script, it allowed him a chance to almost visualise the entire film in his head, meaning that whenever he came to set, everyone would know he would be prepared well in advance.

INTERVIEW

Timothy Bond

Uncredited Co-Writer

Tell us about developing the idea for *Black Christmas*?

I wish I could remember back that far. Roy and I were young, eager and ambitious, and we figured writing a horror movie was a good way to break into the business. I believe there was a news story at the time about a babysitter terrorizing kids in his care, which got us started.

Why did you choose a sorority house and the setting of Christmas for the plot?

The sorority house setting was adopted after I left the project.

How did the writing process begin between yourself and Roy Moore? Did you co-write together or work on different drafts?

We co-wrote for several drafts and then took turns rewriting one another.

Can you tell us why you decided to have your writing credit removed from the film?

Roy and I had formed a film production company and this was to be our first project. We came very close to pulling the financing into place, the idea being that I would direct - (I was a theatre director at the time, with minor film credits). We got financing from a lab, an equipment house, the Canadian Film Development Corporation, and a Montreal based investment company that had some kind of tax advantage to attract investors to the film world. We actually got as far as the closing, lawyers and executives (and little us) around the table, tops off the Mont Blanc pens.

The head of the film development corporation announced he had only one small change to make – delete clause aaa in item xxx of some schedule at the end of the financing contract. The clause said the Canadian Government would guarantee completion of the film – i.e. if we went over budget the investors would not have to pony up more money. Take that clause out and they would be on the hook if Roy and I screwed up. I still have a mental image of the caps being screwed back onto the Mont Blanc pens around the table.

We kept fighting to save the funding, and the lab was very helpful (the government less so). We went to New York and almost closed a deal with an upstart distributor (a name I've forgotten, but it was run by Dennis Friedland and they had just made the movie Joe). When that fell apart, Roy and I decided to go our separate ways, but we had a company with some other properties and some short films. Roy found the deal with Bob Clark and we agreed to give me the company and Roy the script credit.

So there it was...

The original working title for the script was *Stop Me!* - what was the meaning behind this title?

There was a news story about a serial killer who wrote "Stop me before I kill more" in blood on a wall. This figured in our early drafts.

Were there any parts of your script that didn't make it into the film?

Probably, but I can't recall after 50 years in the business.

In your script how fleshed out was the character of Billy?

Very well fleshed out in the sense that we knew his entire back story. I am very keen on fully developing characters after my stage experience.

How close was the finished film to your script?

I can't recall, really. I suspect Bob Clark made a lot of contributions after I was out of the picture.

Were you pleased with the finished film?

Oh yes, and jealous of Bob Clark. But his contributions, especially setting it at Christmas, were stellar.

One of the alleged inspirations for the script was the murder of a babysitter (Janett Christman in 1950) who was receiving harassing phone calls, is this true?

Yes.

Who came up with the title *Black Christmas*?

Not sure. Not me. Roy or Bob Clark or the studio.

Can you tell us when you first saw the film and what your reaction was to it?

I loved it. Saw it in the theatres when it was first released.

When did you realise a film, you co-wrote had become such a cult classic?

A couple of years later. Fortunately, I had my name on another cult classic a few years later; Happy Birthday to Me.

Did you ever consider writing a *Black Christmas 2* script?

No, and I'm sure the rights would be entangled by Roy Moore's estate. But mainly, I think sequels of a great idea are always flatter than the original. Only Hollywood Studios (with insurance company creative mentalities) would ever make sequels or remakes.

Have you ever seen the 2006 remake?

No. Funnily enough I recently had a meeting with Copperheart here in Toronto and saw the poster on their wall. I had no idea there had been a remake. I hear someone is trying to remake it a third time.

Did you ever get a chance to speak to Director Bob Clark about the film?

No, sadly we never met. He was a very talented guy. His movie about the boy who wants a rifle for Christmas is a brilliant classic. Pity he never topped that one.

You directed episodes of *Goosebumps, Friday the 13th* and *Alfred Hitchcock Presents*, amongst other notable shows of the past 40 years, how did you find directing compared to writing?

It's almost 50/50 for me, but I prefer directing. I like working with all the other artists and channelling the experience toward a goal that only exists in my head. Also, you get to work outdoors a lot, which beats on office or a Starbucks.

I made the pilot for Goosebumps, which was a huge hit for Fox TV. I also made half a dozen more episodes. It was creatively a lot of fun. R.L. Stine was interesting. The only adult he ever spoke to on the set was me, I guess because he felt he should. He spent all his time with the child actors.

Friday the 13th was immense fun creatively. We were in the very early days of computer-generated imagery, so we were doing cutting edge work, at least for television. Every episode had to differ from the others before it. Each presented huge technical challenges. A lot of the visual tricks were done in the camera or at least started from shots made on the set.

Some of my favourites:

* The story of a guy who used a magic lantern showing a slide from the US Civil War as a window, to go back in time to rob dying soldiers of artefacts he sold as antiques in the present day. The fun for me was figuring out how he could step into the black and white photo projected on a wall and emerge as the only moving and colour element in the scene to follow.

* The story set in the world of dance, featuring an ancient music box (with a steel disk) that played music that made the dancers dance until they drop. I found a lens on the end of a long steel tube that had its own light source, made to insert into human bodies for a look-see. We were able to make some astonishing shots of the disk turning, sliding down under the disk as it played the music, to reveal gears and levers in extreme close up.

Alfred Hitchcock Presents was another kettle of fish. Here the stories rested solely on actors' performances. I have always loved working with actors since I began directing in live theatre.

You also wrote the screenplay for *Happy Birthday to Me*, tell us how you got involved in this film?

After Roy Moore, I found another writing partner, Peter Join. We had been friends since meeting at a university drama festival a few years before (he acting, me directing). We were approached by John Dunning, head of a Montreal company called Cineflix. He took us to dinner and asked us to write a movie for him. He told us the story he said was "in his head" which was the genesis of the eventual movie.

Peter and I created a screenplay from scratch but incorporating his idea of a campus killer. We did several drafts, never once realizing that there had been another writer before us who had actually created the story that was in John's head. It all came to a climax when the movie was finished, and the other writer precipitated a credit arbitration with the Writers' Guild.

We were very excited to learn that J. Lee Thompson (The Guns of Navarone) would be directing. We went to meet him in Montreal. A lovely guy. With John Dunning, the producer, we sat down to page through the script. Ten minutes in John said we should come up with something better than the accident that injured the girl, Virginia. By now J. Lee was looking dozy, maybe jet-lagged. But I piped up. This is one of the best scenes in the script! The girl and her mom are driving over a lift bridge without realizing it was opening. They end up teetering at the edge. When mom moves to open the car door for her daughter, she changes the balance of the car, which falls into the water, sinks to the bottom, and is run over by a boat, injuring Virginia's head. J. Lee suddenly sat up. "This is brilliant" (he obviously had not read the script). "I know a perfect tank in Hollywood where we can shoot this!!" John Dunning, dollar signs fading in his eyes, weakly protested. But the scene stayed in.

I have no idea how Lee shot it since we were not invited to the set. During the shoot, John Dunning kept agitating for a better ending (our ending was the birthday party and the reveal that Virginia is the killer). He had just seen Carrie and wanted something as good as the hand shooting up out of the grave at the final fade-out. We couldn't figure out how to top the birthday party, though God knows we tried.

We later heard that Lee came up with a "wonderful finale". We were not invited to see the film and had to buy tickets to see it. That ending....!!! What a piece of shit. The only comfort for Peter and I was that the audience, who had been loving the movie throughout, booed the ending. We joined in. Despite the lame finish, the movie did very well.

Of course, Columbia and Cineflix tried to screw us out of our profit participation. How did a movie that cost $4 million and grossed $100 million worldwide fail to make a profit?

Black Christmas is credited as one of, if not the first-ever slasher film, what films did you take inspiration from in the writing process?

None really. Although I sure loved Psycho which I saw in a drive-in theatre. A huge rainstorm broke out during the shower scene. Perfect. My mother was terrified and wanted to go home, but my brother and I insisted on staying to the end.

Was it always your intention to never reveal the identity and motive of Billy?

Yes. There's a full back story embedded in the character, his behaviour and responses. But never revealed.

iii) The Filmmaker

While *Black Christmas* remains arguably the finest work in Bob Clark's filmography, his career in the film industry was diverse, creating a handful of notable features that are still being watched today. Showing his early promise of being able to navigate horror with comedy, Clark's first feature was the 1972 zombie horror *Children Shouldn't Play with Dead Things*. With a budget of just $50,000, he would hire many of his college friends to shoot it across a mere 14 days.

Despite its budgetary limitations, some critics have praised the work of Clark and Screenwriter Alan Ormsby, with the Encyclopedia of Horror calling the work "surprisingly effective". Clark would collaborate with (also Make-Up Artist) Ormsby for *Dead Things* and would re-employ his services later that year for *Deathdream* also known as *Dead of Night*.

Before Clark's untimely death in 2007, there were rumours of a remake, with Gravesend Film Enterprises confirming their intentions to produce in 2010, but a proposed filming date of spring 2011 never materialised. Continuing to dabble into the horror genre, this would be Clark's take on the classic short story *The Monkey's Paw*. Filming in Brooksville, Florida, *Deathdream* stars Richard Backus, John Marley and Lynn Carlin.

Critics were split in the reviews for *Deathdream*, with Chuck Middlestat from the Albuquerque Journal calling the film a "light-weight spooker that starts off pretty slowly and builds into a good nail-biter in the last half hour". After creating arguably his masterpiece *Black Christmas*, Clark took a change of pace with the crime drama *Breaking Point*, starring Bo Svenson.

He would tread on a classic property in 1979, with the Sherlock Holmes tale *Murder by Decree*, with Holmes hunting Jack the Ripper. The late Christopher Plummer (*Knives Out*) would portray Holmes with James Mason (*Salem's Lot*) playing Watson. Clark continued to show his diversity with the 1980's *Tribute*, where a shallow Broadcast press officer learns he is dying as his son from his ex-wife arrives to visit. *Tribute* was also nominated for an Oscar and Golden Globe, with Jack Lemmon nominated for the Best Actor gong from both institutions.

In 1981, Clark would write and direct *Porky's*, which followed a group of horny teenage boys during the 1950s, as they tried to lose their virginities whilst seeking revenge on a sleazy nightclub owner. If you ask most film fans to name a Bob Clark film, after *Black Christmas*, *Porky's* will often be high up the list. It has become a teen comedy classic that set the template for a slew of imitators in the late 90s such as *American Pie*.

He would continue in the sex comedy sub-genre with *Porky's II: The Next Day*, which continues the capers of Pee Wee and co. This time around, Clark would team up with previous collaborator Alan Ormsby and Roger Swaybill, who had worked as an Advisor previously on *Porky's*. This sequel is largely considered inferior to the original, with Clark choosing to step away for 1985's *Porky's Revenge*, which would prove the final entry in the franchise.

Despite the critical failure of *Porky's II*, Clark would continue his relative hot streak with *A Christmas Story*. Again, Clark would direct a period piece, set in the 1940s, following young Ralphie who tries to convince everyone (including Santa) that a Red Ryder BB Gun is the perfect Christmas gift. The irony was not lost on critics that Clark could create one of the scariest Christmas horror films with *Black Christmas*, whilst nine years later creating a seasonal comedy classic that is as much part of his legacy and his sorority house slasher.

Leonard Maltin in his movie guide called *A Christmas Story* delightful plus "truly funny for kids and grown-ups alike". Despite being a sleeper hit on its release, the film has gone on to become a Christmas classic that is on constant rotation throughout December every year. The unique mix of Sylvester Stallone and Dolly Parton would headline his next feature *Rhinestone*, as a country singer teams up with a New York cabbie to win a bet. It would have the dubious honour of winning two Razzie awards for Worst Actor (Stallone) and Worst Original Song with Parton's *Drinkenstein*.

He would reteam with Kim Cattrall (who had previously starred in *Porky's*) for *Turk 182*, a drama where Jimmy Lynch (Timothy Hutton) seeks justice against the city when his older brother is injured during an off-duty fire rescue. Notably, the score for *Turk 182* was completed by Paul Zaza, a previous collaborator of

Carl Zittrer who did the score for *Black Christmas*. After dipping his toes into television with an episode of Steven Spielberg's *Amazing Stories*, he co-wrote and directed 1987's *From the Hip*, where a lawyer is set up with a case he can't win after forcing his law firm to make him a partner under shady circumstances. *Porky's* alumni Dan Monahan would return to Clark's cast list plus an ensemble that included Judd Nelson, Elizabeth Perkins and John Hurt.

Clark would dip his toes into the buddy cop sub-genre with 1990's *Loose Cannons*, starring Dan Akroyd and Gene Hackman. Another notable name in the cast list is *Saw's* Tobin Bell, who had played a minor role in *Turk 182* and portrayed the character of Gerber here.

He would briefly return to the horror genre as a producer for the underrated slasher *Popcorn* in 1991, where a masked killer stalks a group of college students trying to run a horror movie marathon in an abandoned theatre. This was a favour to the previous collaborator Alan Ormsby, who had written the film and was the initial Director before being fired and replaced by *Porky's* alumni Mark Herrier, in his first directing role.

It appeared as if Clark's golden run during the early 1980s was slowly fading away as he moved into directing television movies with *The American Clock* in 1993 and followed this up *with It Runs in the Family*, starring Charles Grodin (*Beethoven*) and Kieran Culkin (*Scott Pilgrim Vs. World*).

A triple whammy of television movies would follow, starting with *Derby*, a vanilla old-fashioned romance feature starring *Kolchak: The Night Stalker* himself, Darren McGavin. Next, was *Stolen Memories: Secrets from the Rose Garden*, starring Mary Tyler Moore and Linda Lavin. Rounding off this forgettable chapter was *The Ransom of Red Chief*, a western comedy starring very young Haley Joel Osment and Christopher Lloyd.

Clark would team up with Lloyd again in 1999 for *Baby Geniuses*, where a super-intelligent baby is being held captive by scientists before being switched with its twin and mild chaos ensues. *Catching a Falling Star* would see Clark return to the TV movie sphere soon after *Baby Geniuses*, for another romantic drama. Haley Joel Osment would return to Clark's stable in 2000 with *I'll Remem-*

ber April, where a young boy finds four Japanese sailors during World War II and struggles with the decision to save them.

The director would be back amongst awards for the right reasons two years later with *Now & Forever*, a romantic drama that won Best Feature Director and Critics Choice Award for Clark himself at the Atlantic City Film Festival.

Maniac Magee, based on the book by Jerry Spinelli, told the story of an orphan boy who searches for a home, with Jada Pinkett Smith as the narrator. A rarity in Clark's filmography would follow in 2004; a sequel - *Superbabies: Baby Geniuses 2*, starring Jon Voight and Scott Baio. Voight would re-team with Clark a year later for *The Karate Dog*, a children's comedy about a dog who can speak to humans plus is a black belt in-waiting in karate.

Clark's final film would be an uncredited directing stint for 2008's *Blonde and Blonder* (released the year after his death), where two blonde ladies are mistaken for international mob killers. Rumours circulated following the release of the

Black Christmas remake in 2006, that Clark was finally going to do a sequel to his original film. Whether this was true was never 100% confirmed, and sadly Bob Clark was taken from the world alongside his son Ariel in a head-on car crash in Los Angeles on 4th April 2007.

"There were two possible routes I could take and still get financing: pornography and horror, or suspense films. Naturally, I chose horror films".

Copyright © 1984 Twentieth Century-Fox Film Corp.
All rights reserved.
Permission is hereby granted to newspapers and other periodicals to reproduce this photograph for publicity or advertising except for the endorsement of products. This must not be sold, leased or given away.   Printed in U.S.A.

Twentieth Century-Fox Presents
RHINESTONE

R-17 "RHINESTONE" director **BOB CLARK**.

Bob Clark behind the camera

PAUL DOWNEY   DAVID HASTINGS

iv) Making the film

Once Clark had given his stamp on the script, it was time for him to begin search-ing for his cast members, the majority of which would fall prey to the psychotic Billy. Speaking in Fangoria 159, Clark himself shared how he approached casting the film; "Sheer believability is my first criterion in casting", he muses. "You're continually dealing with the importance of credibility in a horror film. Comedy, realistic character comedy, need very skilled people to not make it seem corny and burlesque…*Black Christmas* was the first film where I could cast on the basis of aesthetic need as opposed to who I could get for the money".

Certainly, Clark did just this, as he surrounded himself with an ensemble cast of the best in upcoming Canadian talent, as well as also casting further outward bound from the States and beyond. Most notably, Olivia Hussey (who was born in Argentina), still fresh off the hugely successful 1968 adaptation of *Romeo and Juliet*, while US Actors such as Keir Dullea were brought on board to help give the film a wider appeal. While Clark had a vision, he was not one to dismiss sugges-tions and improvise ideas on the set, something the actors all relished with glee it seems, as well as getting involved in set dressing in some cases.

Speaking in her autobiography, Hussey remembers how she became involved with the film and how it came around the right time of her life. "Filming in Canada would take me out of LA for eight weeks, and that I thought was just what I needed". As filming commenced, she recalled how inclusive the shoot was and how she "loved how Bob worked. Quietly and with great care, he went through each day's shooting. He involved us, the actors, in deci-sions about shots and scenes".

Margot Kidder fondly remembers the shoot as well, however, how she came to take

Olivia Hussey and Bob Clark on-set of
Black Christmas

on the character of Barb is something she's not concrete on; "I don't remember how I got the part in *Black Christmas*, but obviously I was summoned to Toronto to do it by an agent, that's all I remember". Despite this, her memories of the shoot are more forthcoming, and she always recalled it fondly, from forming a bond with fellow cast member Andrea Martin to the laughs and partying that went on behind the scenes.

Barb answers the phone to Billy

Speaking in 2006, Kidder noted how while everyone was having fun, the production was still a very professional one, and whilst she never got into Olivia's circle of friends, it wasn't a choice made with any malice. She accepted that people all work differently on a set; some prefer to be a little quieter, while others like herself, could be having a little more of a wild time, not that either avenue was any better than the other. Everyone on set respected each other's boundaries and styles, and it was only after the shoot would finish for the day, that the drinking and partying would commence, which Kidder admittedly found herself sometimes at the forefront of, although it never stopped her and others on the cast and crew from working to the best of their abilities and it never once hindered production.

"I remember being picked up every morning and Olivia would already be in the car and I usually was dishevelled and often slightly hungover whether it be pot or booze, didn't matter one or the other, and Olivia was very straight to me in those days. I thought she was very English and very lovely. She was just as exquisite in person as she was in the movies. But we had very little in common Olivia and I. And I was sort of mesmerised by her. And we'd drive to the set and then Andrea and I would hook up and crack jokes".

Hussey herself comments on the late Kidder always favourably, noting how she was intimidated by her style of working; "I admired – envied, really – her volubility and dedication to the cause. Margot and I got on well (if at a distance), as did everyone on the set", she recalls.

The aforementioned Andrea Martin helped make up more of the sorority sisters but was not originally going to be playing Phyl. Instead, Clark had already cast Gilda Radner, but a month before filming was to commence, she had to drop out of the movie when she was cast for a new TV Show that eventually became known as *Saturday Night Live*. When Radner departed, Clark then auditioned Martin, who immediately took on the role, and who he referred to as "dynamite" in her performance and acting throughout the film.

Jess and Phyl confront Lt. Fuller

Martin also struck up a strong friendship on set with Kidder, with whom she would goof around once the cameras had stopped; "we played off each other a lot and we were definitely the comic relief. I think it was a little competition who can make people laugh the most between Andrea and I, which I expect would be picked up again today if we have work again", enthused Kidder back in 2006.

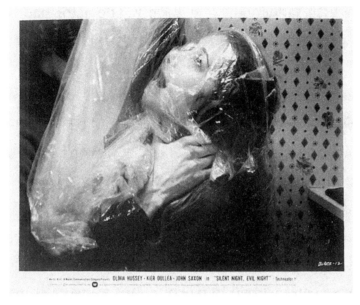

Clare is choked by Billy in her closet with the plastic bag

The celebrated first death role in the film fell to Lynne Griffin, who was making her feature film debut in *Black Christmas*, one that would see her live on in countless promotional materials for the next four decades (and surely more to come), as the ill-fated Clare. Her fixated, terrifying death stare wrapped in plastic became one of the most iconic images from the film, and one that Clark seemingly expected would happen. After discussing the role with Clark, Griffin remembers him saying that "she wasn't gonna last long alive in the film, but her demise would be memorable, and her image be everlasting". Becoming part of the *Black Christmas* family was a fairly mundane journey initially too. "It was a basic audition. With lots of other candidates", remembers Griffin, "however, I might have won the part because I told them what a good swimmer I was and that I could hold my breath for a long time. Which seemed to be a prerequisite for the job. I was also frequently cast as the perennial virgin". Despite knowing her role wouldn't be as substantial as the others, Griffin was thrilled to be working with an exciting cast as well as working with Bob himself.

Rounding out the remainder of the cast were stars such as Keir Dullea, Canadian born James Edmond, as well as cult Actor John Saxon - although the latter only became part of the film after a tragic set of circumstances forced Clark to remove Oscar-winning Actor Edmond O'Brien who was originally set to play Lt Fuller; an event which saddened Clark deeply. The actor had been very excited about being part of the film, but it soon became apparent that he was suffering from Alzheimer's, which was rapidly deteriorating his health. With the cold conditions and intensity of the shoot, it became apparent that Edmond wouldn't be able to work safely, and it was decided that he should be let go and replaced.

Speaking in Fangoria, Clark expressed how "it was one of the saddest moments of my life. I loved him and worked hard to get him for the movie. Edmond came up to do the role and we went to the hotel room to get him and we sat and watched this poor man ramble and try to put his coat on for 45 minutes. He kept telling us how he hadn't worked in a long while and how he was excited to be working again. I might have been inclined to use him, but we were going to be filming in 10 to 20 below-zero weather and shooting was less than a week away. I knew it wouldn't work. So, I finally called his agent and they suggested John (Saxon). It was very, very sad".

Despite the setback, and being called in at the last moment, John Saxon (who had also been approached along with Edmond for Fuller originally), approached the role with the greatest of professionalism still. Although it was a hurried start to his time on the film, mere hours in actual fact, proceedings saw Saxon brought up to Toronto on the same day. He was checked into his hotel and then immediately ferried over to a blisteringly cold park where he began shooting immediately.

Despite the rushed set of events, Saxon remembered it all with fond memories when interviewed a few years back for Bloody-Disgusting; "What happened was after I read the script and liked it very much, I was cast to play 'Fuller' [then] some short time afterwards, my agent Michael Livingston called to tell me that the production had made a mistake: someone else had previously cast another actor to play Fuller. I was disappointed, but oh well. Then unexpectedly, maybe a week later, my agent called again asking if I could get on a plane, I think the same day and fly to Toronto to play the role in 'Black Christmas'. I arrived in Toronto at about midnight, was taken to a Hotel and then was driven out to a suburban location to prepare to do the scene in the woods speaking over a Bullhorn, which was finished at about 3 AM".

The cast and crew all greeted Saxon warmly, and his depiction of Fuller has become another memorable part of the film over the decades, with Saxon bringing a cautious but warm persona to the role.

EMI FILM DISTRIBUTORS LIMITED PRESENTS
BLACK CHRISTMAS x
TECHNICOLOR® DISTRIBUTED BY EMI DISTRIBUTORS LIMITED
This copyright advertising material is licensed and not sold and is the property of National Screen Service Ltd. and upon completion of the exhibition for which it has been licensed it should be returned to National Screen Service Ltd. Printed in Great Britain.

Lt. Fuller addresses the search party in the park in a publicity still for *Black Christmas*

His favourite scene in the film is the infamous 'Fellatio' moment, which he attributes to Clark's sense of humour, as does Kidder herself. "I remember Bob was very specific about what we were doing. As long as we got his dialogue in, if you added something that worked and that added some kind of zip to the character, he was fine with it. Otherwise, he just pulled you right back. *Black Christmas* had the intelligence to have a twinkle about itself. To have a good sense of humour about itself, so it wasn't quite as earnest, and Bob was very clever and smart and a good businessman and great fun. He was absolutely lacking in pomposity of any kind".

The Park and subsequent search party scenes where a young girl is discovered mutilated was filmed at Grenadier Lake in Toronto. On the nights of shooting, temperatures were well below zero according to reports and equally had the most people in the scene alongside Saxon. Clark attributes the night shoot here, as well as the cast and extras to helping him create the reality of the situations happening. Although Clark won't call them extras, "I call them background actors. I think they're as important as every actor. A bad background actor can ruin a scene more quickly than a foreground actor [so] I spent a lot of time with my background people", in this scene and many more.

This shows beautifully within the film, as there is a definite sense of community coming together who rally almost around our core characters, yet seemingly viewed as just as important to these scenes working. Additionally, when the Christmas Carol singers are visiting the house and are hurried away by the parents at the news of the young girl's murder, Clark doesn't allow their inclusion to be minimised, instead of allowing them to inject more tension into the story when the concerned Mother alerts Jess to the horrific crime.

Another Actor who was an integral part of the ensemble was Keir Dullea, who had previously worked with the legendary Stanley Kubrick in *2001: A Space Odyssey*. However, unlike the rest of the cast, Dullea was only scheduled to be on set for a week as he had other commitments. This meant that while he seems to be in a lot of places in the film (with Clark deliciously setting him up to be the potential killer), and always seemed to shy away from interacting with other characters, in actuality, he rarely did in real life, and it is through the power of editing that he only seems too.

His main counterpart is Jess, with who he is in a relationship with and who argues with him over her planned abortion. Despite only being there for a short amount of time, Dullea remembers the film fondly, although not as much of the specifics of the shoot and has discussed it at numerous points when he has been interviewed. "I don't remember a heck of a lot. A lot was going on at the time and I remember that they scheduled out so all of my parts of the film could be shot in a week. This way they didn't need to pay me more than they had to. I never met Margot, I barely met John but with the magic of film it looks like I'm a much bigger part of the story".

Despite this Keir remains very proud of the film and the influence it has carried and built over the decades, citing it as one of the more pleasing performances he has portrayed over his long filmography; "There are only a few films in which I feel bad about my performance or personally hate. One is *De Sade* (a 1969 Roger Corman/Richard Matheson/AIP fiasco), which was so bad the critic for the New York Daily News sat behind me at the premiere and described me in her review sinking down in my seat out of view - and she was right!".

"The other one was a film called *Welcome to Blood City*, with Jack Palance and Samantha Egger, which hopefully will remain in the ash can of history. But I'm proud of my work in *Black Christmas*, " he recalls.

Lobby card image of Peter w/ Christmas tree behind him

Despite the dark nature and tone of the narrative, the injection of Clark's humour spilt out many times into the behind-the-scenes arena on multiple occasions. As Clark himself says, while "it was very, very cold during the shoot, and we were under limitations from the budget, it was a joyful production. The personalities involved in making it were all just precious".

This also extended out to the crew who would find the shoot both creative as well as full of enjoyment, whether they were interacting with the antics of the cast or finding other ways to amuse themselves. But for the majority of the time, humorous antics were led by Clark who always wanted to play pranks and has a laugh on set, despite his role as a focused director. He was merely able to multi-task, much to the enjoyment of the cast and crew.

Clare in rocking chair in the attic of sorority house

Griffin remembers Clark and Camera Operator Albert J. Dunk being mischievous when it was time for them to shoot her dead body in the attic. As she recalls; "I spent a lot of time up in the attic! Bob sat across from me in the rocking chair, and it was he who had his foot on the rocker, rocking me gently through the takes, instructing me to hold my breath, because we figured out that just poking holes for my nose and mouth in the plastic bag wouldn't make it still enough, and condensation would form on the bag".

Closeup of Clare's face in plastic bag in the attic

Bob found all of this immensely entertaining, and made jokes like "Okay, lunch everybody! Lynne, if you could just hold your position and we'll be back in an hour", and then finally saying "That's a wrap on Lynne Griffin!" We all called him 'Uncle Bob'. He was lovely". Hussey remembers the fun usually coming from Clark too when they were filming, recalling how he was "down to doing the voice of the killer and helping to dress the bodies", with a macabre glee alongside the rest of the crew.

Kidder remembers how much fun she was having with the crew when shooting her death scene as well, noting how she was amusingly "stabbed to death by a glass unicorn…in which I was wrapped and stuff and blood and all that! And we were laughing so hard when we were shooting it".

Despite the laughs behind the scenes and seemingly on, there were lots of practicalities to consider throughout the shoot, including the death scenes (even though they had been trimmed back substantially by Clark in his script revisions), as well as formulating a way to almost get into the killer's mind-set both visually and through interpretation. One of the most iconic visual aesthetics of the film is the POV shots which predated *Halloween* by four years, although the latter has been given more attention.

In *Black Christmas'* case, it was down to Camera Operator Albert J. Dunk who also in the process took on the role of Billy by proxy in some cases, something that happened from day one. Dunk remembers how he got involved with *Black Christmas* through the Director of Photography Reg Morris, a seasoned Canadian Cameraman. "Reggie had worked on *Moby Dick* as the Camera Operator and done lots of great British pictures before he emigrated to Canada to work for the National Film Board. Reggie was an excellent cameraman and did an excellent job on *Black Christmas* I thought", Dunk remembers warmly.

Billy climbs up the side of the sorority house

The idea to include POV shots came from Bob himself who had remembered seeing a movie from the 40s where it had been used. However, no one had really noticed the technique to his amazement, so he decided to incorporate the now legendary approaches within the film, to make a statement from the outset. "It was overtly imitated quite a few times" afterwards, states Clark. But for the time "stylistically it was sort of a new direction for thrillers to take. The killer POV shots were new for the time".

Dunk remembers how "the camera was a little under 100 pounds, so it was big. It was me that came up with the idea of strapping the camera to me for the POV shots. The shot going up the trellis outside the house - that was the last shot of the first day of filming. That set the pace for the whole film. I had it mounted on my shoulder and had a special camera rig and everything that allowed me to keep my hands free. So, when I was going up the trellis you never saw the shadow of the camera, you only saw the shadow of me". Clark himself alludes that this technique really helped him springboard the tone of the film onto audiences with the camera work establishing "the whole dynamic of the house, and how the killer has intruded and what the setups will be and that's good in a short amount of time".

With Dunk's technique proving to be a worthwhile approach to getting those POV shots, it was repeatedly employed throughout the remainder of the shoot in more of the film's most memorable sequences, including Clare's death within the first act, with Dunk gleefully explaining that "during the strangulations scene with Lynn, the camera was on my shoulder". With the trellis scene being "probably the easiest because it was mounted on my shoulder, the real trick was just deciding the shots, and Bob and I talked about that a lot. After the first day's rushes, when they saw that shot, that's what dictated how the movie would be shot going forward", he reveals.

Lynne remembers Dunk amusingly too, noting how he "was pretty ground-breaking in use of a body-cam. It was wonderfully intimidating". According to Clark on the DVD commentary, he didn't want to show the killer at all, and this was a way to make that apparent from the outset it appears. "I just wanted the presence of it. This is (an) intensity to me, to see his point of view [watching Clare pack]. The creature is in there!"

Billy watches Clare from her closet

Despite the rooms in the house all being large and comfortable to work within, the actual closet Billy/Dunk jumps out from strangling Clare wasn't so much; "the closet was a real closet but because of my camera rig, it didn't take up any room. The biggest thing was me and the assistant trying to squeeze into the closet. He needed room to pull focus and I needed room to get my hands out and grab Lynn!" recalls Dunk comically.

A lot of fans of the film point to Clark's use of visual clues and movement throughout which create all kinds of additional suspense. No one is more closely linked purposefully to these than Dullea's Peter as he is made out to be the main suspect despite physically not being able to be in practical terms.

A lobby card image for *Black Christmas* showing Jess and Peter arguing

However, the visuals were always designed in a way to align Peter up as the killer continually. Even down to the telephone call between him and Jess, Clark would make sure there were actions both Billy and Peter do, in order to raise suspicion from the audience more. Speaking on the DVD commentary, Clark notes how the camera stays on Jess throughout their entire conversation, stating how "I could have cut as you so often do to Keir Dullea at his location speaking [sic]. Wasn't necessary, but I wanted to purposefully do that to have his disembodied voice too. A very subtle idea but it might plant the idea that Keir is the killer here".

Continually Peter is framed as a silhouette in some scenes, whether outside the house in the chilly temperatures, or even inside when interacting with Jess, and when their discussions become heated.

One of the techniques Clark didn't like using was pulling focus in a static shot, therefore, in some scenes - especially with Peter and Jess, he would block them to go into a position that would bring them into focus themselves rather than using the camera to do so.

Peter watches the sorority house

As Jess sits in her chair contemplating what Peter is saying to her from behind, he naturally moves more towards her eventually and becomes more integral to the framing. As Clark described, "I don't like throwing focus, so I figured this is the more dynamic moment, it's what's happening to her - keeping him out of focus, [there's] a certain dimension to it and how we bring him in", which again allows Peter to have the same shape and outline we've seen from Billy so far, aligning the two characters together once more.

Despite relishing the opportunity to keep the camera on shots, not everyone was fully on-board with the decisions, warier of if they needed backup takes for coverage should they need it in the editing stage. Editor Stan Cole would continually discuss these creative decisions with Bob with a sense of anticipation as the latter comments; there are "so many moving shots that are locking us in and Stan was wondering 'Bob we can't cut'", to which Clark would answer that "we won't need too". Despite Cole's nervousness over these creative decisions, they eventually worked well when the film was screened to Bob and the producers as a first cut, with these long slow methodical takes intertwining nicely with other shocking moments of violence elsewhere in the film, such as Barbara's death cutting to the innocent children outside singing Christmas Carols.

Additionally, these long slow-moving takes would help Clark further place suspicion on Peter, discussing how he just knew a shot would hold, and which at the same time "would put the measure on Keir's involvement. Plenty of time for the killer here to do everything he's done, and Keir can come into the house and wait". He continues arguing how by being "committed to the scene, you can't cut it, but I knew it didn't need to be cut".

For Clark, keeping the camera moving allowed the film to have a naturalness to it, as well as helping to increase the suspense that would come from the silence around the house or the chilly winds from outside. "I would rather make an audience think they'd felt something, fear, whether they felt, whether they anticipate something's coming, rather than throw it at them".

A wide shot of the upper stairs of the sorority house

Certainly, Clark achieves this throughout where silence or the crackling of the fireplace within the house hides a multitude of evils. Shadows behind the characters give a sense that we may have caught a glimpse of someone upstairs as the camera gently floats around the home or down the stairs. "Moving the camera, moving the actors, changing the background rather than just cutting to this, cut to that. It's tough, I know why directors don't do it because it's time-consuming so I spend a few hours setting it up, but I get more pages done", he remembers on the DVD commentary.

Whether subjective POV's, continual takes or moving camera sweeps, all to help incriminate Peter more or enhance Billy's sphere of murderous influence, Clark always maintained these practical techniques to help elevate the film and its themes; from the girls listening intensely to "that killer over the phone, the insane movements of this man just intruding into this house when no-one was aware of him - you see it happen! The camera dictates that it could happen. All of his movements I think are quite plausible" because everything was planned out meticulously beforehand.

Peter leans over the stairs

The production design of the house also allowed a visual insight into all the characters, so that through the lens, we could grasp an overview of each of the girls, all of whom have varying different backgrounds, whether good or bad. Production Designer Karen Bromley worked closely with Bob in the pre-production stage to help convey the lives of each sister through how they would have decorated their rooms. It allowed for a "statement of their lives", asserts Bob who praised the work of Bromley.

Bromley remembers the first time she read the script very fondly; "I found the *Black Christmas* script enthralling. It immerses you in this house and the lives of these young women unaware of their horrible fates unfolding, and as you read, images were happening in your mind with every scene". Bromley immediately began having meetings with Clark to discuss the look, style and feel that he wanted to bring to the film, with Bromley herself citing that relationship as a very robust one. "When the director has a strong vision of his movie, as Bob Clark did, and is a generous collaborator, it is so exciting as ideas start to fly and, at that stage, anything is possible".

"One of the elements we used was the emotional message of colour, as in the Blood Red in *Black Christmas*. Even 'pretty' Christmas lights were red, hung on the front door to portend every entry, however benign it may turn out to be, or not, or seen from outside - 'herein lies something intense'".

Billy approaches the front door of the sorority house

"It was the seventies and colours were changing from the 'happy hues' of the hippies, becoming more intense and were very evident in personal style. Each girl's bedroom was designed using colours reflective of their personality and in some cases to reflect the way they died. The coldness of purples is chosen to set off the sparkling crystals of the fateful unicorn. We had only one of those unicorns so a lot of concern lest it got broken. I do wonder where it is now, but I believe Bob had it. It's unusual but we used boldly patterned bed linens for each girl, no sense of peaceful rest for the close-ups on pillows".

Despite the main location of the house being part of horror legend as a pilgrimage for horror fans worldwide, Bromley notes that the finale in the cellar was not filmed at the infamous location at all. "We filmed the basement scene in another house", she remembers. "It was a fairly large space which we filled with basement stuff to create a sense of being trapped in dead ends. We used odd jangled threatening shapes".

But she assures fans that the attic that Billy hides in throughout the film was very much a part of the main location, adding how "we put a rocking horse in the attic, that romantic image of a happy childhood in the lair of a severely damaged person". Despite her love for the film and being part of its creation, she remembers the cold and the fake snow not as warmly; "One of my strongest memories of filming is having to 'make snow', and then in the scene where the search party is sent out, it was one of the coldest nights of my life on that brutal windy hill above Lake Ontario!"

With cameras rolling on *Black Christmas* from 25th March 1974, most of the filming locations were all situated in Toronto, Canada. The main location is the aforementioned house; a private residence on Clarendon Crescent, which would be used for the majority of shots of the sorority house. North of downtown Toronto, it is also not far from Casa Loma where films such as *X-Men* (2000) and *Scott Pilgrim vs. the World* (2010), were filmed.

The house itself still stands today and is still privately owned, but unfortunately for fans, it hasn't become a horror filming tour holy grail like the Myers House from John Carpenter's *Halloween*. *Black Christmas* superfan Dan Duffin did manage to revisit the location in 2002 for a featurette which would be part of the Tartan Video release of the film a year later and feature original Actors Art Hindle and Lynne Griffin.

Wide image - The filming location for the sorority house today in
Toronto, Canada (credit to Dan Duffin)

Closeup image of attic window of sorority house today in Toronto,
Canada (credit to Dan Duffin)

For additional photography of the interior of the sorority house, Clark used
Annesley Hall, part of the University of Toronto. In 1988 the building underwent
an extreme renovating and restoration project, making it unrecognisable from
when filming took place 14 years prior. Annesley Hall was apparently also used
as a backdrop for scenes at night, including Lieutenant Ken Fuller and his deputy rushing into the car to get to the sorority house near the film's conclusion.

Today this is (appropriately perhaps) an all-female residence for Victoria College, another strand of the aforementioned university.

The University of Toronto, another filming location for
scenes of *Black Christmas* (credit to Dan Duffin)

The University of Toronto in addition would be the other main filming location outside of the residence at Clarendon Crescent. Soldier's Tower at Hart House is used for the scene where Mr Harrison waits anxiously for Claire (whilst being pelted with a snowball by children), to take her home for Christmas; little does he know she is now Billy's companion in the sorority house attic.

Trinity College's Seeley Hall is used for the scene where Jess confronts Peter who is playing the piano, about her pregnancy and controversial plans for an abortion. Seeley Hall is also used again for the scene later on when Peter practices for the University's committee. Trinity College is another location that has been used in a number of Hollywood productions since, including *The Skulls* (2001) and *Tommy Boy* (1995). North Toronto Memorial Community Centre was the location for the hockey game where Jess meets Chris in the middle of the game, to ask if he has seen the missing Claire.

North Toronto Memorial Community Centre which doubled as
the Police Station in Black Christmas (credit to Dan Duffin)

The location used for the police station was at some point an actual real-life police station but at the time of filming, it was the Centre 55 Community Centre based at 97 Main Street, Toronto. Today, Centre 55 hosts community outreach programs such as yoga, senior fitness plus the organisation of senior bus outings.

Once the police are alerted to the presence of Billy being inside the sorority house, a number of cars can be seen quickly zipping across town hoping to get to Jess in time. The stretch of road used is Lakeshore Boulevard near Islington, which has also been used for car chases in 1984's *Police Academy*.

Despite production running smoothly, Clark did look back on one scene in particular with some tiny self-criticism, which revolved around the death of Mrs Mac. Clark wished he had just one more shot edited in to give the impression that the crane actually does hit Mrs Mac when at the moment, you just see her legs disappear into the attic; "I would change that if I could", muses Clark on the commentary.

Despite this tiny oversight, this scene was a memorable one to shoot, with Dunk again providing the murderous guise of Billy for the moment; "Up in the attic, there was a lot of handheld action because it was a clean point of view for the hook attack on Mrs Mac.

Billy waiting to strike Mrs Mac in the attic

That was me, hand holding the camera which I did a fair amount of. We mixed up harnessing the camera or going handheld, depending on how much space we had available. The nice thing about the rig I had for the camera is that it really didn't take up any room and get in the way of anything. Wherever possible I would use that technique".

As the film moved through production, one of the major roles in the film was still missing, albeit formed up most of the time by various crew members, yet never being fully realised on set. Billy was conceived through a variety of ways, whether it be Dunk using the camera rig, or various crew members talking to the girls off camera as they shot the scenes of them receiving the phone calls.

As Hussey remembers, while Billy wasn't a fully formed person on set, his influence could still be felt throughout the shooting; "None of us really knew who the killer was going to be. I think maybe Bob would have a different idea, but we just showed up and we said well is anybody playing the killer, and Bob said 'no no we're never gonna see the killer. Oh, maybe we'll see him at the end when he kills you, I haven't decided yet'".

So that's how we started the film, the killer was maybe somebody that was there, behind a door every day, there was never really anybody cast to play the killer, so it was all in the imagination of the director. So, we just played it really from day to day as it came'. However, whatever guise Billy came on to set as, none of the cast members was prepared for the infamous dialogue that would eventually replace the lines fed to them on the initial shoot when they first saw the film at its premiere months later.

Billy prepares to stab Barb

Enter Nick Mancuso, who at the time was a 19-year-old fresh on the Toronto experimental theatre scene, who had no idea the great shadow this job would cast over the rest of his life. Despite Mancuso being the official voice of Billy, he does acknowledge that Bob himself provided some of the dialogue, as well as another actor, and which were all then mixed together to create the eerie ramblings of our favourite festive slasher. Reflecting on the process; he recalls; "I was only one of the voices of Billy, there were three voices. One was Bob Clark, who did some of the screamings and another was an actress, I can't recall her name, perhaps Mugsey Sweeney. I had actually worked with this actress when I was a stage actor. We worked on a play written by Des McAnuff, who ended up directing the Jersey *Boys* on Broadway".

Remembering the process further, Mancuso notes how he wasn't sure how Bob mixed it all together in the end "but I did most of the voice work. Most of it was done with me standing on my head in order to compress the thorax and give it that 'It's me Billy', kind of rasp. What Bob had made me do was sit in a chair for the audition and he said to just improvise some sounds and so I just started improvising; he said yes you got the part". Mancuso also ended up dubbing two lines for Keir Duella that needed dubbing; "Bob Clark asked if I could dub Keir for two lines, as this would save flying him back over from England", he remembers.

In the commentary, Clark himself reminisces on the initial phone call at the start of the film, as the sisters surround the area to hear Billy. "The guy is quite entertaining and fascinating" chuckles the director, noting further how "we worked very long and hard to create the sound, the personality of this killer. It's made up of 4 to 5 voices, all quite mad", he amusingly concedes.

Clare, Phyl and Jess confront Barb

The scene itself again allows Clark to bring together his roaming camera shots without many cuts as discussed earlier, allowing the killer's voice to "get into their souls", as he describes; "What we hear on the phone is very violent, they're almost under the spell of this madman". On-set, the phone calls were actually from an actor offset piping in the calls from a script. However, none of the dialogue on set matched the much more vulgar sentences audiences would be experiencing.

"The phone calls were a substantial character in the piece" comments Clark in Fangoria Magazine. "So, I knew they had to be good. I wanted them to sound almost supernatural. We were in the studio on and off for two weeks, with many people contributing, including me, Nick Mancuso, and a few women, actually.

None of them was Keir Dullea; we wouldn't cheat that way". Mancuso recollects that at that time he didn't go overboard or in-depth to try and understand the psychology of Billy, and neither did Clark at that point he observed. As far as Mancuso was aware, Billy "was a creep who wanted to kill college girls. That was it", he recalled back in 2019 when interviewed for the British press.

As well as Billy's vulgarity shocking audiences with the use of language that went far against words usually employed in much cleaner, wholesome conservative conversations, another aspect was that while he was kept in the dark and the shadows, he was still being brought to life intermittently by the likes of Dunk with his camera rig. However, one of the more shocking and infamous images in classic horror cinema has been Billy's eye peering out between the crack in the door during the film's finale, watching Jess as she discovers the lifeless bodies of her sisters in the dorm room. For decades, fans have debated and asked each other just who provided that iconic moment, and for the first time, we can officially state with 100% confidence that the chilling eye belongs to none other than Clark himself!

Not only was Clark behind this chilling moment, but he also doubled as Billy in the background as a silhouette according to Mancuso. However, several of the crew have now put the eye mystery to rest including Stan Cole, his wife (and the film's AD) Sandy, as well as Dunk himself, who was there on set actually capturing the shot in question. "Both Sandy and I recall it being Bob's eye" assures Stan.

Billy watches Jess through the door

"Those are definitely his eyebrows; although, his eyes were blue, and, as one can see, the eye peering through the door is brown. Sandy was trying to remember whether or not Bob put in brown contacts, but doesn't recall this possible fact, but he must have". Dunk also corroborates these facts further; "I believe that was actually Bob, as I was photographing the scene. You have to remember when this movie was made there was no such thing as video assist, it was old school cinematography. It was a one camera deal and so I was the guy who got to really see the movie" as well as experiencing who was in the shot at the time it seems, from the cast to Clark himself.

Even many years later, when Dan Duffin was interviewing Clark for the DVD release and was getting to know him as a friend, he had asked Clark directly who was playing the person behind the door, who was behind the eye, to which Bob merely smiled and winked back at him in acknowledgement of his involvement. As Cole muses affectionately, "Like Hitchcock, Bob had a cameo on screen, and/or performing sound effects VO's in his films. He was really just a frustrated actor", he remembers amusingly.

With the film completing the production stage, it had been handed over to Cole who began editing, working closely with Clark, both suggesting and making notes and giving ideas to help the process run smoother and more productive; "The editing process at that time was done by using a Moviola that had a small screen, and one soundtrack. All the film pictures and sounds were broken down into single rolls of 35mm film and track identified with the scene and take a number. I would then run each roll through the Moviola, marking the action I wanted, then remove and run the rolls through the synchronizer, marking my cut point, before splicing them together in sequence", muses Cole.

"When I first started to edit, I actually had to scrape the emulsion on the frame with a razor blade and use film glue to seal the cut. If I had to make a change in a splice, a frame or two would be lost. Before working with Bob, I was glad to have the new splicer (guillotine) using clear tape to make the splice. I would edit each scene separately as Bob would shoot each scene on different days, and of course, out of continuity. I was able to put them in order when I had completed them, and when Bob would come into the editing room, I could only show him the cutscenes on the Moviola until we got a Steenbeck flatbed which thankfully made things much quicker and easier".

Working on the edit took the pair three months, which allowed Cole to stay on working through music, sound effects and ADR. Cole remembers the fond bond he developed with Clark during this time and beyond; "Working with Bob was a pleasure, and we had a great relationship. Bob was easy to work with and was always ready to listen to ideas and various thoughts".

"He had so many ideas of his own, regarding talent, music, and sound effects. He was a very talented, gifted man and had a great attitude with those he worked with. As you can see in the films he did, there are a lot of repeats in the names of the crew, and in some cases, the cast. For instance, Sandy was unavailable to be in all of Bob's films since she was working on others, but she was always the first script supervisor he would call".

One of the most noted aspects of the film is the under-reliance on the violence being seen on screen, something that was scaled back by Clark when he first started redrafting Moore and Bond's script. The original drafts were a lot more like the bloody slasher films that followed in the 80s according to Clark, who was hesitant about going down that route as a way to make the film. Instead, he concentrated on creating suspense from the most mundane of aspects, and while we have spoken about the editing, the camera trickery, as well as actors, another vital component to help build the unnerving feel of Black Christmas, came from Carl Zittrer, who had already begun to create music for the film before cameras had started shooting.

Carl Zittrer composes on the piano

"I read the script first to find out what, if any, music might be needed for the film shoot (like live singing Christmas carols, etc.)" explains Zittrer. "Because this 'on camera' music, things had to be prepared in advance of the shoot. Another reason for reading the script was to absorb the mood of the film and to start thinking about a musical approach". Zittrer's involvement early on in the film's conception came about because of his prior association with Bob. The pair knew each other, and Bob was confident that Zittrer was the right person for the job; "It wasn't so much that I was called for a job, but that I was part of the team. Bob didn't get outside directing jobs back in those early days. No one hired him out of the blue for *Black Christmas*, nor for most of his films. Bob sold the concept, raised the money, produced the film, directed, worked closely with me and his editor, and worked with the distributors of the film on the ad campaigns. If he had waited to be called for an outside directing job, he'd still be waiting".

The music for *Black Christmas* provides a suitably haunting tone, at times almost like a distant wailing. Unlike other later horror films, where the music would dictate the scares and help audiences jump out of their seats, Zittrer's score works closely alongside the work of Cole in the edit as well as Clark's creative choices with the sombre moving cameras, haunting shadows in the background, the silence from within the house in addition to the madness of Billy when he unleashes his murderous rage; "The success of my work depends very much on how well the film works and this depends on a team of filmmakers and no small amount of luck. *Black Christmas* helped my music as much as my music helped the film. It was 'my best work' at the time. A lot of the score music happened differently than I had first planned it"

"I was working with the first portable and affordable synth called the Putney. I first used it on *Children* and learned quickly that it had a wild streak, meaning you never knew exactly what was going to come out of it because the electronic components weren't stable. But by the time *Black Christmas* came along, I had learned how to keep it reasonably tamed. While the Putney was a sound generator, it was also an audio processor. We, (I say 'we' because Bob was an active participant as well), would put his voice and other voices and sounds through the Putney to get inside Billy's head. It was a rich learning experience because we had the freedom to try things that didn't work which is then how we learnt what did work".

With the film seemingly ready, Bob and the producers came together to watch the fruits of their work and labour on the big screen. As the film finished, everyone was happy, and the next stage was about to begin, unleashing Billy onto audiences around the world. "It was a joyful experience", recollects Clark on the DVD commentary. "We felt we were doing something worthwhile, and we felt we'd have a hit with some classical overtones - we thought we had a chance. It was a joy!"

INTERVIEW

Albert J. Dunk

Camera Operator/Billy POV

Bert Dunk's involvement in Black Christmas is two-fold, having worked as a camera operator on the film plus being the POV for Billy, with Nick Mancuso providing the voice for the character. Here is an exclusive interview we conducted with Bert to discuss the legacy of this horror classic.

Who was the infamous eye through the door shot from the finale?

I believe that was actually Bob Clark, as I was photographing the scene. You have to remember when this movie was made there was no such thing as video assist, it was old school cinematography. It was a one camera deal and so I was the guy who got to really see the movie, so in those days. You got paid good money and you could decide if filming could carry on because the shot was fine.

How heavy was the camera that was harnessed to you?

The camera was a little under 100 pounds, so it was big. It was me that came up with the idea of strapping the camera to me for the POV shots. I got hired before the director of photography, as initially, they were going to hire a British DP who I had previously interviewed and got along well with, but in the end, we ended up hiring Reg Morris, who was a Canadian cameraman. His background was that he was a camera operator and his brother was Oswald Morris who shot many great British movies.

Reggie had worked on Moby Dick as the Camera Operator and done lots of great British pictures before he emigrated to Canada to work for the national film board. Reggie was an excellent cameraman and did an excellent job on Black Christmas I thought.

The shot going up the trellis outside the house, that was the last shot of the first day of filming. That set the pace for the whole film. I had it mounted on my shoulder and had a special camera rig and everything that allowed me to keep my hands free. So, when I was going up the trellis you never saw the shadow of the camera, you only saw the shadow of me.

During the strangulation scene with Lynn Griffin, the camera was on my shoulder.

Was the trellis scene the hardest to film for you?

Actually, that was probably the easiest because it was mounted on my shoulder, the real trick was just deciding the shots and Bob (Clark) and I talked about that a lot. After the first days rushes, when they saw that shot, that's what dictated how the movie would be shot going forward.

The killer POV is very unique for the time period, was there any indication of how innovative you were by using this technique?

Later on, I was doing a lot of work in Los Angeles and one of my key grips on one of my movies does a lot of Tarantino films. It turns out that Black Christmas is one of Tarantino's favourite movies that he watches every Christmas. I guess John Carpenter liked it too, as I know he spoke to Bob about it and asked what you would have called a sequel and we know that idea became Halloween. I think the POV shot started a trend and a lot of filmmakers caught onto it and thought it worked really well. It is always great never to see the person that is doing the killing. The BBC are actually great at using this technique if you watch any of the classic Father Brown or Inspector Morse they have what I call 'The BBC Lurker', the guy who just comes into frame who have bad intentions.

What can you tell us about the attack on Mrs. Mac in the attic?

Up in the attic, there was a lot of handheld action because it was a clean point of view for the hook attack on Mrs. Mac. That was me, hand holding the camera which I did a fair amount of. We mixed up harnessing the camera or going handheld, depending on how much space we had available. The nice thing about the rig I had for the camera is that it really didn't take up any room and get in the way of anything. Wherever possible I would use that technique.

How did the crew find the sorority house for filming?

This was taken care of by the location scout, and we were looking for a nice big house to film in. It was based right across the street from a family called the Gundey's and their kids used to come to the set and watch us film and befriended the film crew. It turns out the family had a company called Wood Gundey which was a big financial institution.

It was a beautiful house; the Production Designer Karen Bromley (who I still keep in touch with) had a great time working there.

How cold was it filming as it appeared to be bone-chilling for the outdoor scenes?

Not really as the snow on the front yard was actually produced by the fire department as it was actually foam.

I think it was the fall and we were shooting up in Guelph. The park we shot in was Hyde Park that is based here in Toronto, and those scenes were actually John Saxon's first scenes as he brought on to the project. The guy who was originally gonna play that role was Edmund O'Brien, and he was basically too old and couldn't remember his lines.

John flew in and came straight from the airport to that location, but he did a great job and was such a nice guy.

Tell us about working with Bob Clark?

Bob was very organised and had a series of little index cards with every shot from the film on them. He would come to work in the morning with his cards and he would know which shots he wanted, how they were gonna be filmed and where.

I thought he was doing great and after the first week's rushes, he showed us a movie he did called Children Shouldn't Play With Dead Things. It was the worst movie I'd ever seen (laughs), so I thought oh my goodness, but anyway this was much better. I think he was surrounded by better people on Black Christmas and he had learnt from the experience. Filmmaking is a never-ending learning process.

I met up with Bob years after the film in Vancouver where I was doing a film and I went over to see him as he had called my agent and put me in touch. We were tentatively planning to work together, and I was spending a lot of time in Los Angeles going back forth between there and Toronto. So, we were going to plan it out once I got back to Canada and he and his son were sadly killed on the pacific road highway in a head-on collision.

Do you ever see any other members of the crew?

We had a reunion at a Comic Convention in Toronto, and we had a panel with Art Hindle, Lynn Griffin and a few others.

One of the most fascinating scenes from a filmmaking point of view is the plastic bag strangulation, what can you tell us about filming that?

The closet was a real closet but because of my camera rig, it didn't take up any room. The biggest thing was me and the assistant trying to squeeze into the closet. He needed room to pull focus and I needed room to get my hands out and grab Lynn.

Do you have any funny anecdotes from life on set?

It's how it looks on the screen that counts but when they say 'cut' is another story. There was lots of joking and lots of camaraderie and everyone was working to the end to get this film finished. I think everyone was quite pleased with how it went because we used to dailies after work every day. So, we go and see how the previous day's shots went and make any corrections. I can't recall us having to do any reshoots.

During the scene where Margot Kidder gets stabbed with the glass unicorn, the little glass trinkets in the foreground start to have a shake to them as the attack starts. That was actually a mistake.

What happened was my camera operator threaded the loop on the camera a little too tight, so the frame was getting blurred on the pull-down and that is why you got this jumpy picture. It turned out perfect for what we were doing, it's one of those accidents that work in your favour but you never know at the time.

I can't recall if it was Bob who was the silhouette of the killer in that shot. It was more likely it was Keir (Dullea) but I don't remember.

Going back to the crew, the continuity girl Sandy actually ended up marrying the Editor (Stan Cole) and I saw her around 10 years ago.

Were there any other scenes of Billy that never made it into the final cut?

I don't know that there was really. Bob had it all down on his index cards, so he knew what he wanted to do and of course, film stock is expensive so we were being as economical as possible.

Do you think the film works better as the killer is never formally identified?

I guess it must help it and although we have the misdirection of it being Keir in the end, but alas it is this mysterious Billy character.

Was there a cast and crew premiere for *Black Christmas*?

There was a screening I just can't remember the location, but we did all see it before it got a wide cinematic release. It was most likely at the film lab owned by Finn Quinn who had invested in the film. When I first saw it I thought Bob had done a great job and I enjoyed the experience of working on it.

Were you aware of some of Billy's colourful dialogue when filming these scenes?

No, no idea as that was all happening during post-production. I am sure Bob got a few words in there somewhere, making at least one obscene phone call.

Did Bob ever talk to you about a *Black Christmas* sequel?

No, he told me they were making one, but it was awful (referring to the 2006 remake). You have got to be careful with remakes, as it better be a whole lot better than the original otherwise you are in trouble as you have so many people who like the original. It is a hard task to create a remake that is better than the original, but there are some, but not a whole lot.

What does *Black Christmas* mean to you 46 years later?

Obviously, it has kept people's interest because people are still watching and talking about it, so it has stood the test of time. What can I say? Other than we must have done a good job.

INTERVIEW

Karen Bromley

Production Designer

What attracted you to want to be an Art Director/Production Designer? Who were your influences?

I was searching for something more creative and fascinating than a life on a prairie farm. I studied Interior Design and Architecture at the University of Manitoba. Winnipeg had a rich theatre culture and I fell under its spell.

My first step in was to volunteer as an usher at The Manitoba Theatre Centre where John Hirsch was Artistic director. I helped with sets for the University Theatre group and talked my way into an apprenticeship at Vineland summer stock theatre in Southern Ontario. I had found a community that I was thrilled to be a part of. I designed sets for various theatre companies in Canada and Vermont US for a few years.

I was very fortunate to freelance with a design construction company that provided sets for everything imaginable. We did commercials for TV, Industrial shows, variety musical shows for television, movie theatre interiors, stores, and the Canadian Centennial Train full of Historical exhibits that crossed Canada ending up at Expo 67.

In between movies, I spent many seasons inspired by the exacting demands of designing the public affairs shows for the CTV Network. The big cumbersome studio floor video cameras were challenging, as a few degrees angle on an anchor's desk made a huge difference to all those close-ups with the background screens and their emerging VFX technologies. I called it a precision design sabbatical when doing those shows.

I was fortunate to have such an astonishing variety of experience, to hone skills, and design challenges that served me so well when designing for the big screen. There, the whole world is our pallet! Who wouldn't love this profession!

I can't point to any one movie designer who influenced me; there were so many movies that were full of inspirational images. We were called art directors then, and in the later 1970's the title of production designer began to come into use, because of the somewhat management creativity, most art directors currently provide. I wonder if people understand that in earlier films the 'art director' was filling basically the same role as today's production designer.

When you're starting a new project, what is your process? Do you read/go in-depth with the screenplays, dialogue, details and characters? Do you pursue your own independent research or is it a major collaborative effort? What was this journey like when approaching *Black Christmas*?

To get an understanding of the peculiarities of the story setting, I do my preliminary research, before my first creative conversations with a director. If it is a particular world with unique physical, technical or historical qualities, research assistants are invaluable.

As you research and become immersed into a place or a time, details begin to reveal their power in the reality of that world. You find elements you can pull out of that world to use, such as colours, spatial relationships, kinds of light, certain shapes, or symbols that are consistent. These details when used carefully, or exaggerated, or even subverted, form part of an underlying visual message to help create a certain sense of place.

One of the best parts of designing a film happens in those conversations working with the director where you start to see how to visually support their vision of the film. As a style, a certain ambience, a visual approach begins to evolve, and you see how to enhance or manipulate all the visual elements to contribute to that Director's intentions for the drama.

What was it like working on the film and what challenges did you face (if any), while making *Black Christmas*?

Christmas lights look their best set against white snow beside the evergreens. We worked against that pretty image with shadows, dense foliage and dark undefined shapes, and in our case, we had to work with a lack of natural snow. Sometimes, nature rarely co-operates with film makers on that level. We had to find an artificial snow that wouldn't leave a nasty residue on house lawns. Those were very early days, and our options were limited. We ruled out Instant potato mix sometimes used and ended up using the white natural based foam that was sprayed on runways when aircraft are in danger at landing, perhaps causing sparks that may ignite and start a fire.

We also assured homeowners that being biological it was good fertilizer for their lawns. There was a very green lawn the next summer! I was out there before dawn, on many bitterly cold mornings with the SPFX crew as they sprayed snow for that day's shoot, hoping it would survive wind and sun, not collapse before the end of the day's shoot. If it froze hard, it was more durable and real looking. We had to watch for fluffy foam stuck to actor's trousers or boots.

The house is a leading character in Black Christmas. It is perhaps a refuge, but we wanted to project that it is, in its very being, a killer. The search for the perfect house was a long one and when Bob first saw it, he sensed it was right. Inside, the geography for blocking shots and actors was exceptionally good. The dark heavy wood, to set red lights against instead of bright walls, the busy, small paned, not large windows we shrouded with curtains to control the view and amount of daylight. A closed place. Seen from outside at night, red Christmas lights, like a warning, hung in the middle of the glow from the windows, hampered the usual sense of a safe welcoming place.

The dark powerful staircase dominates the space at the entry and into the living room. With the telephone at the bottom of the stairs, below the first landing it can be shot from above, and so increase the sense of the danger from within the house. As if the house was talking to you. Bob used this setting brilliantly. Jess gets a call from the deranged killer Billie and is terrified, as are the audience, by the voice of her boyfriend immediately above her. The mistaken identity of the killer is set up so strongly right then.

Do you remember who played Billy's iconic eye in between the door frame?

I don't remember much about who was in the 'eye shot'. I do remember having carpenters re-hang the door to allow just the right width of space for the eye.

But I remember we put a trellis up the side of the house, set out from the wall to become a ladder for the camera man with camera on his shoulders who portrayed Billy there. We had to take care in attaching it to the house so to not leave permanent damage. I remember relief when Bert got down safely.

What are your thoughts when you think back to working on the film?

It was a wonderful experience working on Black Christmas. We were a young industry here in Canada at that time and anything was possible. Even so, I don't think any of us, with the possible exception of Bob, had any idea the film would become a cult hit for decades to come. It's been a great source of pride for me to have contributed to such a successful film. Not many have that enviable record.

It's also been interesting over the years to have various requests for interviews or my thoughts about making the movie. I never imagined being recognized for a horror film! It is a film that touches primal fears in all of us and has endured as such.

My husband, now producer, John Eckert was an AD on Black Christmas. We live not far from the Black Christmas house, which is protected as an historical site built for Sir Adam Beck, builder of the Niagara Electrical Power Generation System. The house has changed very little over the years. We often wonder as we pass by 'how does a family go upstairs to sleep each evening having seen our movie?'

P.S. John thinks it was Jerry Arbeid's eye in the door.

Have you seen any of the remakes and what did you think?

I have not watched any remakes of Black Christmas. Well, I got a short while into one recently and stopped. A pale imitation. Bob Clark was an original and his movie is exceptional.

INTERVIEW

Carl Zittrer

Composer

Did you strike up a working relationship with Bob Clark on *Children Shouldn't Play with Dead Things*?

My working and personal relationship with Bob went back to years before Children. There wasn't really a difference between our personal and professional relationship. We were in University together and were active in local (Miami area) theatre. We went to movies together and listened to music (classical, electronic, jazz, experimental, etc.) together. We also talked about the movies we wanted to make.

You worked with Bob quite regularly for a number of years, were you one of his first calls once he got a directing job back then?

It wasn't so much that I was called for a job, but that I was part of the team. Bob didn't get outside directing jobs back in those early days. No one hired him out of the blue for Black Christmas nor for most of his films. Bob sold the concept, raised the money, produced the film, directed, worked closely with me and his editor and worked with the distributors of the film on the ad campaigns. If he had waited to be called for an outside directing job, he'd still be waiting.

Tell us your reaction to reading the script to *Black Christmas*?

I read the script first to find out what, if any, music might be needed for the film shoot (like live singing Christmas carols, etc.) because this 'on camera' music things had to be prepared in advance of the shoot. Another reason for reading the script is to absorb the mood of the film and to start thinking about a musical approach.

How early did you get involved in the project?

I was involved in the project from pre-production, maybe even pre-pre-production.

Black Christmas **has some of the most haunting music in any horror film; do you feel it is your best work?**

The success of my work depends very much on how well the film works and this depends on a team of filmmakers and no small amount of luck. Black Christmas helped my music as much as my music helped the film. It was 'my best work' at the times. A lot of Black Christmas score music happened differently than I had first planned it. I was working with the first portable and affordable synth called the Putney. I first used it on Children and learned quickly that it had a wild streak... meaning you never knew exactly what was going to come out of it because the electronic components weren't stable.

But by the time Black Christmas came along I had learned how to keep it reasonably tamed. While the Putney was a sound generator, it was also an audio processor. We, I say 'we' because Bob was an active participant as we put his voice and other voices and sounds through the Putney to get inside Billy's head. It was a rich learning experience because we had the freedom to try things that didn't work which how we learn what DOES work.

How hard was it to essentially subvert the themes of Christmas into something really unsettling for the score?

Christmas themes held it all together. Christmas was the canvas on which I could paint. Christmas carols were the counterpoint to my admittedly discordant atmospheres.

What was the hardest piece of music to work on for the film?

The most technically challenging was Peter's piano recital. Keir Dullea heard the piano piece before and during the film shoot. This helped him move and react accordingly, but his hands and fingers (in the shot) are mine. Stan Cole made it visually smooth, then I edited the music far into the night to make the playing as smooth as possible, but still having to keep Keir's body language, my fingers, and the audio both visually and musically believable.

When was the last time you watched the film?

Maybe a couple of years ago at a horror film convention.

The film has become a massive cult hit amongst horror fans in the years since its release. When did you first realize how popular it was?

It's interesting to me that the film is popular with fans who weren't even born when the film was made, but I think it's also interesting to ask why its fan base is growing. Certainly, the film has aged. Not a cell phone in sight. No pop tunes. Old cars, old moral attitudes. But it has honesty and energy, and you can see that the actors had fun playing off each other. There are no (pardon the expression) dead spots in the film.

The elusive character of Billy is one of horror's most memorable killers, do you think it's better we never found out his identity and motive?

NOT seeing Billy leaves it all to our individual imaginations. We 'see' in Billy the thing we fear most... and that's different for each of us.

Six years later you worked on *Prom Night* with Paul Zaza, I guess that was a very different experience to *Black Christmas*?

Yes, different, but not so different. Didn't use the Putney, but our method was the same: find the mood of the picture and try to score, not so much what you see on the screen, but what you don't see.

During the slasher boom of the 1980s, were you surprised no one decided to revisit *Black Christmas*?

No, not surprised because I learned some time ago never to be surprised at the logic, or lack thereof, of the movie business culture.

Did you ever get the chance to watch the 2006 remake?

The answer is 'no'. I never saw a remake that I liked, and I try not to watch them. They usually copy all the superficial things about the original and leave out the life and breath of the original. No offence to the filmmakers, but the reviews of the 2006 Black Christmas tell me I didn't miss much.

v) The Would-Be-Victims of *Black Christmas*

One of the most resounding opinions on the film is the appreciation audiences have for the characters, as well as the cast inhabiting them, setting the template up for numerous horror films to follow. Though they do not follow every trait, Clark invested a lot of time in making the sorority girls themselves both vulnerable, yet strongly independent.

Unlike the majority of horror films to follow, bar a few classic examples (looking at you Laurie Strode), *Black Christmas* did not settle its narrative on forgetful knife fodder, instead, allowing the film's danger to intertwine and gel with some of the lighter moments, as well as moments of deep psychological repercussions which Billy couldn't even claim credit for.

At the time of writing, readers only have to search for the film on Google and you will find a wealth of immediate websites that review the film or give an editorial on its legacy, all the while making note of these characters we are immediately thrown into the mix with. Ian Sedensky via Culture Crypt notes that the film "may be the only horror film where sorority girls are not mere bubble-headed bimbos, disrobing and dying purely for the pubescent pleasure of teenage boys". Over at Bloody-Disgusting, Meagan Navarro writes that by Clark taking such time to allow each of the girls (as well as the rest of the supporting act), time to breathe without diluting the main evil presence of Billy throughout additionally, "means we care about what happens to them".

Clare and Phyl in the sorority house

And therein lies one of the strengths of the film, its attention to those who are integral to the narrative moving along. Unlike the slasher triumphs of the 1980s which swelled and bloated into the early 90s, previously being seen dead on its ass before *Scream* came along, *Black Christmas* avoided the infamous emphasis on over-the-top death pieces and gore, a reliance that often came into odds with the MPAA.

While Jason impaled and decapitated, Freddy sliced and diced, and while Michael went into a full-on cult mode, massacring whole swathes of rarely important and diminishing Haddonfield residents, Billy was playing an altogether different game of cat and mouse. But with characters who would not be going without a fight, it would seem, even when potentially blind-sighted by their own insecurities (alcohol, sexual escapades and even abortion).

Clare Harrison (played by Lynne Griffin)

Over the years, Griffin has never shied away from her love of being part of the legacy of *Black Christmas*, even assisting in the various new behind the scenes supplements on a variety of home release formats over the past 20 years. From Toronto originally, Griffin's filmography includes other horror delights such as *Curtains*, battling Martians in the TV adaption of *War of the Worlds* in 1980, while she also dipped her feet back into the festive time of the year in *Santa Baby 1 & 2* playing Mrs Claus, a far cry from the horrors of Clark's film.

As well as being a movie actress, she is also an experienced stage performer appearing in a number of Shakespearian ventures such as *King Lear* (playing Cordelia), as well as Viola in *Twelfth Night*. Her mother represented her in her emerging career, and this eventually put her on a path with Clark when she found herself auditioning for the part of Clare Harris.

Lynne Griffin who played Clare

65

Speaking with Terror Trap website in 2011, Griffin reminisced what her impressions were of Bob and working with him; "He was a very lovely, jolly person. As far as I remember, at that point, I was always being cast as the ultimate innocent virgin. I'll say no more about what was really going on in my life! But I was being cast that way a lot because I had this sort of innocent, virginal look. It really worked well for the role [in *Black Christmas*]. It's funny because I wasn't really that way in person!"

Indeed, Clare Harrison initially may seem to be looking more like a mere footnote in the film, set up to be the obligatory first death to get the murderous chaos started quickly, as she is the first character to be killed by the mysterious Billy in a horrifically-filmed and equally unnerving scene where she is suffocated by a plastic bag via two grubby hands that come flying out at her from behind her clothes rail in the closet. All the more sinister is the juxtaposition of her terror and lingering muffled death moans coupled with the killers too, while the rest of her sisters downstairs are all cheering and presenting Mrs Mac with her Christmas present. Griffin recalls how being grabbed by Billy was "a total shock because I didn't really know when to expect him to jump out! As I recall, we didn't do a lot of takes for that scene either".

One aspect she does reveal though is who played Billy in that specific scene; Dunk, who was in the closet, found with the camera attached to him still via his shoulder which allowed him to both capture the action (or screams), as well as interact with the cast. Griffin does agree with this, and to her knowledge "I think it was just the cameraman who was holding a hand-held camera. Yes, you're right. He did have some sort of black cloth over his head. I remember Clare's death scene was shot in a real closet in that house. The cameraman was squeezed in behind the dry-cleaning bags -- so tight -- and there was only room for him and maybe the focus puller!"

However, while Clark directs the scene with intense, quickly cut violence and POV shots, Clare's death takes on an even more emotional tug even after her demise when not only are we continually reminded of her lifeless corpse in the attic but we are also reminded that she is so close to being discovered as her life-

66

less face, frozen in terror sits comfortably by the highest window in the house, for all to see if only they looked up. Additionally, so horrific is this image, that it became one of the main thrusts of the advertising campaign, with Clare's demise adorning posters, DVD covers as well as custom fan art over the years.

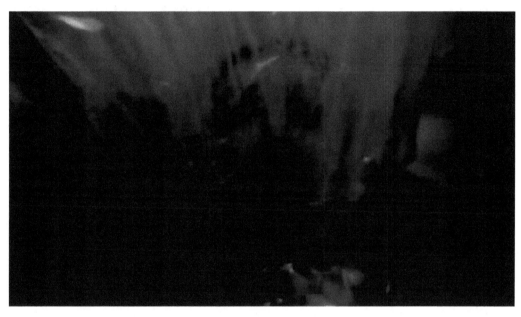

Clare being strangled by Billy in the closet

Despite her small screen time (alive), Griffin enthuses Clare with an authentic vulnerability from the outset, completely opposite to some of her sisters in the house, namely Barbara, who takes as many chances as she can to seemingly humiliate her for her more reserved persona. Yet later in the film (again a fantastic skill to unravel more traits for a dead character), Mr Harrison's tour of his daughter's room reveals a hint that some of this innocence she arrived with has since eroded, with the various posters on the wall (a naked hippy couple having sex covered up not so subtly by Mrs Mac providing the start of the humour that Clark gleefully works in between her and Mr Harrison), allows him a glimpse into his daughter's new life that he disapproves of immensely.

This particular moment seems to allow Clark to provide a social commentary on the differences of opinion between the older generations; while Clare's relationship with Chris is more mundane and routine, a fact the more liberal-minded Mrs Mac attests to and supports, it is seemingly at odds with the more conservative, well-spoken and proper Mr Harrison, who dismisses it still ("I didn't send my daughter here to be drinking and picking up the boys"). Maybe Clare finally began to break free of her parent's restraints while living away from home, and although not as graphic in her exploits, and still having a responsibility to herself unlike say Barbara (again, maybe where that tension comes from "this is a sorority house, not a convent!"), this opening herself up to new opportunities as well as experiences, something she may never have had the chance to do before, makes her violent demise and subsequent visual revisits, all the more impactful on the audience. A girl just starting to find her place in the world, cut short by Billy.

INTERVIEW

Lynne Griffin

'Clare Harrison'

What can you remember about auditioning for *Black Christmas*?

It was a basic audition. With lots of other candidates. However, I might have won the part because I told them what a good swimmer I was and that I could hold my breath for a long time, which seemed to be a pre-requisite for the job. I was also frequently cast as the perennial virgin.

How did it feel to be in your first feature film?

I was delighted to be with such an extraordinary cast of actors! And with a great director like Bob Clark, who made it such a happy experience, even though the subject matter was pretty spooky.

What did Bob Clark tell you about the character of Clare?

She wasn't gonna last long alive in the film, but her demise would be memorable, and her image be everlasting

Were the cast of sorority girls close on set?

We were all very chummy during the party scenes, however, I didn't really hang around long enough to get to know anyone all that well. I did chat with Olivia about playing Juliet in Zeffirelli's Romeo and Juliet, which was a highlight for me.

Margot Kidder's Barb is quite something in this film, was all her dialogue already in the script, or was some ad-libbed?

Margot approached this role, it seemed to me, as a, um, method actress. I know she had some substance help with her drunk scenes. I don't think she ad-libbed that much. But she certainly owned and embellished what was written.

You were theatre trained so what was the transition like into television and films?

I learned quickly, mostly from television work as a teenager, to keep things authentic and real when you are in front of a camera, and to project my little head off when I was on big stages like the Stratford and Shaw festivals. However, both require truth.

What appealed to you about going into acting?

I was a very shy child, so my mum thought it would be a good way to bring me out of myself. And I loved playing pretend, and particularly loved the dress-up part. And I still do.

Did you know of any of the cast prior to filming?

I certainly knew of Olivia, from Romeo and Juliet, which was the most exciting casting news, pre-filming. But I also knew of Margot and Andrea Martin, and Keir Dullea. I had never met Art Hindle before, but I certainly got to know him, as I shared my first screen kiss with him, and we have been life-long friends ever since.

Can you recall the first time you saw the film?

You know, I actually can't! I don't think I went to an initial screening. My most impressive memory is Bob showing me what the poster would be! And little did I know that the image of me would become so iconic.

We have to ask about your death, what can you recall about filming this scene?

I spent a lot of time up in the attic! With Bob and Bert Dunk. Bob sat across from me in the rocking chair, and it was he who had his foot on the rocker, rocking me gently through the takes, instructing me to hold my breath, because we figured out that just poking holes for my nose and mouth in the plastic bag wouldn't make it still enough, and condensation would form on the bag. Bob found all of this immensely entertaining and made jokes like 'Okay, lunch everybody! Lynne, if you could just hold your position and we'll be back in an hour.' And then finally saying 'That's a wrap on Lynne Griffin!' We all called him 'Uncle Bob'. He was lovely.

Was it Bert Dunk with the plastic bag or someone else?

Yes, it was. Bert was pretty ground-breaking in the use of a body-cam. He was actually the one climbing the trellis at the beginning of the film, and also it was his hands strangling me in the closet. He and Bob were inventing the 'killer' camera POV throughout the film, which was wonderfully intimidating!

How did the film crew get the cat to work within the scene?

Bob was responsible for throwing the cat, Claude, onto my lap. Claude was a very pretty cat, but not a very willing participant. So eventually the bag on my face was sprayed with catnip.

Tell us about playing 'dead' in the attic, was this tricky?

Along with what I've already said, it was surprisingly comfortable and light-hearted, as Bob and the crew treated me very well and joked a lot.

How did working on _Black Christmas_ compare to _Curtains_?

Well, for starters, on Curtains I was alive at the end of the film! Also, it was a total trip to play a stand-up comic, (and I don't want to be a spoiler), but to have many more scenes, and to playing a more aggressive character, both funny and dramatic, and to work with the likes of John Vernon and Samantha Egger. And to be called to set a lot more and to earn more money.

The atmosphere on set was quite different on Curtains because it was filmed in a studio, whereas Black Christmas was filmed in the actual house. And Richard Ciupka, who had a European style of working and was becoming a budding film auteur. Also, Curtains required a lot of re-shoots a year later and quite a bit of reworking and plot revisions.

It was particularly fun to spend so much time working with all the women in the ensemble of Curtains. We were all very friendly even though we were all playing competitors.

Black Christmas **wasn't a massive financial hit when it was released but has become this cult classic, can you recall when people started talking to you about the film?**

Yeah. It all came about with Facebook. Once I had joined the social network, fans seemed to find me from all over, and interest in the film, when it was released on DVD, exploded! Since then, I have been frequently asked for screenings, Q and As, and special appearances which I am delighted to do, to promote the newfound interest in the film.

I have been told that it is Quentin Tarrantino's and was Elvis Presley's favourite film to watch at Christmas time! In fact, many fans tell me it is their favourite Christmas movie. Mine is Bob Clark's other Christmas film, A Christmas Story. Which I watch every Christmas!

What is the strangest request you've had from a fan at conventions?

I don't think it was a fan's request, but I decided, as a photo-op, that I would put the plastic bag over my head and take pictures with the fans. It actually turned into something that people now request. So, I always bring a plastic bag, and I'm happy to oblige.

Was it strange to revisit the sorority house from the film for a DVD documentary all those years later?

No, it was great! It remained so much the same, except for the attic. Which had been, obviously, converted into a very nice and tidy bedroom. But both Art and I fully enjoyed running up and down the staircase and re-enacting some of the scenes. The house is a great attraction to fans who visit Toronto. I am not sure how the new tenants receive them, although I had heard that a fence had been put up.

Were you surprised there never was a sequel?

No. What surprised me was that Bob Clark decided to leave so many questions unanswered and leave the ending ambiguous. That certainly seemed to me that there could be a possibility of a sequel. However, they wouldn't need me, as I assume, Clare would be severely skeletal had there been a sequel. I believe there are now two remakes of the film.

You would have been perfect for Mrs. Mac in the 2006 remake; would you have revisited *Black Christmas* if the offer came in?

I would have jumped at the chance; had I been offered! I will still put out there, to anyone who might want to make a sorority house horror film like Black Christmas; I am available and interested in playing the house mother!

What is the scariest part of *Black Christmas*?

The part that always makes me jump out of my skin? Not my own death, but when the killer sneaks down the stairs as Olivia runs past and he grabs her hair. That's the scary part to me! The reason I think Black Christmas is so successful is that a lot of the scariest parts are what we don't see, rather than what we see. Psychological fear to me has always been the most frightening. Which is why I'm such a Hitchcock fan.

***Black Christmas* is lauded as the first 'slasher' film but it's probably one of the first Christmas themed horror films, is this something you are proud to be part of?**

Yes, I'm very proud and humbled at its continued notoriety and success! I would never consider Black Christmas a 'slasher' film, and I am not a fan of the actual slasher films that followed. Black Christmas set and holds a standard of creating terror without the use of gratuitous blood, gore, and sex. It is still lauded as one of the best of the genre, which makes me very proud.

Chris Hayden (played by Art Hindle)

Art Hindle headshot

Art Hindle has been gracing the small and big screens for a long time, appearing in TV shows such as *Friday the 13th* and *Poltergeist: The Legacy*. He got his first big break in film in The *Proud Rider* (his first role in 1971), while after working on *Black Christmas* with Clark, remained a loyal actor to the director by appearing in *Porky's 1 & 2*. His career is still going strong today and looking at his IMDB page alone, reveals that Art has no intention of truly slowing down for the time being.

Art recalls how he "wanted to be an actor", singling out his aunt who suggested that he 'should just go and find a local theatre group and learn to act'. In Toronto in those days, there were not a lot of theatre groups to speak of, so that sort of squashed that idea". Being pressured to make a living, after happily having his first child at 19, he began working in the world of business and quickly became a top stockbroker, which while providing financial security made him "very unhappy". Still wanting to be an actor, Art proclaimed he would "do anything".

Chris speaks with Jess about the missing Clare

His involvement with *Black Christmas* was like any other acting job. Speaking on the Shout Blu Ray release, he recalls how he'd "like to say I was discovered in a play or something like that, but it was just another audition with somebody named Bob Clark. So, I met him in a hotel room. He gave me some scenes to read, they weren't actually scenes that my character would be playing, there were scenes that Keir Dullea would be playing. So, I read those, and Bob pretty much told me at that moment that I was terrific, and I got the part. Not that part though!"

However, his role as Chris Hayden in the 1974 original remains a fan favourite, a young man in love with Clare, who becomes fiercely concerned about her well-being when no one can find her. His concern as well as relentless independence to discover his missing girlfriend allowed Art to embed a positive depiction of mature students, one that goes against the grain of all-night drinking and parties. When we do see him in the film, he is always attempting to better a situation (even playing on the Ice Hockey team, or challenging the Police with their lack of procedures and efforts). In one of the more interesting 'meet the parents' routines we all have to go through, Chris meets Mr Harrison in the worst of scenarios as they both become increasingly more desperate for answers and helps search the nearby park for clues on the young girl in the narrative who was missing.

Recalling the initial time of pre-production, Art notes how "I wasn't a big horror film fan, so I hadn't heard about *Children Shouldn't Play with Dead Things* [Clark's previous horror], and didn't know anything about Bob Clark, didn't know who he was. For me, it was another job, another gig, another chance to make some money at the time".

Chris berates the deputy at the police station

75

The experience of shooting the film and gearing up for production is one Art looks back on fondly. Originally, Clark asked him to step in for Keir who couldn't get to rehearsals with Olivia who wanted to run scenes with him. Due to Keir's unavailability, Art stepped in and read those scenes with her instead. "He had the house ahead of time, so I had a chance to not only work with Olivia, but work in the house that became the sorority, and to watch Bob Clark right up-close talk to all his film crew. They would come in and interview for jobs too".

Chris and one of the police officers help a distraught Mr Harrison

While Clark was interested in adding subtle humour to the roles, Chris' character is one of the rare few within the film not given that material to work with. Furthermore, Chris is there at the end when Jess has been discovered, and the police are seemingly wrapping up. In his own world, seemingly unable to grasp the implications of what the events unfolding could mean for Clare's wellbeing. A touching moment is again his concern for others, as Mr Harrison collapses and he valiantly helps get his (potentially) would-have-been grief-stricken father-in-law out of the house for medical treatment.

Speaking about his fictional missing partner, Art remembers warmly that "Lynne was very quiet, but a very good actor [and] it's a very innocent kiss", between him and her at the beginning of the film, again helping to highlight the maturity and conviction of not only his character but also the more vulnerable, flourishing Clare. "I gave her her first film kiss, and since then we've become good friends. She's got a tremendous sense of humour as does everyone on the show, so my relationship to her and everyone on the set was just A1".

Mrs Mac (played by Marian Waldman)

Mrs Mac gives Mr Harrison the finger

Speaking on the original Tartan DVD commentary release in the early 2000s, Clark speaks very fondly of the character of Mrs Mac, and especially Waldman who brought her to life so well, noting that she was always "loosely based on my aunt". Although she alludes to this with a slightly cheeky demeanour, the fact that Mrs Mac was one of the few characters carried over into the 06 remake, as well as the love the character has had from fans since the film's release, shows that she is a fascinating one to warrant inclusion within the film. On the outside, she can be cranky and sarcastic, and frankly is very much an alcoholic, if you peel back the layers, there is actually a distinct warmth and love for the girls she looks after and vice-versa. While there are hints of a sad backstory where she herself had dreams of being on stage that for whatever reason, never came to be, perhaps almost making her drinking and other notable innocent flaws all the more acceptable.

If it was not for her age, and her own dreams not bearing fruition years earlier, in someone else's hands, the character would have been instantly dismissible, but Clark makes Mrs Mac just as important a part of the houses' inhabitants as the younger girls. Their affection towards the older lady (even when knowing about her drinking and other foul-mouthed escapades), makes this family unit Clark creates all the more real and important, one which does then impact how we feel when characters are dispatched by the always lurking Billy.

Born on December 16th, 1924 in Toronto, Marian Waldman began her career on stage as a choir girl before taking on more active actress roles in further stage plays. She was the daughter of her Physician father while her mother was a Professor, and despite experiencing a childhood under their non-artistic careers, she was determined to remain in the arts and was not prevented from doing so either. When not on stage, Waldman found herself acting in some other horror film projects such as *Deranged: Confessions of a Necrophile*, which was loosely based on real-life serial career Ed Gein, playing the real first victim of Gein's crimes, Ezra Cobb, whilst her final film role was in *Phobia*, playing Mrs Casey. However, while dabbling in film, she was also a screenwriter and had written episodes for TV series such as *High Hopes*, *The Starlost* and *Dr Simon Locke*.

After originally offering the role to Bette Davis who subsequently turned it down, Clark offered Waldman the role, who evidently made the role her own, evidenced in that she is almost certainly referred to in various retrospectives, one example being warmly penned by writer Oliver Pfeiffer in scifinow.com who describes Waldman as bringing "literal high jinks with her portrayal of [the] drunken sorority housemother Mrs Mac, who spends a considerable amount of screen time secretly scouring the house for hidden booze".

Additionally, cast members still today think very fondly of Waldman and their experiences of working with her, such as Griffin who has remarked on "what a wonderful character performance that is". Griffin continues in her admiration when discussing how "not long ago I went to a Q & A and they asked me to sit and watch the film and little did I know that they were going to show it on an IMAX screen. [Therefore] I noticed things that I never had before. This included some of the subtleties in Mary's performance and some of her subversive drunk scenes were particularly hilarious. She was just a very sweet woman and not like Mrs Mac at all. She was quite the lady!"

Mrs Mac talks with Mr Harrison

Warm, lovable, a bit of a foul-mouthed rogue but one who is ultimately very protective and very fond of the young women in her care, Mrs Mac continually defends their wellbeing and privacy with much assertiveness (although whether it always works is very much down to Clark's frequent use of cheeky humour). Showcasing this down to earth persona while all the time still presenting her with very human flaws that point to a saddened past of dashed hopes and dreams, Clark succeeds in making Mrs Mac one of the many highlights of the film (as well as a modern meme queen), so when we do experience her death halfway through the film, it helps Clark remove the initial metaphorical plaster that we hoped would shield the girls from the horror of Billy for much longer.

Waldman's portrayal delivers a multitude of emotions, which initially, viewers could easily dismiss as just for pure amusement, but when we look deeper at the character further, Mrs Mac has allowed Clark a chance to address these layers to present further opportunities that we can only theorise on within Waldman's unforgettable performance.

For example, re-watch the film and compare how while she is initially very annoyed at Mr Harrison's continual complaints about the house, the girl's attitudes and how she herself is running the home, later on when Barbara verbally attacks her in a drunken outburst – Waldman's face and characterisation exhibits a much more saddened persona, devoid of the sarcasm seen earlier and now seems to have much more of a weight on her shoulders as the circumstances around them get ever more chilling and tense.

Waldman's face imbues regret, guilt at her own role in not keeping more of an eye on the girls, which again maybe signals her own failed artistic desires and dreams more? It is all the more saddening then, that Waldman wasn't able to see the further appreciation of her work and the love fans have for her character, as she, unfortunately, died peacefully in her home in Toronto in 1985 after an unsuccessful battle with breast cancer.

Lt. Ken Fuller (played by John Saxon)

John Saxon is no stranger to cult cinema exploits and is arguably known to horror fans more as Lt. Thompson in Wes Craven's unforgettable classic *A Nightmare on Elm Street*, while others may know him as Roper who faces off against Bruce Lee in *Enter The Dragon*. Even if you haven't seen him in those two films, you will have seen him pop up somewhere on your screens since his filmography spans over 200 films and TV shows up until 2017 (even *Dynasty!*).

John Saxon in *Nightmare on Elm Street 3: Dream Warriors*

Originally born as Carmine Orrico on August 5th 1936 in Brooklyn, New York to Italian-American parents, he was eventually discovered by the infamous Talent Agent Henry Wilson, who was then known for representing (and some say creating) Rock Hudson. After seeing Saxon on the front cover of a magazine, Wilson got him to relocate to Southern California and after changing his name to John Saxon, helped to launch his lasting career.

Throughout the early 60s Saxon found himself appearing in film projects out of Italy, and in a 2002 interview for The Flashback Times, remarked on his decision to take this route, commenting how "At the time Hollywood was going through a crisis, but England and Italy were making a great many films. Besides, I thought the European films were of a much more mature quality than most of what Hollywood was making at the time". As well as this, Saxon appeared in the Western genre as well, so by the time he was offered the role of Lt. Ken Fuller in *Black Christmas*, he was a well-known name across the world. However, getting the role had stemmed from unfortunate circumstances beforehand for Clark.

Originally (and even though Saxon was the first choice for the role), Lt Fuller was to be played by Oscar-winning actor Edmond O'Brien. Unfortunately, his declining ill health at the time with ever-worsening Alzheimer meant the latter could not participate in the film at all. "It's one of the saddest moments of my life," remarks Clark, who remembers his experiences with the then 59-year-old actor. "I loved him and worked hard to get him for the movie. Edmond came up to do the role and we went to the hotel room to get him, and we sat and watched this poor man ramble and try to put his coat on for 45 minutes. He kept telling us how he hadn't worked in a long while and how he was so excited to be working again. I might have been inclined to use him, but we were going to be filming in 10 to 20 below-zero weather, and shooting was less than a week away. I knew it wouldn't work. So, I finally called his agent and they suggested John. It was very, very sad" a remorseful Clark remarked on the website The Master Cylinder.

"I remember flying up to Toronto" Saxon continues on the same website, who recollects, "arriving at midnight, being driven to the set and doing a scene right then and there. I don't remember if I had read the script at that point". The scene in question was from the very cold Park scenes where Fuller, police and authorities are beginning to make a search for the missing local young girl. He remembers being at the "suburban location to prepare to do the scene in the woods speaking over a Bullhorn, which was finished at about 3 AM". It was all done very quickly, and while the production was saddened about the loss, they equally made the role and film work still and with as much energy with Saxon now in the role. O'Brien featured in a few numerous projects before his heart-breaking death from the disease on May 9, 1985, in California, aged 69.

Lt. Fuller answers the phone

Fuller is presented as a seasoned officer in the film, a man who has seen a lot of the bad side of life, but not necessarily enough to have made a negative impact on him, instead, actually allowing him to elevate and evaluate events much more closely - that he can tell when something doesn't add up, that things in life are not just mere hearsay or coincidence. And these skills, which he has no doubt developed over the years, allow him to become the first authoritative figure in the film to start putting all the parts of the jigsaw together and determining that something is not right, and thus needs investigating. Not to say that Fuller is lifeless and devoid of soul, in actual fact, because of the crimes in life he has had to investigate and become accustomed to, he does still find the funnier aspects of existence to help counterbalance this negativity. Nowhere is this exhibited more so than in the scene where he begins to call the sorority house for the first time, and finds the extension written down by the dim-witted Sergeant Nash as FE for fellatio.

Again, arguably stemming from Clark's cheeky humour, Fuller is shot via profile in the foreground, while his colleague (known only in the credits as the Laughing Detective, but played with great humour by actor John Rutter), who is already in on the joke, beautifully plays the impending comical chaos, bouncing off Fuller's bewildered expressions to further enhance the scene.

Fuller and the 'laughing detective' have a good laugh about Barb's fellatio joke

His laughter echoes throughout as Fuller himself becomes more and more aware of the perverse gag and confronts the innocently uninformed Nash ("It's summat dirty ain't it?!"). It is actually one of these author's favourite parts of the film, because of how the scene is played and how it allows Clark to flesh out the opposing nature of these characters in such a short amount of time, showing them briefly outside the roles they are employed to deliver, to serve and protect and humanise them more, and in a film covered by an overwhelming sense of evil, it is welcoming but never outstays or feels unwarranted within the film's narrative.

Over the years since the film came out, Saxon has enjoyed participating in a number of fan events and conventions that have celebrated the film and never waned from discussing the movie and his role in it, remembering the experience very affectionately as well as how it has continued with audiences. Reflecting on the film in 2006, he commented on how he appreciated the film, even more, every time he watched it. "You know you have an interesting idea, but sometimes you don't realise how interesting it is until much later in life. I just finished watching *Black Christmas*, a film I was in 27 years ago and I'm not speaking from my own participation, [but] I liked what I saw of myself".

"But the film itself made more than an impression on me. It created feelings in me that I wasn't probably capable of having at the time I made the film. A sense of participation and I think this is something that happens with age and maturity, you understand greater depth about things. Each and every development in the film and each and every character in the film, particularly (Olivia) Hussey, her sensitivity, her pain and conflicts, and so on, I identified and felt a great deal for her. And the whole development of the situation, the plot and the way it was treated. I wound up having an experience that, well it triggered an experience in me that was horror or anguish that I think is involved. It is the emotion that I think is the undercurrent of horror films".

Speaking about Clark's directing and storytelling further, Saxon was impressed by Clark who he refers to as being part of a small sample of directors at the time, including Wes Craven whom he also worked with on *Elm Street*, who he regarded as a true "craftsman who was very careful, and they worked very hard. [Bob] was very particular, and he had everything quite worked out and it was a mosaic that he had planned. When I read the script, I immediately sensed the whole dynamic of the story, how good it was, woven together. And that there were lots of switches and unexpected turns". *Black Christmas* was the only film Saxon worked on with Bob Clark, but the two continued to appear together in numerous film screening Q & As that were held, while Saxon himself continually praised the film with his own unique enthusiasm which continued up until his sad death brought on by pneumonia on July 25, 2020, in Tennessee. He was 83 years old at the time.

Mr Harrison (played by James Edmond)

Just when we think Billy's rampage cannot get any crueller, we are introduced to Clare's helpless and innocent father, Mr Harrison, a frail man who has come to pick his daughter up for the holidays, and who is initially greeted by a snowball accidentally hitting him in the face. While responding to this with some sarcastic assertiveness, Clark straight away places the character visually and narratively in a position that continues throughout; seemingly lost and out of his depth.

James Edmond was born on 7th February 1924 in Walkerton, Ontario, Canada. And while most recognise him as the prude, pompous, but by no-means unsympathetic Mr Harrison in *Black Christmas*, his filmography warrants mentioning, as he worked on other numerous projects including *Alfred Hitchcock Presents* playing Philip Chase in the 1987 episode *The Impatient Patient*, while appearing in a host of TV movies such as 1985's *The Hijacking of Studio 4*, while his acting career went back further to the likes of 1954's film *Devil Girl From Mars*. He was also married to Shirley Faessler.

Mr Harrison's character initially seems to be a secondary plot ploy played out to allow Mrs Mac's visual gags and coarse personality to play off, but while Clark does position him this way in the first act, a man who is "very disappointed in this atmosphere", when observing his daughter's bedroom, this demeanour becomes more fragile and eventually heartbroken with grief when events unfold by the finale.

As mentioned earlier in this chapter, there is a slight impression given that Clare felt restrained at home by her more conservative parent(s), whose idea of academia is to merely focus, fit in with head down to study. Whereas Clare's introduction to this Sorority house evidently had begun to allow her the opportunity to explore herself, take more risks, have more fun even, yet all the while still doing well in her studies (which seems to be the origin of the contention between her and the very much more laid back Barbara), the former aspects alarming Mr Harrison who remarks; "I intend to do something about it".

Mr Harrison speaking on the phone as Barb continues her mischievous ways in the background

However, while not a main player, Mr Harrison is a constant throughout the story, often being allowed to reiterate his growing concerns for his daughter as well as his impending collapse. He is there when Barbara and Phyllis first report Clare's disappearance to the police (under the foolhardy Nash), not only expressing a seemingly now more sympathetic observation of Barbara's excessive drinking problems while she is still trying to help him but also employing his sarcastic assertiveness again, only this time in solidarity with the girls at the Polices' inept response to their concerns. As Nash tries to debunk his fears, he merely responds with "thanks, that's not much conciliation".

Again Clark's attention to his characters and their story arcs allow for how they eventually end up being more believable than merely occurring more for shocks or drama, and as Mr Harrison sits listening to Barbara in her drunken state later in the film, there is a hint in his face of interest, not out of snobbery now, but now of some empathy. This is only broken when Barbara tactlessly remarks that "if she's dead you'll blame me", and the realisation of those words take hold of him. It is a definite turning point for his character, but not one that will also end well, as events further pile around him, with Clark giving him specific attention at certain moments of horror.

An example is the proceeding scenes where the young girl's body is found in the park; Clark first gives the scene to bystanders and the mother, her screams echoing throughout the scene, yet Clark juxtapositions Mr Harrison into the foreground while the young girl's mother screams continue. Again, while not the main character, Clark gives particular attention to Mr Harrison, positioning him and not forgetting his emotional attachment to the events, so while we are not given the chance to see the poor girl's remains, Mr Harrison does, and this parallel with losing a daughter, and his ever-increasing concerns thus runs a lot more powerful, so that when he does eventually collapse in the final scenes from shock, it never feels too dramatic or out of place.

Instead, because Clark has given Edmond the time to let his character breathe beautifully amongst the nightmare, becoming ever closer to home, it becomes a much more emotional moment in the finale. Mr Harrison allows Clark to demonstrate the tragic and emotional consequences of the slasher film on the human psyche we very rarely see, through Edmond's increasingly haunted performance.

After seemingly retiring from acting in 1988 with the TV movie, *Breaking All The Rules*, being his last role, Edmond sadly passed away on November 4th 2000, in Paris.

Peter (played by Keir Dullea)

Keir Dullea was born May 30, 1936, in Cleveland, Ohio, USA, and is arguably most known as the infamous David Bowman in Kubrick's *2001: A Space Odyssey*, but his career has spanned a multitude of decades and has seen him play a huge range of roles including spots in *Murder She Wrote*, *Law and Order*, while also coming back to the role of Bowman in *2010: A Second Odyssey*.

Keir Dullea in *2001: A Space Odyssey*

He is still going strong too, appearing recently alongside Josh Hartnett and John Malkovich in the 2019 film, *Valley of the Gods*.

Speaking in 2016 with Filmizon at Trekonderoga, Keir describes the filming of *Black Christmas* as "a pleasant experience, if not a high point in my life", but nevertheless, his role as Peter provides the film with a thrilling and unnerving decoy that Clark purposefully torments so that we are never quite sure if Billy could just actually be Peter instead. Clark enjoys himself too much throughout the film by laying down just enough clues and deceptive filmmaking techniques throughout the narrative to create a sense of unease from the audience towards the character, to create that slightly nagging feeling of further doubt in their minds.

An example is when Jess speaks with Peter on the phone, which takes place after the audience and the characters in the house have already been subjected to the first of Billy's calls. So, when Peter then calls for Jess later, as Clark explains; "I could have cut as you often do, to Keir Dullea at his location speaking. It wasn't necessary, but I wanted to purposefully do that, to have his disembodied voice too. A very subtle idea…but [it] might plant the idea that Keir is the killer here".

However, Clark has mentioned on numerous occasions that while he incorporates a lot of doubt on Peter's character, "there are so many clues that he could not be…Keir could not be the killer if you look carefully", he muses. Speaking on the DVD commentary track, Clark remarks further on Keir's acting, acknowledging that "he brought with it a certain madness, [so] it becomes more and more possible [he] is [the killer]. But we never cheated on the film, you can watch it very carefully and clearly know from the audience point of view, if you really hear and watch that it can't be Keir".

Additionally, his role helps the film become quite a political tour-de-force as Peter continually argues with Jess about her wanting to abort their child. This was quite a revolutionary subject to discuss and make light of in 1970s cinema, especially a horror film. However, while this plot device may seem like some sort of exploitative cheap narrative ploy, Clark never allows this to happen, instead, giving the discussion the time and space within the film to be played out with growing maturity, despite Peter's way of handling it afterwards which ultimately leads to his downfall in the finale.

What is interesting to note is that Peter never really interacts with the other members of the cast, and visually becomes more and more isolated in the frame and scenes as the film progresses, perhaps allowing Clark to signify his decline in mental well-being. Certainly, we hear him later on again with Jess on the phone, crying (another example of Clark not cutting to him to further inject that doubt), while also being alone when he smashes up his precious musical equipment and piano. Such scenes you may feel are never needed or should end up on the cutting room floor, but they are integral to not only Peter's characterisation, but also help set up the finale.

As the film progresses and Jess continues to deny Peter their child, he becomes increasingly violent in his threats. "You selfish bitch! What are you trying to do to me?", this demonstrates the character at his worst, helping raise his demanding persona as if Jess' body is for him to obey and command. When she refuses to marry him further, she reignites Clark's earlier desire to allow these girls to show more leadership and maturity than their male counterparts within the film. It additionally aligns Peter more and more with the mannerisms and anti-female stance that Billy has been demonstrating, their language almost intertwining with one another as both become increasingly desperate when discussing babies, much to Jess' horror.

Accompanied by Clark framing of Peter's thin frame, which also is not that dissimilar to the glimpses of Billy's body we see as well as his skulking in the shadows (watch Peter's shadow come down the stairs immediately after Jess gets another phone call from Billy), and you'd be hard done by to not think it was our favourite Christmas killer coming for her.

Peter outside the basement as he tries to reach Jess

All this time spent on making Peter the decoy, while knowingly saying it simply cannot be him though, allows the audience to continually feed doubt into their viewing of the film. This helps set up the finale, in which Jess kills Peter as an act of self-defence, at this point completely convinced it was him all along (Clark deliberately framing Peter's similar shadowy frame that we've seen Billy exhibit beforehand in the film).

Keir's performance, which is always quite mild-mannered from the beginning, but which becomes increasingly more disillusioned and threatening as the film goes along, helps Clark to not only give Billy an out but also allows the political analogies in the film to become more realised too. As Kelcie Mattson in her blog, Women in Horror Films concludes, Peter becomes "an instantly recognizable and despicably truthful representation of white male privilege".

Phyllis (played by Andrea Martin)

Andrea Martin has a notable connection to the *Black Christmas* universe, originally starring in the 1974 classic, before returning for the 2006 remake playing what is essentially a role that brings her full circle, as the now ordained Barbara 'Ms. Mac' MacHenry, in a loving nod to Marion Waldman. However, her role in the original as Phyl, loyal friend to Jess, and referee extraordinaire in trying to keep Barbara alcohol free, while still sometimes enjoying the cheekiness of those outbursts at times, places her character in a wonderful position. Her assertive nature is matched only by her concern for her fellow sisters, and she is often the one who senses all may not be well in their surroundings, questioning everything and with good reason.

Andrea Martin's career has seen her develop a vast filmography of work, her voice talents being associated with the likes of the legendary *Batman: The Animated Series*, *Sesame Street* and the marvellous *Earthworm Jim* as Queen Slug-For-A-Butt. Whilst her physical presence has graced other celebrated projects such as the *My Big Fat Greek Wedding* films and having guest turns in shows such as *Will & Grace*, *Star Trek: Deep Space Nine* and *Modern Family*. She is still going strong today, having been cast in the recent series, *Elena of Avalor* as Queen Abigail.

Phyl having a good laugh at the sorority Christmas party

Martin's appearance as Phyl though suggests a timid woman who is equally level-headed and like the aforementioned Clare, still able to indulge her books and study long into the night. It is quite apt that Martin should take over Waldman's role in the 2006 remake, as Phyl here essentially almost shadows Mrs Mac, by being the one trying to help life run in the house a lot smoother, which isn't always an easy job when your house mother is a not so subtle alcoholic, and your fellow sisters all come with varying competing personas. However, Clark never allows Phyl to just be pigeon-holed into a one-dimensional caricature, instead of allowing Martin the chance to explore a range of emotions and characterisation throughout.

An example is when Phyl and Jess are startled by the volunteers from the search party at the back of the house, resulting in the two girls having a much welcome momentary giggle between the nightmarish events going on around them. It allows Phyl (and Jess), a temporary release from her concerns and worries about her friends, and is a welcome one, compared to her more assertive tone when dealing with Barbara earlier in the film as she lashes out at her sister, essentially forcing her sister to realise she has had a few too many drinks and that she is embarrassing herself in front of Mrs Mac and Mr Harrison. The former scene of Phyl giggling is all the more tender when a few moments later she is savagely killed off-screen.

Some writers have made a point of the strong independent women *Black Christmas* proudly displays, and often signal Jess as a major part of their subjective analysis. However, Phyl arguably also can be given equivalent focus in this area, perhaps even more so than Jess. While Kelcie Mattson commends *Black Christmas* as remaining "a smart, restrained film that centres the desires of women and approaches its topics with frankness", she additionally honours its abilities to show its central girls as "active and confident…discussing reproductive rights with impressive practicality. There's no shaming, punishment, or piss-poor redemptive arcs for 'bad/dumb' girls who like sex; their deaths are inexplicably tied to their womanhood, but it springs from the Moaner's disgust for women in general rather than a moral condemnation".

One would argue then that this emphasis could be placed on the shoulders of Phyl more than the other girls, with her initial doubts ignored continually by the authorities, which in turn harbours her growing suspicion of Peter. While being sensitive to Mr Harrison's concerns, and her own frustrations with Barbara as well as the growing threat she suspects, cements her as a more pivotal focus within the confines of Clark's world he is crafting. Let down by ignorant males, misogyny and threatening male calls, she uses her womanhood life skills to try and keep one step ahead of the problems despite their ineffectiveness by the film's end.

Martin leads all these juxtapositions with relative ease and it is a testament to her talents, which she can showcase a wide variety of depth and emotion strong enough to instil within the outwardly looking bookworm persona that Phyl depicts. It is all the more chilling then, that Phyl is one of the deaths we do not see occur on screen. For that reason we feel it a lot more as an audience since Clark has allowed us time with her, to get to know her, understand her frustrations when she goes to the Police station to report Clare missing, her genuine support for Mr Harrison, her challenging of Barbara's behaviour, her questioning of Peter's motives and Jess' abortion dilemma, for which she is sympathetic too (and loyal to her friend's wishes).

All of these varying displays of character then hit hard when, with her face frozen in fear, she is quickly cornered in Barbara's room and confronted by Billy, who quickly slays her with ease behind a closed door, a madman she has ironically done her best to keep the other sisters safe from by being the voice of reason in the background.

Barbara (played by Margot Kidder)

As with his other characters in the film, Clark encourages us to look beyond what he is showing and listen also to what is being said. Barbara is really a great advocate of this technique he employs, because what you do hear in the initial first act from her, despite its somewhat brash tone, actually hides quite a heart-breaking backstory that on re-watching the film adds many more layers to her character. As well as this, it justifies her behaviour to those around her as well as when she is attempting to reflect on her own inner demons and loneliness.

Barb on the phone to her mother

Whilst we hear the big gathering and chatter within the house, Barb is ushered away to the phone to take a call from her mother. Evidently, her family are well off, but taking another moment to read between the lines, she is effectively being abandoned by her family at the one time of the year she should be celebrating with them. Being actively welcomed home after a time away in education to catch up, open presents, eat merrily and enjoy some time to relax in less academic surroundings. Instead, we hear the following;

BARB

Oh, come on. You've got to be kidding! Why couldn't I come with you? Well, who the hell is he? Oh, Christ Mother! You're a real gold-plated whore, you know that… Rude? I was trying to be a bit more than rude Mother.

As an audience member picks up on this brief exchange, it suddenly changes our initial perceptions of Barbara, from loser delinquency, to actually someone a lot more fragile, whose only good escape is the continual booze she surrounds and engulfs herself with. Clark and Moore's script provides just enough hints here to make evident a broken home that panders to wealth and gluttony rather than close family ties. It's even more idyllic than that while her sisters can be assertive with her, to remind her she is being cruel or out of tone, that they all equally still show great care and affection to Barbara; a young woman who in reality, really is quite desperate inside, shunned by her mother who favours the company of her new beau, leaving her daughter wanted nothing more than to feel loved.

It is quite something then, that Clark places the character more towards the supplementary fun and frolics side of the narrative in the first half, a woman who swears around children seeing Santa, all the while with a glass in her hand, and who berates Clare for her more vested leaning stance, one we suspect Barbara would want nothing more to be like as well. However, the continual rejections from home (as well as maybe from other men) have forced her down another, less academic path, one down a bottle or five. As Kidder recalls, "I remember I was attracted to her because she was wild and out of control and not the conventional leading lady which was always the boring part. If I got stuck with that part, it was always really dull".

"I do know that my character was already written as quite wild and outrageous because that's why I took the part, that's why I thought it was fun" recollects Kidder.

Margot Kidder headshot

Margot Kidder was born on 17th October 1948 in the Northwest Territories, Canada, and is known famously for her role as Lois Lane in the Christopher Reeve *Superman* films. However, she was no stranger to horror films having also appeared subsequently in the original *Amityville Horror*, while continuing to work throughout the rest of her career on film and TV appearing via notable guest spots in *Tales From The Crypt*, *Murder, She Wrote*, *Earth Final Conflict*, and *Law & Order: Special Victims Unit*, while also returning to her beloved *Superman* roots in *Smallville*.

Additionally, she had also made a name for herself north of the US border on the Canadian film scene. "I didn't even get that I wanted to be an actress at that [early] point although I did love acting, so on a personal level it was a matter of what was the best part, and what happened was that I got to, for some reason, do slightly more eccentric characters in Canadian movies than I did in American ones, so I accepted a lot of work in Canada. I think that's because the commercial considerations were not as great as they were in LA" she muses.

Barb's most infamous scene is her exchange with Nash. "Where I spell fellatio?" she recollects. "I remember that we were all laughing hysterically when we filmed it, thinking we were being outrageous". Unsurprisingly it was a testament to Kidder's acting skills that Barb's comically drunken image means some people today think she could have been actually drunk on set for real to do the scene. "Was I drinking beer? No, I don't think so. I think even in those days we knew that you didn't get drunk on the set". She goes on to say how the scene, "that was all written by Bob, [needed him] having to shut me up, to reign me in, to have me stop improvising. That has also not changed in my life" she laughs.

Kidder remembers the boldness of the particular Fellatio joke, attributing it more to Bob's wicked sense of humour and how it probably wouldn't get past censors in more modern times; "People were much less uptight in those days than they are now, but it was the late 60s, early 70s. We were saying and doing anything. I think these days you'd have all the damn Christian's down your throat you know. You couldn't do that scene that these days, [there are] organizations that would have you banned from being on the air, much as they'd ban *Saving Private Ryan* for using obscene language, we couldn't get away with it".

Barbara's drunken antics do become more of a heavier emotional burden it seems later though, as the self-inflicted realisation she comes to about how people will blame her for Clare going missing bring about a less than enthusiastic audience she once held earlier, making her sisters laugh in the most awkward of situations for fun. Now that awkwardness allows Kidder to return to the lonely woman we saw briefly at the beginning, bruised and scorned by her own mother, and instantly going for the drink. Again, the themes of solidarity in sisterhood and womanhood come full force as Phyl demands she go to bed, but in a way that Barb realises the error of her ways and that her sister is just being cruel to be kind.

Barb realises the error of her ways

It is all the more tragic that Barbara has one of the more violent and visually disturbing death scenes as Billy stands over her repeatedly stabbing her with a unicorn while Jess stands at the door downstairs listening to a group of children singing Christmas Carols. Despite this horrific death, Clark does allow us one more time to sympathise with Barbara and remember that she has been abandoned when she has an Asthma attack and Jess goes to calm her down. To reassure her that the nightmare she was having (or was she, was Billy playing games with her in the room before Jess entered?), was just fake and that she is safe and looked after. A surrogate set of mothers she has in Jess, Mrs Mac, Phyl and the other girls it seems.

Despite the bloody, eerie undertones of the story, Kidder remembers, however, the fun she had making the film citing co-star Martin as the funniest who made her laugh endlessly. Despite "a lot of shrieking, a lot of changing the script on the spot, and who could be the most outrageous", everyone was still so professional and always committed to making the best film they could. Even her death scene she remembers with a smile; "Yeah, stabbed to death by a glass unicorn! I had never figured out when we were shooting it quite what was happening. You know, the ending of these horror movies can always be a little confusing and I had no idea till I saw the movie what had happened. One of them was a scene in which I was wrapped and stuff and blood and all that! And we were laughing so hard when we were shooting it".

Despite the popularity of Kidder's performance and Barb in general, it is perhaps saddening that out of all the women in the house, she is actually the most vulnerable one, one who presents a strong front and glint in her eye, when inside there is a continual emotional turmoil and confusion (sadly a parallel within her own life, as she battled manic depression), which makes her lumber almost from one scene to the next, attached to her other sisters in hope for the next rise she can give them in laughs, in the one way and style she can, alongside her trusty drinks.

Kidder does a wonderful job keeping Barb a very grounded and tragic character, and who like most of us, can keep some of our problems well hidden, allowing them a slim chance sometimes to be witnessed in an attempt to gain the help we need. Despite the girls in the house evidently acknowledging her emotional trauma, and not being able to care for her in a medical sense, they nevertheless do what they can to make sure she is safe and loved. Kidder remained passionate about her involvement in *Black Christmas* and defended it always, even up until her sad passing on May 13th, 2018 in her sleep. Tragically, and even more upsetting, her death was recorded by the coroner as "a result of a self-inflicted drug and alcohol overdose".

Jess (played by Olivia Hussey)

Before we delve into the final girl that is Jess, brought to life with a great vulnerability, but equally with fierce independence by Olivia Hussey, it is important to note the uneasy social and political events that were in the air in both the States and Canada at the time. A year before the film came out, in 1973, there had been a major case in the Supreme Court, Roe v. Wade (410 U.S. 113), which essentially ruled that a woman could choose to have an abortion without the interference of excessive restrictions from the government. This had been a revolutionary piece of legislation that triggered a huge response from both sides, especially as abortion had been outlawed by the early 1900s.

This momentous verdict meant that even by 1974, it was still a decision to some they would fight against, while others welcomed the ruling. Therefore, tensions were rife, with Pro-Christian Church and Planned Family/Parenthood groups being very vocal in their opposition to the ruling while other groups campaigning for the outcome were equally as vocal in their win. It is not only bold but also a landmark in itself, that both Moore and Clark factor in the subplot between Jess and Peter who fight and argue over her plans to terminate their child. Considering the climate the film was coming out in, and that this subplot inadvertently plays into the finale and the outcome of the investigation seemingly, the fact *Black Christmas* gave the subject so much attention was a milestone, although Hussey herself doesn't give the themes too much credence; "it was just a subplot wasn't it, it wasn't that big of a deal. I mean it certainly explained my weight. I was eating these Chinese pancakes with Bob every night after shooting and my waist was expanding!"

Jess takes a disturbing phone call from Billy

Additionally, this sub-narrative also helps us understand as well as demonstrate Jess as a strong woman, capable of making sound judgements, that put her at odds with the more male-dominant masochism displayed by the increasingly unhinged proxy prime suspect, Peter. Jess' popularity as well as status as the early prototype final girl is still discussed and celebrated even today in many editorials online. As recently as December 2019, Bloody Disgusting wrote how she is "a complicated heroine [who] left an enduring imprint on the genre, one that played a significant influence on the slasher subgenre in particular and still offers up valuable lessons in storytelling and characterization 45 years later". Indeed, Jess is the blueprint for Laurie Strode who arrived only four years later and through the more commercial success *Halloween* received, the latter became the final girl template which in turn inspired countless other slasher films to follow.

However, while this may be the case, it is ignorant to dismiss the appeal and character of Jess Bradford, who is equally as tough a fighter as Laurie, hitting Billy with a good door slam after trying to discover her friends to save them. Her bravery is also more apparent with the background soundscape ever enforcing the demented screaming and frightening aggression of Billy who is in pursuit. Speaking in 2007, Hussey recollects how "I'd never done a scary film and Bob approached me and I just loved the whole idea of getting away from home, leaving the baby for a month, going there and doing something I'd never done before and being the heroine of this very frightening plot". From reading the script alone she thought it was fantastic; "I said oh my god, this is so frightening and then you know, Bob wanted to do two alternative endings and we didn't know if I was going to be killed or not so I think he left it open at the end. But in one of the versions, they were going to kill me and then he said it's better that we just leave her in the house with the phone ringing".

Hussey is quick to dismiss the age-old complaint about the victims in horror films doing all the wrong things and not getting out the house immediately, away from danger, citing a number of the cleverly embedded subplots for helping validate Jess' actions; "through Jess's mind, she was thinking maybe it was her boyfriend that was harassing her and I'm sure in her head she was thinking to leave me alone and then she got these horrible things [happening]. I thought who could that be? I mean if you start getting threatening calls, you don't just pack a bag and leave, you deal with it. I mean women are stalked every day aren't they, so it was a form of stalking [but] this man stalked the sorority house, instead of just one person".

Jess' unassuming nature means that for a majority of the film, while unnerved by the calls at the beginning, she does begin to suspect more and more that Peter is the culprit, but after he is dismissed from her mind, she begins to suspect something is definitely amiss. However, with the calls seemingly not revealed to be coming from within the house until the finale, the sanctuary of the sorority house brings her some assured sense of safety.

Rejecting the horror genre critics, Hussey does protect her role and the character of Jess very much it seems, as she comments further that "when you're watching a horror film, you always want to say, don't go in there, don't go in there, don't be stupid, but if they don't, there's no movie, so you have to really be the one, the actor that goes in that door so everybody can turn around and say don't go in that door you fool, don't you know what's waiting for you know? You just have to do it and it's part of what makes the audience feel like they're involved and gets the hair rising up on their arms".

However, in reality she amusingly notes that "I'd get out of there, if that really happened to me, I'd be out of that house so fast you wouldn't be able to say, Olivia!

I'd be gone! I mean they stay; all these murders and things, disappearances and these girls stay there! I'd be gone, long gone!"

Olivia Hussey was born on 17th April 1951 in England. After appearing on stage in London in the early part of her career, she was eventually successful in securing the role of Juliet in Franco Zeffirelli's 1968 *Romeo and Juliet* gaining awards and international recognition thereafter. After appearing in *Black Christmas*, she returned to work with Zeffirelli in the hugely ambitious event television series, *Jesus of Nazareth* in 1977, while also appearing in other films globally. She also never forgot her horror roots when she appeared in the 1990 adaptation of Stephen King's *IT*, and also took on one of the most infamous characters in horror cinema history, that of Mrs Norma Bates (aka Mother), in the prequel/sequel *Psycho IV: The Beginning* where she worked alongside the seminal and late Anthony Perkins.

Olivia Hussey in *Romeo and Juliet*

She has also been a prolific voice actor lending her skills to many of the *Star Wars* video games including *Star Wars: Force Commander*, *Star Wars: The Old Republic* and *Star Wars: Rogue Squadron*.

Jess hides in the basement from Billy and Peter

Despite her long and distinguished career, she finds her title as a Scream Queen a lovable one which she accepts wholeheartedly; "why not?" She cheekily muses when asked how she feels about such an honorary title. However, she has noted how "I didn't get to scream much in it did I? I just looked terrified, it was the phone calls! It's really hard because you're doing four different phone calls in a day and you've got to make the different expressions and you can just be the same, the repetition, not her again going 'huuuhh, huuuhh', you know, so you've got to make it vary a little bit". But nevertheless, her scream queen title she has happily accepted.

Jess is a progressive and radical character, one who did not merely accept herself as a part of her boyfriend's life, the conservative family ideology so to speak. But someone who had her own dreams and ambitions and wasn't afraid to pursue them. Even by today's standards, the character can still be seen as a strong independent voice in female progression. She is steadfast in her decisions that fly in the face of those that Peter is demanding of her and not once does she falter or regret her actions, while she is also sympathetic to his feelings as well in the process. Clark does this no more so in the scene in the University, where Jess is positioned to the foreground of the frame, her face determined yet hurting for Peter, who is not asking, but downright demanding again what he wants to do. However, with Jess, the prominent person in the frame (therefore with the power balance in her favour),

Peter's threats make a pathetic little impact as he is visually smaller in the frame. This does not make Jess unsympathetic to an audience at all, as one could initially colour her as cold and unfeeling (or a "selfish bitch" as Peter so gracefully remarks about her). She has a genuine concern for not just Peter, but all those in the house, her sisters, their wellbeing, their faults and their attitudes, altogether allowing her to keep peace within the four walls along with Phyl, who seems to co-inhabit the mother role with her that is usually accommodated by the rarely sober Mrs Mac.

You care about these characters, and Jess' plight is one given considerable attention, especially the more the film runs along. At various points, she becomes more and more alarmed by the telephone calls, especially when the voice says exactly the same as she did earlier in her fight with Peter. Despite her intelligence here, her loyalty kicks in and she stays to look after the comatose Barbara, all the while with her wit about her.

This allows Clark to paint her as a deeply loyal member of the sisters within the house, sympathetic to Barb's increasingly volatile behaviour in some cases, while also helping her later in the film when she suffers from her asthma attack. Such compassion and devotion to her friend, as well as concern, have helped endear Jess to fans over the decades and are some of the main reasons why she is still remembered so fondly within horror fan circles and audiences in the genre.

Jess consoles Barb after her nightmare

Additionally, Hussey gives a credible and unpredictable performance, using her talents as an actress to show Jess feeling the weight and guilt of her decisions and actions with the planned abortion and how they intertwine with the plot as it goes along. By allowing Jess to show her sister's flaws and that they themselves have their own personal demons, makes her friend's deaths all the more traumatic and potent when they do happen, even off-screen.

When the evitable occurs and Sgt. Nash reveals the infamous line that the calls are coming from inside the house, Hussey's face expresses a genuine horror of the danger closing in around her all the more. While the threat of Billy has been continually there (even visually in some clever cases), he has until now, been at a distance, merely prowling. However, now he is closing in, and yet Jess still doesn't leave the house, instead of looking for her friends, her concern echoing through the now silent and dimly lit house. Ultimately, as she is unable to save her friends, her determination to stay alive storms through as she rams the door back into Billy, and heads for safety. And while not stopping the real killer, and attacking Peter in his stead, Jess' wellbeing is still of paramount concern for the audience.

Final girls are human, flawed but human. They all deal with some kind of trauma in their lives, sometimes even before the story we see, but the fact that these events allow them to ultimately triumph in some way, even just by surviving or helping others to survive too, means we accept them even more. While the evil is secretly gliding in and out of the shadows of the house, forever watching, Clark gives Jess space to make an impression. Even in the finale, when those shadows are closing in, trapping here more than ever.

As Bloody Disgusting argued in 2019; "Jess set a precedent; her complicated relationship status and decision to terminate an unwanted pregnancy played a direct role in the film's final act. It also made her feel like a human being, rather than merely a character. Not least of all because she made one final, fatal error in the film's conclusion". While not given as much commercial limelight as Laurie Strode, Jess is still a vitally important character in the horror genre.

Billy (played by Albert Dunk, Bob Clark, Nick Mancuso)

One of the very first things you notice about Billy is just how protective Bob Clark is of him, which is slightly ironic when the character is pretty much a shadow. For a murderous killer that Clark very rarely lets us see, it is a testament to his directing skills and Moore's script that we are still talking (and obsessing) over the mysteries surrounding him nearly 50 years later. While he was initially imagined by Moore's script, it was Clark who arguably nurtured the character more into the one we all shiver to think about today. It's all the more testament to the cast and crew that Billy is made up from an assortment of people in reality, yet they all gel together to create one consistent and demented persona that we know simply as Billy. As Clark commented back in 2003, Billy "is quite entertaining and fascinating", noting how "we worked very long and hard to create the sound, the personality of this killer. It's made up of 4-5 voices, all quite mad".

The man billed as the primary voice of Billy is Nick Mancuso (as The Prowler/ Phone Voice), who was born on May 29, 1948, in Mammola, Calabria, Italy. Still working today, Mancuso fondly remembers recording the voice of our favourite festive killer still now, but is quick to note how he wasn't the only one dubbing Billy in post-production; "I was only one of the voices of Billy, there were three voices. One was Bob Clark, who did some of the screaming and another was an actress, I can't recall her name, perhaps Mugsey Sweeney. I had actually worked with this actress when I was a stage actor. We worked on a play written by Des McAnuff, who ended up directing *Jersey Boys* on Broadway".

While not seen for years and even realising the film had become a cult classic, Mancuso remembers the rather interesting way he developed the voice of Billy, musing that "I'm not sure how Bob mixed it all together, but I did most of the voice work. Most of it was done with me standing on my head in order to compress the thorax and give it that 'It's me Billy', kind of rasp. What Bob had made me do was sit in a chair for the audition and he said to just improvise some sounds and so I just started improvising and he said yes you got the part". In addition to Billy, Mancuso also "ended up dubbing Keir Dullea, as there were two lines that needed dubbing. Bob Clark asked if I could dub Keir for two lines, as this would save flying him back over from England".

However, while still a complete mystery nearly 50 years later, Moore did, however, give Clark lots of information to playoff though throughout the script, describing Billy with some explicit writing that makes evident his unholy actions and persona which transfer well to screen and which are complemented later in post-production by the aforementioned Mancuso as well as others. Firstly, there is the description of the voice of Billy himself, whom Moore refers to in the script as THE CALLER on numerous occasions throughout;

Suddenly the voice changes from that of a woman's to something that sounds almost sub-human. It wails.

Later in the script, he describes more variations with detailed modes of address such as;

CALLER

(talking quietly as a child)
Don't you tell, Agnes. You'll be sorry. Please don't tell. Please Agnes. I won't do it again. There now Agnes. It's okay. It won't hurt. That's a nice Agnes. Pretty Agnes go to sleep. Go to sleep.

Then with more hostility in tone and address denoted by the CAPS in the screen-play;

CALLER

NASTY BILLY!

Clark comments on the intensity of these phone calls, describing them as "very violent", but while that may be the case, they almost seem to put the girls "under the spell of this madman". He comments further on how they took what Moore had written in the script and then worked to create a more detailed persona for the killer; "we literary wrote a progressive story for the killer, telling the story of Billy, and clearly Billy had done something to his baby sister, or there was a thought that he had. Whatever it was, the madness that he carried, we were trying in a subtle way to create humanity even for this nameless, senseless killer".

One of the more descriptive moments which we can compare here is the scene where Billy momentarily loses his inhibitions more so than before and begins smashing up the attic. In the script Moore writes;

There is the sound of heavy breathing which becomes louder and heavier until it is almost deafening. The subjective camera growls and shrieks and then rages through the attic violently.

Mrs Mac's hanging body is smashed aside and swings in a broad arc. The camera feels and sounds like a ferocious trapped animal.

It slams up against a wall and turns careening through the attic again with an agonized wail, knocking over a chair and breaking the rocking horse with almost superhuman strength. It crashes viciously in a corner with the sound of breaking glass and gags and hisses and growls. It shakes about on the floor and whimpers until the sounds become more human, like a man crying.

Clark discusses this scene and the persona of Billy in length during the DVD Commentary, noting how he was troubled whether visualising and showing his rage would "weaken the character in a way" He goes on to reflect that; "I felt strongly that this man suffers and he's maybe mad, he may be even cunning. He's the killer, but clearly the thing about Billy and his acting out, if we didn't have that going on, he wouldn't be doing those phone calls, acting that out and trying to experiment in some ways. So, I felt that pain should be shown [and] when we shot it, they agreed".

It is quite interesting too that Moore uses a variety of strikingly dramatic words such as "hissing", "growls" and a "ferocious trapped animal" to describe Billy in that same moment. What may be a coincidence on his part, allows his writing and characterisation to have parallels with Clinical Lycanthropy, which often can see an individual exhibiting behaviour that resembles animal characteristics such as howling, crawling and even growling, even more, noteworthy then that Moore describes the sounds as reverting back to 'more human' at the end of this outburst.

This can be brought on by extreme psychosis which also has links to halluci-nations and other mental health conditions such as Schizophrenia and Bipolar Disorder. Certainly, with how Billy is written and visualised, one does wonder what he is potentially seeing in his own mind. Is he hallucinating? Is he reliving a traumatic moment from his youth when he "killed the baby!"? Are the calls and the excessive conversing to the ever-increasing dead bodies' manifestations in his mind of Agnes, or even 'Mommy'?

This makes more sense when a viewer realises that he seems to address these unseen people when he kills his victims, addressing them not as Barb, Mrs Mac, Clare or Phyl, but as Agnes etc. - communicating (or hallucinating), with them from a bygone time, even trying to defend his twisted actions? Despite never under-standing him fully, these characteristics have made Billy survive over the years as "our favourite, foul-mouthed lunatic", chuckles Clark, who makes assumptions that Billy may even think of himself as a guardian to Agnes' legacy, maybe har-bouring some perversely twisted guilt over his actions with her. "If Billy harmed his sister accidentally, taking out Mrs Mac and horrible girls who misbehave and swear at him", could seem justifiable muses, Clark.

As a physical presence, Moore and Clark wisely keep Billy as an unseen menace mostly throughout and wisely so. This allows all the information given to us via his actions and vocals, to allow Clark to mystify the elusive killer even more visually, bringing even more unease to the proceedings and to his apparent declining state of mind. An example is a scene where Barb is brutally murdered in her bed, Moore writes Billy (we must note that Moore refers to him in the script as the CALLER) as "a shadow [who] crosses Barb's face", all the while employing a child's voice (one that cleverly juxtapositions against the children singing carols at the front door to Jess in that same moment). Moore continues that "we get our first glimpse of the caller. His eyes…only his eyes", which are seen through only "a break of light reflecting from the glass animal", that falls upon them, which he notes are "horri-ble", and which are additionally "fierce and animal-like" in the moment.

Even when he is not explicitly on-screen Clark provides a few moments where keen-eyed viewers can see Billy's shadow or silhouette in the background of shots, obscured or deflected by characters in the foreground. While chilling in itself as a visual, it also increases the dangerous nature of him when he is clearly listening to conversations in those moments. As Clark elaborates, "he repeated the line about the wart, that Keir had said something similar earlier. But my explanation for that is if you go back to the scene where he's arguing with [Jess] by the Christmas tree, you'll see a shadow back in the corner; the killer is there, listening to that scene. A lot of people really gave us high kudos for that – 'damn, you're right, it couldn't have been Peter, he's in the house, why wouldn't he come down to listen to them?'". This adds a layer of extra horror to the film, as you suddenly realise Billy has not been confined to just the first floor but has been all around the house it seems, hiding in the shadows, observing his prey.

After concentrating so much in the first act on the phone calls and POV shots, Moore and Clark take a great time progressively intertwining this voice and behaviour with some limited visible attributes of Billy being revealed, which help advance more and more just how terrifying this unseen persona really is. This is until, by the end of the film, we understand we are truly seeing evil incarnate in human form. In the finale, for instance, where Jess ultimately discovers the bodies of Barb and Phyl, and we come to that infamous shot of Billy's eye watching her through the gap in the door, Moore talks about the voice dramatically again, linking it back to those "fierce and animal-like" eyes earlier described in the script.

Suddenly, chillingly, she hears a voice. It cuts right to the bone.

CALLER

(childlike)
BILLY'S A BAD BOY! BILLY KILLED
THE BABY!

Jess looks up.

From Jess' point of view, we look up at the door and there, in the crack between the door and the door frame, the eye of the killer glares out at us.... After a beat, the door starts to swing toward us slowly...

Interestingly, Moore continues to use Billy's eyes as the focal point of his madness and instability, perhaps drawing inspiration from Shakespeare who once wrote; "The eyes are the window to your soul". Such an interesting approach to use here when it seems Billy's soul seems utterly absent, yet his eyes show us the madness embedded within him, a vessel of psychotic murderous rage, yet the premise rings wholly true to these proceedings and the character himself.

While post-production helped enhance Billy's distant antagonistic vibe via Mancuso primarily, on set, no one knew the killer would sound as vulgar as he eventually did. "When I took the phone call" remembers Hussey, "the voice they put in afterwards wasn't the voice that I was hearing, that was added during the looping and so I didn't really hear the really horrible things that were being said. I heard Bob Clark reading back to me, you know things like 'I'm gonna get you', and I had to react and be terrified but then when you actually see the film, some of the things are horrible and I wasn't hearing those, so they were not in the script. And Bob Clark improvised them and then added them afterwards".

Billy climbs into the sorority house attic

One of the lingering and fascinating parts of Billy's legacy is that by the time the end credits roll, we are still none the wiser as to just who he is or his backstory. And while this is seen as one of the film's strongest elements, it wasn't always the case. In one of the earliest drafts of the script written by Moore and Bond, the latter insists that the whole identity was always there, but the mysterious elements around his behaviour were brought in more and more with later drafts after he had departed the project. Speaking in 2020, he confirmed that Billy was originally a "very well fleshed out [character], in the sense that we knew his entire backstory. I am very keen on fully developing characters after my stage experience", muses Bond.

Clark elaborates that "we actually wrote a history for Billy. I think he would have come from a town, I think there was some incident with his baby sister, where he killed her, or probably not, he damaged her severely. He was a disturbed child, and we got a lot of tension from his behaviour, was probably jealous of his baby sister and created that schism between him and women. You could write a whole history on him if you wanted, there were enough dynamics, but we never really did".

However, while he explains that there was "a full back story embedded in the character, his behaviour and responses", it was never the intention to reveal his identity. Something which is still debated, discussed and theorised about even today by fans as well as other filmmakers who have provided in-joke what-if scenarios to explain Billy and even what happened next. One of the more entertaining notions was from the writers behind 2003's *Behind The Mask: The Rise of Leslie Vernon*, which tells the story of a serial killer in the making who is followed around by a film crew as he gives away his secrets while preparing for his first massacre. However, in the film, we meet his mentor, Eugene, played by the late Scott Wilson.

Scott Wilson and Nathan Baesel in *Behind the Mask: The Rise of Leslie Vernon*

Speaking with Icons of Fright several years ago, co-writer David J. Stieve confirmed that he intended Eugene to be Billy, seen now later in life. "I can confirm that Eugene has always been Billy in my mind. Scott (Wilson) would be the right age for him, and it always fit for me that Eugene would have that 'old school' nostalgia and slight professional jealousy that even though he was a pioneer in the business of fear, he never achieved the fame or notoriety of his successors (Michael, Jason, etc). That's just me, however. It was never explicitly written into a draft, it was always just lore that Scott Glosserman and I carried with us!" It's then interesting to hear Eugene reminisce about his earlier exploits, especially the following part of his speech.

EUGENE

> It was a whole different world back when I was in the game. I had a good portion of my success in the late '60s, '70s. Back then, it was about the quantity of work – how many jobs can you fit in a year, how many places can you hit?... We just hit hard, wiped everybody out, and disappeared as soon as we could... without ever giving a thought to coming back.

As for Bob Clark, would he have continued the story of Billy? "I would make it the following fall. Somehow in the interim, the killer had been caught, he had been institutionalised and I would have him escape one night and now he's free in the community. Nobody knows it at first and he starts stalking them again at the *Black Christmas* sorority house. And I was going to call it *Halloween*".

After viewing *Black Christmas*, what is always evident is the attention given to all these characters as well as a passionate attempt at developing them above and beyond the usual non-descriptive victims we would become accustomed to in so many later slasher films. From the sisters themselves, there is unity, there is heart, and while there are flaws, there is a sense of comrade between them all, despite their conflicting backgrounds, ideals and personalities. Clark insists that he "spent a great deal of time establishing the reality of these young people who lived in this sorority house. It isn't enough to just simply make a film that scares people. If it isn't about people we relate to, who we believe in, who act like it's 1974, [well] prior films telling the story of teenagers have often been quite silly", he remarks.

Certainly, over the last few years, more and more editorials on horror blogs and websites have acknowledged the strength of Clark giving this time and space to allow the characters to evolve, especially since it worked also in the favour of the actors who were then given the time to equally allow their performances to imbue a warm sensibility that audiences could appreciate.

As Clark concludes, the "dynamics were very important to the story. [The first act] pretty much established the whole dynamic of the house and how the killer has intruded and what the setups will be". The fact that by about 1/3 into the film we feel strongly for these sisters, as well as Mrs Mac, the ever more sympathetic Mr Harrison and other characters, mean when they are targeted by Billy, their deaths (even those off-screen), hit us so very hard.

INTERVIEW

Nick Mancuso

'Billy' (Co-Voice)

Have you had the chance to see either remake?

No, I've never seen the remakes. I've heard they're not very good.

Is *Black Christmas* the first slasher?

Ostensibly one of the first of the slasher movies and it opened the door to all the other ones that came shortly after, the Friday the 13th's and the Freddy films that went on for over 20 years leading up to the Rob Zombie films.

It's a little bit like science fiction being reinvented with the introduction of Star Trek, creating an entire genre that birthed Star Wars and all the rest of it.

Black Christmas in a sense set off the parting shot.

I went to one of those fan conventions about Black Christmas in Toronto, and there was like 200 people there in the room, and I asked, "Why are you here?" And someone responded by saying that Black Christmas is the greatest film made in the 20th century, and I thought, what?

What happened to the Exorcist and Rosemary's Baby?

Anyway, it clearly somehow touched some unconscious fabric of the social experiment, kind of like a bad dream. A recurrent nightmare, a social nightmare. If I looked at it I'd say, I think it has something to do with the rebirth of growing up and creating relationships.

Were you the only voice of Billy?

I was only one of the voices of Billy, there were three voices. One was Bob Clark, who did some of the screaming and another was an actress, I can't recall her name, perhaps Mugsey Sweeney. I had actually worked with this actress when I was a stage actor. We worked on a play written by Des McAnuff, who ended up directing Jersey Boys on Broadway.

I'm not sure how Bob mixed it all together, but I did most of the voice work. Most of it was done with me standing on my head in order to compress the thorax and give it that 'It's me Billy', kind of rasp. What Bob had made me do was sit in a chair for the audition and he said to just improvise some sounds and so I just started improvising he said yes you got the part.

I actually ended up dubbing Keir Dullea, as there were two lines that needed dubbing. Bob Clark asked if I could dub Keir for two lines, as this would save flying him back over from England.

Was that an odd experience as an audition?

I was a stage actor and had hardly done any film (at the stage), I think the only work I'd done was some CBC shows, a show called The Great Detective and series called Police Surgeon. I was around 21 years old and being from the stage we were doing a lot of experimental performances during the 1960s such as Peter Brooke, the Living Theatre out of New York.

There was a theatre revolution going on in the 60s, impacted as well and we threw out the fourth wall and audience participation became greater. We were into street theatre, so to me it was all part of this conceptual kind of experimentation with characters, voices and sound.

There is kind of a twisted internal landscape that this guy, Billy, obviously based on Psycho, which is the real precedent. Anthony Perkins and his mother, his dead mother in the attic, mirror Black Christmas with Billy spending most of the film in the attic.

Bob Clark definitely took some elements from Psycho, in a sense he brought it down into the masses. Psycho was a kind of heightened psychotic experience for a refined taste and Black Christmas is shall we say less refined.

The fact it is less refined is certainly one of its appealing elements.

Exactly, it is like going into a really simple but well-run family restaurant and having mom's apple pie.

In terms of the script, there is a backstory for Billy in the original script and was this ever presented to you?

Hell no, I never went to the set and went to a studio. I never worked with any of the other actors; I was in a studio with Bob. I didn't really have any contact with the cast. I did know Art Hindle, having worked with him before because he was Canadian.

Did Margot Kidder know that you did the voice of Billy when you worked together later?

We had never met until we worked together many, many years later. She didn't have a clue it was me doing the voice of Billy; I don't think it was discussed in our conversations.

How do you see Canadian actors?

I knew John Candy, and so many other great Canadian actors and comedians at the time. There was an air of revolution going on at the time.

What is interesting is that Bob is not Canadian, he was from Texas and ended up doing one of the most successful Canadian films ever made; Porky's, which was a huge hit. He also ended up working with Harold Greenberg, who I also worked with when I did a film called Death Ship, another horror extravaganza that was also remade. We had a cast that included George Kennedy and Harry Raskey.

Did it ever concern you doing such a dark role early in your career?

No, when you do theatre like I did, such as Shakespeare and Checkov and many of the classics, I became part of a theatre movement in Toronto. We did all kinds of plays and experimental shows and I was surrounded by so many creative people who went on to have very great careers, people like Des McAnuff who went on to become one of the great Broadway directors with Jersey Boys and Tommy. We would meet on street corners and just start riffing, a bit like jazz musicians.

Some went onto musicals but dark Latin types like me went into the dark Latin roles. I did go through the five stages of an actor's career, defined as starting off playing the lover, you play the hero, the villain, the loser and finally, you play the monster. So I started off playing the monster and went full circle and now I am starting all over again.

Do you have any films coming out soon?

I did a wonderful film recently called The Performance, about an old actor who returns to the theatre he began in when he was 21. The Executive Producer was actually, Peter O'Toole, who was originally meant to be doing the part but he passed away and I ended up stepping into the role.

That film is currently stuck in the world of legal disputes, but I am hoping it will get released because it's some of the best work I've done in 30 years.

Have you ever visited the *Black Christmas* house?

Yes, it was off the back of an interview I did with The Telegraph newspaper in 2019. I was really surprised they got in touch, and it was about Black Christmas.

I knew where it was because it is based on a well-known Toronto Street, and I met a Black Christmas fan (Dan Duffin) and he actually came to Canada on his honeymoon and to see the house.

What do you make of *Black Christmas'* place in horror notoriety?

I think when you think of Frank Capra's It's A Beautiful Life, which is a White Christmas, and it's interesting because it became part of the fabric of Christmas. That all became part of the Christmas spirit, and during the late 60s and early 70s when things started to go awry, White Christmas took a little twist and it became Black Christmas, and it's been black ever since.

I think there is a lot of references, and I remember re-watching it and feeling like I was saying hello to an old friend, who happens to be carrying a dagger.

There is also the running theme of assault on women, and teen angst that was hungover from the 50s and 60s. This again was shown in Norman Bates in Psycho, a character who can't let go of his mother.

I knew Melanie Griffiths and her mother was Tippi Hedren, and Hitchcock had a thing for her and she told me this bizarre story where there was a birthday party. Hitchcock presented Melanie with a gift and he had this elaborate box and she opened it up and it was a coffin with a perfect portrait of her mother. That's twisted, genuinely twisted.

Tell us about the commentary track you did for the 40th anniversary of *Black Christmas*?

I did do a commentary, and it was pretty crazy. I've never heard it. I never got a cent from the film, but never got credit as I wasn't part of the actor's union.

There is some heavy-duty dialogue in the film. The language at times was quite shocking in the film, especially for the time. I think Bob Clark did that on purpose, in order to turn the audience into the sorority girls. It triggered the disgust of the audience.

How do you prepare for roles?

I was going to be a research psychologist, but I was acting all the way through this time, meaning I have a deeper interest in some elements of the industry. When I see a character, I try to analyse all sides of them, but it is hard as most of the writing, unless you are doing the classics, doesn't really warrant that much analysis.

How Does Bob Clark rank in terms of the directors you've worked with over the years?

I put him right up there; Bob had an incredible sense of humour. I was a scared 21-year-old kid, living on stolen tomatoes when I was doing theatre.

He was incredibly kind and made you feel at home. He had a paternal quality to him and was very funny and we just spent our time laughing. We were doing all these horror scenes but away from the camera we just laughed. He was one of the directors where you had a ball, and that is a rarity. The whole film is tongue in cheek, it's not satire - it's kind of a parody of itself.

How did you re-discover *Black Christmas*?

I didn't even know it existed until about 20 years ago when I got a call from a fan to do an interview. I didn't have a clue; it was this cult classic. I'm just blown away by the fact that Black Christmas has had more response to any film that I have done, and I've done almost 250. That little film done in 1974, where I was the voice of Billy has been remade twice now, it's crazy!

vi) Essay

Christmas Carnival

An academic reading of *Black Christmas*

During the commentary track on the original Tartan *Black Christmas* (Clark, 1974) DVD release in the UK, Director Bob Clark mused "this isn't really a horror, it's more a thriller" (Clark, 2001), commenting further how he never made "any slasher. You don't see anybody slashed in my films, even *Murder by Decree*" (Clark, 1979). And while he himself carried on with this view, there is no doubt that *Black Christmas* nevertheless transgressed his honourable assumptions, instead of becoming a classic staple of the horror genre, one it has never found itself escaping from.

Certainly, critics would agree with the label, proclaiming the film as still "one of the better slasher movies 40 years after its original release" (Scullion, 2014), while The Los Angeles Times in 1975 referred to the film as a "smart, stylish Canadian-made little horror picture that is completely diverting" (Thomas, 1975). In more modern times, critics and audiences have been reassessing the film much more fondly, arguing how it "is a rightfully beloved and thought-provoking piece of horror cinema that is still extremely relevant to the women of today" (Alvey, 2019).

Unlike *Halloween* (Carpenter, 1978), which quickly bounced back from its initial bad word of mouth, *Black Christmas* took a longer journey to be seen in a much more favourable light and to cement itself into the classic horror hall of fame. Instead, seemingly lost in the wake of Carpenter's success, and with it, losing its right to claim it had included the original slasher film prototype, something Carpenter has never disputed. Despite this, academics have continued to dismiss Clark's use of POV techniques and emphasis on pacing, instead frequently charging *Halloween* instead with changing the landscape of the horror film since its release, with academics identifying the picture as prime for generating "the prototypical slasher film" (Staiger, 2015: 214), and in effect "the golden age of slashers" (Kerswell 2010: 9).

Significantly, the film's use of the point-of-view (POV), camera techniques and mise-en-scène have been cited as both "powerful and stylish, setting the scene – both thematically and visually – of what was to come" (Kerswell, 2010: 78), not only within *Black Christmas* and *Halloween* but for the consequential slasher films that followed such as *Friday the 13th* (Cunningham, 1980), *Prom Night* (Lynch, 1980) and *The Burning* (Maylam, 1981). One wonders if these theorists and academics have ever acknowledged their glaring omission in the years since.

Additionally, scholars such as Pat Gill have elaborated on the deeper meanings of these technological and thematic achievements in the horror/slasher film, linking them to a text's power to make the suburbs an unsafe haven, a place where it "not only fails to protect its children, [but also] has become the breeding ground of living nightmares" (Gill, 2002: 16). *Black Christmas'* antagonist, the cackling, obscene and rarely seen Billy, could also embody Freudian attributes, such as his sharp improvised unicorn weapon against Margot Kidder becoming a symbol of male empowerment, "the phallus" (Bloch and Ferguson, 1992: 211), which is only taken away by what Carol Clover titles the Final Girl, she who removes Billy's power by employing her own weapon against him (a fire poker stick in this case). As Clover comments, "she specifically unmans her oppressor [presenting] the castration, literal or symbolic of the killer at her hands" (Clover, 1992: 49).

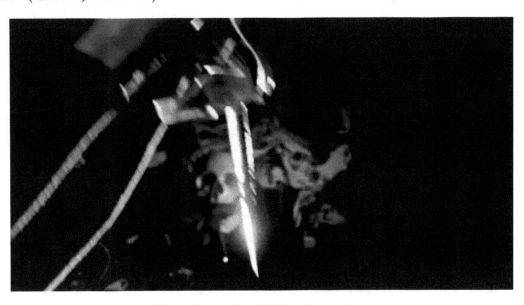

Billy stabs Barb with the glass unicorn

121

Nevertheless, while there have been some loose connotations made between *Black Christmas* and academic thought, such as Kat McCollum, who gave the film a feminist reading in 2020, not much else has been discussed on Clark's film, again with it appearing always in the shadow of *Halloween*, which has been discussed fiercely over the years. One of the more frustrating elements is how *Black Christmas* can easily fit into a lot of the academic thought on the genre but has yet to be given such an effort.

One area, for instance, that seems to have been less explored is the connotations the film intimately has with the nature of the carnival spirit as well as celebrations of circus culture itself that would temporarily come to town. Similarly, not unlike the festival of Christmas with its German Markets, late-night shopping and the Santa's Grotto experience all seemingly accompanied by laughing, drinking, Santa and Elf cosplaying and smiling tree decorations. This is nonetheless all epitomised by a momentary "feast characterised by the ritual transgression of the social order habitually persecuted by the political and religious authorities of the day" (O'Donnell and Foley, 2008: 108). *Black Christmas* highlights (especially through its lighting techniques), particular attention to Billy's evil persona, use of obscene voices and language, and the idea of how this seemingly playful and sexualised behaviour is what helps him blend in with the sexual awakening of the sorority house and like other slasher characters such as Michael Myers, can then "walk among society as an individual who fits in" (Francis Jnr, 2013: 37).

Mrs Mac and Clare displayed in the attic

This strengthens the connection between carnival culture and text, as Billy's obscene behaviour "not only confronts physical threats to normative boundaries but [also] suppresses social and psychological issues" (Cooke, 2017: 85). Through not only its antagonist, Billy's ever unnerving presence in the town, but the ever widening and ongoing "conflict between order and chaos, stability and change…the struggle between authority and licence" (Craig, 1995: 162), he imposes on the people there too, this article posits that *Black Christmas* not only perform a process of carnivalization within its structure but also extends on its ideals through the rebirth of a new order. This is especially illustrated by the deceased victims of Billy who present a form of "grotesque realism" (Cohen, 2011: 176), a component of carnival theory, temporarily around the Christmas holidays.

According to Russian Theorist - Mikhail Bakhtin, the notion of carnival theory and of carnivals themselves represented a "temporary suspension of all hierarchic distinctions and barriers among men…and the prohibitions of usual life" (Bakhtin, 1984: 15). In *Rabelais and His World*, "Bakhtin suggests that in the Middle Ages, the carnival played a much more prominent role in the life of the ordinary people, who inhabited a dual realm of existence: one official, characterised by the authority of the church, the feudal system, work, and one unofficial, characterised by reversal, parody, song, and laughter" (Vice, 1997: 150).

Vice describes further how, for Bakhtin, this folk carnival humour is a "boundless world of humorous forms and manifestations [which] opposed the official and serious tone of medieval ecclesiastical and feudal culture" (Vice, 1997: 151), and which consisted of elements made up of "folk festivities of the carnival type, the comic rites and cults, the clowns and fools, giant, dwarfs, and jugglers, the vast and manifold literature of parody" (Vice, 1997: 151). These features, argues Bakhtin, can be traced in examples of carnivalesque literature and within paintings such as *The Battle Between Carnival & Lent* (Bruegel, 1559), and can still be observed in more contemporary film and TV products, because, as he encourages in *Problems of Dostoevsky's Poetics*, similar notions can continually be allowed to present evolving transportation of carnival's pageantry so long as a text demonstrates "a language of artistic images that has something in common with its concretely sensuous nature" (Bakhtin, 1984: 122).

Bakhtin was explicitly interested in two factors that he believed make-up overall carnival nature, that of the grotesque body and also what he called "marketplace speech" (Gardiner, 2002: 49), a type of wording and dialogue that is only apparent when a normal societal structure is placed into the chaos that carnival culture brings with it. Robert Stam elaborates further that Bakhtin "audaciously recasts the unconscious/conscious distinction as one not between two orders of psychic reality, but rather between two modalities of verbal consciousness" (Stam, 1989:4).

This article contends that within *Black Christmas*, such opposition is manifested between the almost duelling nature of the authorities with the sorority girls, their friends while accompanied by Mr Harrison, as the former's seemingly blatant disregard for the missing Clare and increasingly sinister phone calls are initially dismissed by Sgt. Nash through his ideals. As Alvey contends "It's nothing new for the police to shrug off the concerns of women only for there to be deadly results. Most of the film features Jess's fraught pleading with the police to be taken seriously. She is aware that there is something desperately wrong, and so are her sorority sisters and those associated with them. But there is very little outside help to be found for the young women" (Alvey, 2019).

Additionally Clare's disappearance as well as "the sorority sisters [receiving] continuous vulgar and threatening phone calls…are constantly disregarded and brushed off" (Alvey 2019), with comments such as; "90% of the times, girls reported missing from the college are at a cabin with their boyfriend", a statement that immediately discards all professional responsibility the police/authorities should be exhibiting when being informed of a potential missing person and in the process, places the younger characters as an "alternative to those oppressive constructions" (Hyman, Malbert and Jones 2000: 15), as well as being at odds with how a police force (an official consciousness), should be dealing with these worrying circumstances.

The authorities (bar Lt Fuller played by the late John Saxon), in effect, are this official consciousness, a correlation of all that is normal within society including the town setting itself and how it is supposed to operate; an official consciousness that symbolizes "that which social and ideological structures allow one to express openly, while unofficial consciousness expresses that which deviates from socially accepted norms" (Stam, 1989: 4).

An example of the latter can be observed through Margot Kidder's Barbara, who in frustration (as well as aided by drunken conduct), attempts to humiliate Nash comically, listing her exchange as "Fellatio". As this occurs, it suggests evidence of carnivalization occurring not just through Billy's actions, but also equally through the sorority sisters who resort to unofficial language in their desperation to be heard and taken seriously before it is too late.

Barb talks fellatio at the Police Station

If the young victims are providing a process of carnivalization occurring through a language that "expresses alternative or conflicting perspectives" (Cohen, 2011: 179), in that they are maintaining the narrative that something is terribly wrong with the status quo and that someone is out there making threats on their lives, This article posits Billy also as an agent of carnival process, though through the grotesque body instead, which is accompanied by "strange moans and screams and violent, sexually explicit mutterings" (Shaw-Williams, 2017).

This is achieved not only in that of his own rarely seen façade glimpsed through clever lighting and which twists and contorts but also exemplified in his victim's corpses which have been stashed away "in a grotesque display" (Shaw-Williams, 2017).

The latter is "whole and mutilated, followed by an array of bodily wastes such as blood…salvia, sweat, tears and putrefying flesh" (Creed, 1986: 67), all attributes of Bakhtin's grotesque body, that which draws from an "exaggeration of the body, particularly its degradation" (Magistrale, 2005: 173). However, Billy's actions also suggest an extension on these ideals, as he penetrates not only the lower area (mocking Jess' baby), that which was defined as only "the bodily lower stratum" (Bakhtin, 1984: 20) but also the upper regions, signifying a greater scope of carnivalization to "redraw the boundaries" (Brottman, 2004: 168) while allowing society to "be undermined and challenged" (Neale, 2004: 367) on a much broader scale.

Barb is stabbed to death by Billy

Cohen remarks, "Bakhtin suggests that the ambivalence of the carnival experience manifests itself in laughter, feasts and images of the grotesque body", (Cohen, 2011: 178), all of which are found in the horror movie regardless of its overall intent, with the latter being an instantly recognisable trait of the genre and which will be addressed in more depth through Billy's persona and actions at a later stage. However, as previously stated, this form of carnivalization in literature and media can be identified when a narrative or plot follows an oppression-type structure, and which voice ideals that invert the standard make-up of our society, a "temporal rationality" (O'Donnell & Foley, 2008: 107), an idea that this article proposes is present within *Black Christmas* and its bastardisation of the season.

As previously suggested, Jess, Barbara and Phyl's roles throughout the text are to offer up a version of Bakhtin's carnival illustrated by an ideological language discourse and atmosphere that runs oppositional to a more official dialect that imposes "hierarchic distinctions" (Bakhtin, 1984: 15), one which ultimately "forms a solid ring around man" (Bakhtin and Medvedev, 1985: 14), and which is conceived and constructed by power structures such as Government institutions. From the outset, the girl's dialogue is at odds with this mandate and immediately presents a "different point of view, a different way of seeing the world" (Mitchell, 2006). Certainly, in their first scene receiving Billy's call, some of the other girls are unnerved by not just his crudeness, but equally of Barb, who challenges the madman there and then with language also not permissible by society's terms it would seem.

JESS

It's him again! The moaner!

BILLY

(inaudible sounds)

BARBARA

He's expanded his act.

CLARE

Could that be one person?

BARBARA

No, Clare, that's the Mormon Tabernacle Choir doing their annual obscene phone call.

BILLY

Let me lick it! Let me stick my tongue on it and lick it! … You… You pig cunt! Yeah, you pig cunt! You pig cunt! Let me lick it! Lick it! Lick it! Let me lick your pretty piggy cunt! Pretty pig cunt! I'll lick your pretty pig clit. I'm like a tuna farm, baby!

BARBARA

Mmm, not bad.

BILLY

Suck on my juicy cock! I'll come over. I'll come over and you can… You can suck it. Suck it! Okay?

BARBARA

Listen, you pervert! Why don't You go over to Lambda Chi? They could use a little of this!

BILLY

You piggy cunt, you want my fat cock.

BARBARA

Oh, why don't you go find a wall socket and stick your tongue in it, that'll give you a charge.

BILLY

I'll stick my tongue up your pretty pussy!

BARBARA

You fucking creep!

BILLY

I'm going to kill you (ends call)

CLARE

I don't think you should provoke somebody like that, Barb.

BARBARA

Oh listen, this guy is minor league. In the city, I get two of those
a day.

Arguably evident is that Barb's immediate attitude towards Billy (as well as those
displayed later on by the girls continually to both Billy further and the Police), can
be realised as "taboo, beyond the pale, a kind of mental carnival" (Stam, 1984: 4),
deemed as not of the norm, not of rational society and certainly not expected of
students who should be there to study, yet to Bakhtin, the sorority sisters' dialect
is of equal merit despite its somewhat worrying variance from official courses of
communication.

    To Bakhtin, despite their offering an alternate view to combating the situation
they are in, it is still part of a "plurality of fully valid consciousness" (Bakhtin,
1984: 8), while also demonstrating that carnival language does not discriminate,
locating this "ideological combat at the pulsating heart of discourse whether in
the form of political rhetoric, artistic practice, or everyday language exchange"

(Stam, 1989: 8), the latter seen further throughout the remainder of the film when Jess and the authorities continually disagree over what to do about the situation (more so since Clark highlights Peter as a solid red-herring throughout).

Such an approach indicates a far greater degree of carnivalization within the film in that while Billy simultaneously hides in the house and carries out his carnivalesque killings, Phyl tries to alert her sister, Jess, by imprinting a dire warning later in the film stating, "I just know Clare's dead, I can just feel it". "Impressions [that] do not coincide with the reality perceived by the majority" (Telotte 1982: 145). The situation creates what Bakhtin categorised as heteroglossia, "whereby language becomes the space of confrontation of differently orientated social accents, as diverse sociolinguistic consciousnesses fight it out on the terrain of language" (Stam, 1989: 8).

Sobbing Phyl is consoled by Jess

These differing languages and voices are what "intervene between the history of society and the history of language" (Stam, 1989: 8), and that while a "dominant class strives to make the sign uniaccentual and to endow it with an eternal, supraclass character, the oppressed, especially when they are conscious of their oppression, strive to deploy language for their own liberation" (Stam, 1989: 8). In essence, what is being observed and noted in *Black Christmas* is that the girls are becoming more and more aware of their vulnerability and the threats to their wellbeing, so begin to operate with other modes of communication, other ways to be vocal that begin to create alternate divergences of speech that defy what has been laid down as the norm, because "to speak of dialogue without speaking of power, in a Bakhtinian perspective is to speak meaninglessly in a void" (Stam, 1989: 8).

Only when we reach the climax of the film when the crimes of Billy have been revealed, does the unofficial carnivalized vocabulary of the girls become fully realised and accepted. An unofficial discourse has temporarily become the norm and infected the town's inhabitants, as their own speech has become at one with carnival patterns, albeit until after Christmas and after Billy has successfully evaded capture, taking his world view and order with him.

Not only has Fuller adopted the same ideals that the girls used to describe what they perceived were happening to them, but the latter's attempts to warn authorities in verbal exchanges that were originally perceived as a threat to officialdom have now not only been undermined, and even destroyed "the hegemony of [an] ideology that [sought] to have the final word about the world" (Bakhtin, 1989: 9), but it has also renewed, "shed light upon life, the meanings it harbours, to elucidate potentials; projecting, as it does an alternate conceptualisation of reality" (Mitchell, 2006). This continues to occur until Billy disappears into the night, allowing the process of carnivalization to begin only then to rescind, putting back into place the "official life subjected to the hierarchy of the social order and everyday existence" (Cohen, 2011: 178), since Peter has been wrongly named as the killer.

With the aforementioned reference to Billy and as previously hypothesised in this article, attention must be given to the suggestion that he himself possesses some traits of Bakhtin's carnival theory, namely, that of the grotesque body, with greater emphasis on this notion placed on his victims as they lie "dismembered" (Jefferson, 1989: 215), yet all the while sharing with their attacker a loss of "individual definition" (Jefferson, 1989: 215), in the process. This permits *Black Christmas* to complete the circle of conveying full carnivalization to occur temporarily within the town, its boundaries, as well as on the inhabitants. Already it is suggestive in this article that the prominent sorority sisters have functioned in a way so as to bring about the process through "marketplace speech" (Bakhtin, 1984: 10).

Conversely, the grotesque body has also been on display in multiple ways throughout the film, not only through Billy, a "monster" (Alvey, 2019), himself as Alvey suggests, but his victims, and achieved through brutal displays of violence that also carry with them a certain "play, mockery [and], inversion…all elements of Bakhtin's carnival" (Babin and Harrison, 1999: 135).

Billy watches outside the sorority house

In the first instance, Billy consequently signifies minor yet recognizable manifestations of Bakhtin's grotesque body, in his adult state, exhibited persistently by Clark as a shadowy figure, never whole, who has crazed looks, but which the majority are concealed in darkness, yet offers "a temporary suspension of all hierarchic distinctions and barriers among men" (Bakhtin, 1984: 15). Additionally, his gait and posture are continually unnatural in tone, he remains silent, and stands out of place against typical suburban mise-en-scène, (such as his demented eye peering out from behind the door), acting as "alternate" (Jefferson, 1989: 214), to the mundane of everyday life, a "clear oppositional message" (Stam, 1989: 158), to the status quo, suggesting a demonstration of what Bakhtin would define the grotesque body as; a "flesh of new life, conceived but as yet unformed" (Jefferson, 1989: 216), and whose irregular "body movements contain something of…carnival" (Cohen, 2011: 185).

Billy is always looking at the normalcy of existence around him, a duty that ultimately turns him against such a structure and into his own "utopia that rejects all traditional definitions and characterizations" (Drexler, 2000: 227), planning instead a temporary overthrow of them. He exercises his now arguably carnivalesque form and ideals over a Christmas break by murdering victims and presenting their bodies in a new form, one where flesh all over (and not just in the lower stratum as Bakhtin expressed), has been penetrated, and is now a greater "collectivised jumble of protuberances and orifices: bellies…buttocks…mouths, guts and so on" (Jefferson, 1989: 216).

In so doing, Billy, the Father Christmas of Bakhtin's carnival, becomes "a vast nothingness that seeks to usher in a totalizing unaversive of empty, static homogeneity" (Fawver, 2011: 10), and further seeks to initiate a new view of life since "bodily fluids such as blood, mucous or urine are signs of health when they are within the body, but [now are] signs of a dangerous transgression of boundaries [now] they are on the outside" (Vice, 1997: 164).

Phyl and Barb in a bloody display of Billy's carnage

The culmination of these intentions occurs when Jess discovers the mutilated bodies of her friends in the house. Her friends Barbara and Phyl are laid out as "grotesque parodies of feminist types" (Leeder, 2015: 16). Interestingly also, the once sexually promiscuous Barbara, in particular, has been halted from further sexual advances against others, degendered in a word. Billy's depowering of their sexuality and sexual organs furthermore support Bakhtin's notions that carnival "implicitly exalts the blurring and shifting of gender distinctions, a release of the boundaries of socially imposed sex roles" (Stam, 1992: 163), forced upon by a dominant ideology.

Billy in essence has allowed his victims to regenerate into a new mocking form (Agnes even?), through an aesthetically presented grotesque nature in death, proving his macabre craft so to speak, a trait Bakhtin similarly attributed to carnival behaviour and which *Black Christmas'* antagonist further associates with his grotesque body ideal, all working together as a perfect alternative to thrive and oppose an official consciousness.

Through a combination of carnivalesque ideals and activities, the murderous Billy and his unwitting accomplices, the sorority sisters offer a macabre notion of "rebellion…satire and playfulness" (Cohen, 2011: 178), through cooperation with an ever-shifting heteroglossia of voices. These voices express "alternative or conflicting perspectives" (Cohen 2011: 179), while a "grotesque absurdity" (Magistrale, 2005: 167), encroaches on the town the film is set within at Christmas as this madman begins an attack upon the boundaries of "official state" (Holquist, 1984: xxi), a chance to temporarily "redraw the boundaries" (Brottman, 2004: 168), by murder.

Ultimately this is achieved through the psychopath's mindset, one that is uncomfortably denoted by Clark as an almost "playful mockery of hierarchical order by individuals oppressed by it" (Cohen 2011: 178). After Billy enters the house, seemingly already carrying some trauma and oppression from his past, he exhibits an almost childlike curiosity with the place, watching the inhabitants, listening to their private conversations, as well as unnaturally observing and singing to his victims after killing them, as if revelling in their new carnival forms. By the climax of the film, he now populates the local landscape with an atmosphere of overturned meanings through "fools [and] costumes" (Bakhtin, 1984: 5, 40), as well as a deadly persona that "is related to transition, metamorphoses, the violation of natural boundaries" (Bakhtin, 1984: 40).

The chilling final shot of the sorority house as the phone continues to ring

Under his distinctive, never whole physical state due to various mise-en-scène, Billy offers those who either fall under his weapons or narrowly evade it a "radical transformation of [the] perception of reality" (Telotte 1982: 147), via continual physical or mental torment. Bakhtin's notion of the grotesque body has been employed within *Black Christmas* by Billy, alongside an unwitting addition of diverse communication on the sister's parts to offer "the chance to have a new outlook on the world, to realize the relative nature of all that exists, and to enter a completely new order of things" (Bakhtin 1984: 34).

In *Black Christmas*, such a process has been primarily achieved through the eyes and actions of a madman. And while carnivalization will rescind by the end of Christmas morning, and some natural order will be resumed, we only have to wait until any proposed next sequel to see a new process of carnivalization occur again. Or if we answer the phone that continues to ring out over the end credits, when all seems well again it seems on the outside. Whichever way, both will allow Billy to come back and continually "twist, mutate and invert standard themes of societal makeup" (Mitchell 2006).

References

Alvey, Jamie (2019), *The Radical Legacy of Black Christmas (1974), Morbidly Beautiful,* https://morbidlybeautiful.com/radical-legacy-black-christmas/, Accessed 4th July 2021.

Babin, Edith and Harrison, Kimberly (1999), Contemporary Composition Studies: A Guide to Theorists and Terms, London: Greenwood Publishing.

Bakhtin, Mikhail (1984), Rabelais & His World (trans. Helene Iswolsky), Bloomington: Indiana University Press.

———————————(1984), Problems of Dostoevsky's Poetics (trans. Caryl Emerson), Minneapolis: University Of Minnesota Press.

Bakhtin, Mikhail and Medvedev, Pavel (1985), The Formal Method in Literary Scholarship: A Critical Introduction To Sociological Poetics, London: Harvard University Press.

Bloch, Howard and Ferguson, Frances (eds) (1992), Misogyny, Misandry, and Misanthropy, California: University of California Press.

Brottman, Mikita (2004), 'Mondo Horror: Carnivalizing the Taboo', in S. Prince (ed.), The Horror Film, New Jersey: Rutgers University Press, pp. 167-188.

Bruegel, Pieter (1559), The Battle Between Carnival and Lent, Vienna: Kunsthistorisches Museum.

Carpenter, John (1978), *Halloween*, USA: Compass International Pictures.

Clark, Bob (1974), *Black Christmas*, Canada: August Films.

Clover, Carol J. (1992), Men, Women and Chainsaws: Gender in the Modern Horror Film, Princeton: Princeton University Press.

Cohen, Lynn E. (2011), 'Bakhtin's Carnival and Pretend Role Play', American Journal of Play, 4:2, pp.176-203.

Cooke, Anthony C. (2017), Moral Panics, Mental Illness Stigma, and the Deinstitutionalization Movement in American Popular Culture, Statesboro: Palgrave Macmillan.

Craig, Kenneth M. (1995), Reading Esther: A Case for the Literary Carnivalesque, London: John Knox Press.

Creed, Barbara (1986), 'Horror and the Monstrous-Feminine: An Imaginary Abjection', Screen, 27:1, pp.44–71.

Cunningham, Sean S. (1980), *Friday The 13th*, USA: Paramount Pictures.

Drexler, Jane (2000), 'Carnival: The Novel, the Wor(1)ds, and Practicing Resistance', in D. Olkowski (ed.), Resistance, Flight, Creation: Feminist Enactments of French Philosophy, London: Cornell University Press, pp.216-235.

Fawver, Kurt (2011), 'Massacres of Meaning: The Semiotic Value of Silence and Scream in The Texas Chainsaw Massacre and Halloween', The Irish Journal of Gothic and Horror Studies, 10:2, October 2011, pp.49-57, https://irishgothichorror.files.wordpress.com/2016/04/ijghsissue10.pdf, Accessed 29th December 2017.

Francis Jnr, James (2013), Remaking Horror: Hollywood's New Reliance on Scares of Old, Jefferson: McFarland.

Gardiner, Michael (2002), The Dialogics of Critique: M.M. Bakhtin and the Theory of Ideology, London: Routledge.

Gill, Pat (2002), 'The Monstrous Years: Teens, Slasher Films and the Family', Journal of Film and Video, 54:4, pp.16-30.

Holquist, Michael (1984), 'Prologue', in M. Bakhtin, Rabelais and His World, (trans. H. Iswolsky), Bloomington: Indiana University Press.

Hyman, Timothy and Malbert, Roger and Jones, Malcolm (2000), Carnivalesque, London: Haywood Gallery Publishing.

Jefferson, Ann (1989), 'Bodymatters: Self and Other in Bakhtin, Sartre and Barthes', in K. Hirschkop and D. Shepherd (eds), Bakhtin & Cultural Theory, Manchester: Manchester University Press, pp.201-228.

Kerswell, Justin A. (2010), Teenage Wasteland - The Slasher Movie Uncut, London: New Holland.

Leeder, Murray (2015), Devil's Advocates: Halloween, Leighton Buzzard: Columbia University Press.

Lynch, Paul (1980), *Prom Night*, USA: AVCO Embassy Pictures.

Magistrale, Tony (2005), Abstract Terror: Surveying the Modern and Post-Modern Horror Film, Vermont: Peter Lang.

Maylam, Tony (1981), The Burning, USA: Miramax Films.

Mitchell, Angela (2006), 'Carnavalesque', Weekly Journal of Postmodern and Critical Thought, Devoted to Cross-Disciplinary Academic Discourse, April, http://www5.csudh.edu/dearhabermas/carnival01bk.htm, Accessed 3rd January 2018.

Neale, Steve (2004), 'Halloween: Suspense, Aggression and the Look', in B. K. Grant and C. Sharrett (eds), Planks of Reason: Essays on The Horror Film, Maryland: Scarecrow Press, pp.356-369.

O'Donnell, Hugh and Foley, Malcolm (2008), Treat or Trick? Halloween in a Globalising World, Cambridge: Cambridge Scholars Publishing.

Shaw-Williams, Hannah (2017), *Black Christmas* Original Movie Ending & Killer Identity Explained, ScreenRant, https://screenrant.com/black-christmas-movie-ending-explained-billy-killer-identity/, Accessed 5th July 2021.

Scullion, Chris (2014), *Black Christmas* 1974 Review, The Revenge of that was a bit Mental, https://thatwasabitmental.com/2014/02/10/black-christmas-1974-review/, Accessed 4th July 2021.

Staiger, Janet (2015), 'The Slasher, the Final Girl and the Anti-Denouement', in W. Clayton (ed.), Style and Form in the Hollywood Slasher Film, Houndsmills: Palgrave Macmillan, pp.213-229.

Stam, Robert (1989), Subversive Pleasures: Bakhtin, Cultural Criticism & Film, Baltimore: John Hopkins University Press.

_____ (1992), New Vocabularies in Film Semiotics: Structuralism, Post-Structuralism and Beyond, London: Routledge.

Telotte, Jay P. (1982) 'Through A Pumpkin's Eye: The Reflective Nature of Horror', Literature: Film Quarterly, 10:3, pp.139-149

Thomas, Kevin (1975), Gothic Tale of a '*Black Christmas*' in The Los Angeles Times, August 6th, 1975, Pg.12.

Vice, Sue (1997), Introducing Bakhtin, Manchester: Manchester University Press.

vii) Release and Critical Response

Filming concluded on *Black Christmas* on 11th May 1974, with the film now set to be pieced together in the editing suite of Co-Financier, Findlay Quinn. The film would be released on 11th October 1974; exactly five months to the day filming ended and gathered a worldwide gross total of $4.1 million off the back of a budget of $620,000. Given inflation, this would be an overall taking of $21.6 million in 2020. Back in 1974 horror was certainly still the evil stepchild of cinema with critics rounding on *Black Christmas*, dismissing it as "hardly worth the effort of all concerned" according to the New York Times.

John Carpenter's *Halloween* would suffer a similar initial fate before critics would round on it as a modern (for the time) horror masterpiece. One of the first reviews comes from The Ottawa Citizen's 21st November 1974 edition, with the unnamed staff writer decidedly unimpressed.

"Black Christmas is a film of routine horror and no great surprises".

Michael Walsh for The Province appeared torn on the film in his 27th November 1974 review, saying;

"Clarks wants to please both the mystery-thriller and the straight horror fans. Black Christmas arrives at a kind of middle ground by toning down both intelligence and sensationalism. The package that remains won't completely please anybody".

There were some that saw the genius of the film though, including Kevin Thomas from The LA Times (6th August 1975 edition), who said;

"Black Christmas is a classy, stylish horror picture...strong on atmosphere and captures an uninhibited campus milieu with accuracy and often raunchy hilarity! Performances are superior right down the line. Writer Roy

Moore, director Bob Clark, cameraman Reg Morris and editor Stan Cole, all very able and confident craftsmen, are adroit at creating mounting suspense and terror with a typical ladies-in-distress predicament".

This article also featured a quarter page advert for *Black Christmas* alongside smaller ads for *Jaws* and *The French Connection 2*, which in itself is a fascinating time capsule. The Boston Evening Globe echoed this praise, saying;

"Black Christmas is the best chiller of the year, a creepy, murderous suspense film with an ending guaranteed to rattle what's left of your sensibilities after the movie's hour and 45-minute onslaught".

Regis Philbin was also glowing in his assessment of *Black Christmas* for ABC TV;

"The purpose of this film is to frighten the audience - and I mean it really scares them. Just the shrill ringing of 'Black Christmas' is enough to raise the hackles on your neck...really well done".

Calgary Herald - 23rd November 1974

Closer to home The Toronto Sun compared the film to Alfred Hitchcock's *Psycho*, saying,

"Black Christmas is a winner, all gift wrapped and ready for starved scare fans who haven't had a really good shriek since 'Psycho'...a page right out of the Hitchcock handbook!"

John Saxon was the subject of a feature article in the 23rd August 1975 edition of the Evening Herald, with the actor explaining some of the marketing campaigns from Warner Bros for its US cinematic release. "Warners are going in for some unusual forms of exploitation on this," he says. "There have been some Santa Clauses walking around in black suits, some provocative sky-writing and a number you can dial to listen in on some of the obscene phone calls - from the film's soundtrack. The original title was *Silent Night, Evil Night*, but it was bulky for a theatre marquee and *Black Christmas* sums it up better".

The Calgary Herald edition for Friday 28th August 1975 also published an article to celebrate *Black Christmas* breaking the $1 million mark at the box office. The report stated,

John Saxon featured in the 23rd August 1975 Evening Herald

"The film's gross, 10 months after initial release stands at $1,274,000 - second among Canadian-made films only to the record of $1.8 million of The Apprenticeship of Duddy Kravitz, which was directed by Ted Kotcheff (First Blood and Weekend at Bernie's) and starred Richard Dreyfuss".

Black Christmas was also revealed to have made $1 million of sales at the Cannes Film Festival and officials responsible for the federal government-sponsored Canadian participation at the festival confirmed that the movie did more business than any other Canadian-produced feature that year. The film was predicted at this time, with a $7 million box office gross. Warner Bros, who were also announced as dealing with the US release of the film, ensured the film with 600 more theatres set to take on screenings.

Edmonton Journal 28th August 1975

Bill Thompson, Entertainment Writer for The Philadelphia Inquirer reviewed *Black Christmas* in the 2nd October 1975 copy;

> *"Black Christmas is a surprisingly interesting film that will keep you squirming in suspense until the last scene ends".*

Gene Siskel in the 6th October 1975 edition of The Chicago Tribune, however, was certainly less complimentary about the film stating;

> *"The picture has only one kind of cheap thrill. It's women who repeatedly walk slowly into certain death, and the director plays out the suspense for more than it's worth. A few laughs are generated by the college girls talking dirty".*

The Miami News' Bill von Maurer though reversed this review, heaping praise on the film, calling it;

> *"A mindless fun horror picture, that undoubtedly will have great appeal for the 18 to 25 and let's have a beer after the show set".*

Bob Keaton, Entertainment Writer at the Fort Lauderdale News reported on 12th October 1975 about the re-release of *Black Christmas* in South Florida. Clark (a former resident of Fort Lauderdale), was interviewed as part of the article, discussing the marketing campaign alongside Warner Bros, stating that "actually Warner Bros have been great all along. When their approach didn't work (the original title of *Silent Night, Evil Night)*, they were perfectly willing to try my way. You know when you don't have a big budget and you can't hire a box office star, then you really have to work hard to sell a picture. Now with a national re-release, we don't expect the picture to be a giant, but we do expect it to be a moderately strong hit".

And indeed, while the film still received some lukewarm responses, it was with The Red Deer Advocate reporting on 15th October 1975 that *Black Christmas* had gone on to win three awards as part of the Canadian Film Awards on 12th October. Margot Kidder won Best Supporting Actress for her portrayal of Barbara in a feature, Stan Cole bagged Best Editing for his work on the film, while Ken Healey-Ray won Best Sound Editing for the film, all of which are still rightly remembered by fans even today as major highpoints of Clark's chiller.

Fort Collins Coloradoan Sun 14th December 1975

The New Jersey Record were blunt with their assessment of the film in the 24th October 1975 edition, saying;

"The film is a workmanlike product that knows its cliches well, but it can't be recommended to anyone with taste".

Lisa Tuttle in the 29th October 1975 edition of The Austin American Statesman wrote;

"Black Christmas provides a few chills and strains (usually unsuccessfully) for a few chuckles. Most noteworthy and commendable is the director's restraint".

While not wholly positive, Stanley Echelbaum did have some praise for the film in the 30th October version of the San Francisco Examiner;

"Black Christmas nonetheless provides a number of effective moments of nerve-wracking suspense".

Bill Benton was full of praise for Bob Clark and *Black Christmas* in the 14th December 1975 edition of the Fort Collins Coloradoan, even comparing Clark to Hitchcock;

"If Clark keeps improving, he just might rightfully inherit the mantle of Master Alfred Hitchcock," he noted.

David Brandon reviewed the film for the 19th December 1975 edition of The La Crosse Tribune, and was largely positive, saying;

"The tale terrorising but the casting is beautiful".

Black Christmas a money maker

THE BRANDON SUN, Friday, August 29, 1975   13

TORONTO (CP) — Black Christmas, a Toronto-made film thriller, has become English-speaking Canada's number two domestic box office champion and the second to crack the $1 million barrier.

The film's gross, 10 months after initial release, stands at $1,274,000 — second among Canadian-made films only to the record $1.8 million of The Apprenticeship of Duddy Kravitz.

Warner Brothers has opened the movie in selected U.S. markets under the title, Silent Night, Evil Night. The title was changed because it was felt white audiences would stay away thinking Black

Christmas was for blacks, said producer Gerry Arbeid of August Films.

Black Christmas made $1 million worth of sales at the Cannes Film Festival and officials responsible for the federal government-sponsored Canadian participation at the festival confirm the movie did more business there this year than most of the other Canadian movies combined.

Dick Schouten of Vision IV, an associate of the project, said the film has been making a profit since last December.

Producers talked Warner Brothers into a 50-50 proposition to go with them on costs of a simultaneous, multi-

theatre Los Angeles opening under the original title backed by an already successful advertising campaign prepared by its Canadian distributor, Toronto's Ambassador Films.

Warner Brothers changed its mind and was soon taking advertisements in Variety, the international show business newspaper, to announce that starting this fall Black Christmas would be shown in 600 theatres across the U.S.

Mr. Schouten said Warners Brothers is predicting a minimum $7-million U.S. box office gross.

The film features Keir Dullea, Olivia Hussey, John Saxon and Margot Kidder.

STEWART N. KING OPTICIANS
BRANDON SHOPPERS MALL
728-4955

**BACK BY POPULAR DEMAND
EDWARD BEAR IN CONCERT
WESTERN MANITOBA
CENTENNIAL AUDITORIUM
TOMMORROW NIGHT**

The Brandon Sun - 29th August 1975

Indeed, while receiving some lukewarm resistance in its initial outing and subsequent re-release in the mid-1970s, *Black Christmas* would seemingly ascend these minor opinions, and become more and more popular with audiences as well as the newer generations that would grow up alongside it within the horror community. Even those who branched out their love of horror to run mainstream sites such as Dread Central who in 2017 with the film receiving a new 2k scan on Blu Ray, they continually praised it, stating that while;

"Black Christmas was a reasonable success upon release, more so commercially than critically, time has been kind to this old gem and many now view it as an outright horror classic. For the uninitiated, however, let me say that I cannot overstate how exceptional Clark's film is – never giving the killer an identity, an entire subplot concerning abortion, a palpable sense of grief for Claire's father, a cast of interesting, unique people who don't ever feel like archetypes, and a potential downer of an ending. Fans will agree that the unsettling events portrayed don't diminish with repeat viewings; if anything, subsequent watching serves to reinforce that it is a standout among a sea of imitators"

145

Only question in mystery is why movie was made

By A. H. WEILER
New York Times News Service

NEW YORK — "Black Christmas," which landed on local screens a year after its release in Canada where it was produced, is a whodunit that bets the question of why it was made.

The answer is hard to come by. This moody depiction of the Christmas slayings of university sorority sisters and their housemother, among others, is as murky as the script, which dotes largely on obscenities that are no more pointed than the violence, dull direction and pedestrian performances.

Radio club sets a break

The South Texas Citizens Band Radio Club will hold a coffee break and dance Saturday at the Knights of Columbus Pavilion, 5525 S. Alameda, to raise money for a building fund.

The coffee break, from 1 to 6 p.m., will feature refreshments and games for adults and children. The public is invited.

Rod Crittendon and the Country Men will play for the dance from 8 p.m. to midnight. Admission is $5 a couple and $3 for singles.

Why this skulking psychopath is driven to making explicitly obscene phone calls in a variety of crazed voices to the girls before dispatching them remains a fairly foggy business. The slightly comic, alcoholic housemother, Marian Waldman, and Margot Kidder, who is also a drunk and as blatantly outspoken as the killer, and Andrea Martin and Lynne Griffin as the other victims, are obvious in perfunctory portrayals.

Olivia Hussey, as the pregnant, sole survivor, is properly confused and terrified by the bloody events. But Keir Dullea, the neurotic music student-lover she rejects, does little but rant about the prospective child she doesn't want and smash his piano in a fit of rage.

After several witless murders, John Saxon, the film's flustered, if perplexed, detective, cynically asks a dumb cop, "Don't you think we ought to look into it?" Considering the ersatz tension and plotting, "Black Christmas" is hardly worth the efforts of all concerned.

The Corpus Christi Caller Times - 31st Oct 1975

Chris Coffel over on Bloody-Disgusting recently re-examined the film embedded within his UK Blu Ray release editorial citing it still as "one of the best and most influential horror films ever made. It essentially created the blueprint for all other slashers to follow". He continues on how "maybe the most impressive part about the film is that here we are nearly 44 years later and it still holds up…and every time I find it to be suspenseful and utterly terrifying. Not many films can recreate the first-time viewing reaction on multiple viewings, but *Black Christmas* succeeds every time".

And with more and more fans discovering the film over the last few decades, especially with the release of the subsequent remakes, it seems Billy, Jess, Phyl, Barb, Fuller and the rest of the ensemble will continue to find praise where it is due under Clark's careful directorial approach.

viii) TV Premieres and Video Debut

Saturday 28th January 1978 was the original date for *Black Christmas'* US TV premiere, but this was thrown in controversy following a double murder at a sorority house in Tallahassee which was later confirmed to be the work of notorious serial killer Ted Bundy. The content of *Black Christmas* was deemed too close to the real-life murders, so NBC President Robert Mulholland requested the showing be cancelled.

Black Christmas on Betamax Video

Warner Home Video finally released *Black Christmas* on VHS Betamax in 1986, using the iconic image of Claire in the rocking chair, surrounded by a wreath as the main cover art. The back cover features headshot images of Barb, Jess and the ill-fated Claire (whilst being suffocated in the closet).

The tagline used on the reverse states – "A Christmas of another colour brings a killer on the loose".

Black Christmas' UK television debut was promptly pulled in August 1987, as the film was set to screen on the same day as the Hungerford Massacre, where a man shot dead 16 people before killing himself. The Guardian reported on 22nd August 1987 that the film would be replaced with a Dick Emory comedy. A BBC spokesman told the newspaper; "When there has been any major tragedy, we look at our schedules to see if there is anything which is not appropriate".

BBC blacks out TV violence

THE BBC acted yesterday to expunge violence from the television screen in the wake of the Hungerford massacre.

It barred last night's BBC-1 late film, Black Christmas, about a psychopath killing college girls. It was replaced by a Dick Emery comedy

A BBC film, Body Contact, due to be shown at the Edinburgh Festival yesterday and on TV on September 20, has also been removed from the schedule. It has been described as a "stylish pastiche with echoes of Bonnie and Clyde."

The corporation said it has no plans to show again Rambo, First Blood, which started the craze for the fictitious killer.

"When there has been any major tragedy we look at our schedules to see if there is anything which is not appropriate," a spokesman said.

But clean-up campaigner Mrs Mary Whitehouse was not satisfied. She had already protested about ITV going ahead with Thursday night's episode of The Equalizer.

She said : "It is sickening that it has taken a tragedy of this magnitude to bring the BBC to the point when it has finally accepted the power of television to affect how people behave."

London Weekend Television has cancelled its planned showing tonight of the Western Nevada Smith, directed by Henry Hathaway, because it features a gunman avenging the murder of his parents.

The Hungerford Massacre featured in the
22nd August 1987 edition of *The Guardian*

Montreal-based Malo Video would release the film again on VHS in 1990 as a re-issue with the tape featuring trailers for *Backstreet Dreams* (1990) and *The King of the Kickboxers* (1990).

ix) DVD Release and Beyond

In 2001 *Black Christmas* would get the first of many DVD releases from Critical Mass. After this, another version was released via the Tartan Video range, released on 8th December 2003. Tartan would re-issue their version of the film with brand new artwork three years later on 4th December 2006, presumably to coincide with the Glen Morgan remake and hopefully garner more slasher fans.

The first UK DVD release of *Black Christmas* from Tartan Video

American and Canadian audiences were also treated to a Special Edition of the film just a day later, on the 5th December 2006.

Black Christmas expert Dan Duffin oversaw this release alongside studios Sommerville House and Critical Mass, with new interviews from Olivia Hussey and Margot Kidder. The same release would be replicated for the film's first Blu Ray release in 2008, which was overseen by studio E1.

When Tartan Video folded in 2008, it was taken over by Palisades Tartan, with the next release of *Black Christmas* in shops from 18th October 2010 from the Metrodome Group, in what can only be summarised as a 'bare bones' DVD with no special features.

Another now-defunct studio, the legendary Anchor Bay Entertainment, would release a 'Season's Grievings' Blu Ray edition of the film on 24th November 2015. Two hours of bonus material included a commentary by Actor Nick Mancuso as Billy, plus a panel discussion with the cast and crew from FanExpo 2014 and various documentaries that had featured on previous releases.

Seasons Grieving's Blu Ray edition of *Black Christmas* from
Anchor Bay Entertainment

Cult physical media favourites Scream Factory would be the next studio to release a Collector's Edition of *Black Christmas*, with a deluxe 2-disc, set released on 13th December 2016. The first disc contained a new 2K scan of the film plus three commentary tracks from Nick Mancuso as Billy, Bob Clark's commentary which originally featured on the Tartan Video release in 2003 plus John Saxon and Keir Dullea teaming up for another. The only other unique feature on this release was a new interview with Actor Art Hindle.

On 20th November 2017, UK *Black Christmas* fans' prayers were finally answered as 101 Films proudly released a dual DVD-Blu Ray set of the 1974 film, being labelled as the first time in the UK in this format. The dual release also featured the 40th-anniversary panel with the remaining cast plus a previously released interview with Art Hindle and Lynne Griffin ported over from the previous Scream Factory edition.

In other worldwide territories, *Black Christmas* has equally found itself on numerous home release formats, with German fans finding the film released by Capelight Pictures, and which also licenced previous bonus materials onto the disc, the majority found on the Critical Mass Blu Ray release from the US, but still a welcome addition for German fans.

x) The Novelisation

In 1976, Author Lee Hays was commissioned to write a novelisation of *Black Christmas* by Public Library, a New York paperback publishing house. Hays' most famous work would come eight years later when he penned a novelisation based on the screenplay for *Once Upon a Time in America* (1984). The film, starring Robert De Niro and James Wood, would go on to become a gangster classic. Hays would also pen 11 other novels, which include four books on the popular *Columbo* television series.

The rare *Black Christmas* novelisation by Lee Hays

Although the book follows the film's storyline pretty faithfully, it does add the odd anecdote, including more inner dialogue from Billy. We begin with Billy looking at ways to enter the house and are immediately transported into his clearly fractured, mentally damaged mind. Although never confirmed, the film and this novelisation hint at a multiple personality disorder, which could explain the multiple voices he uses in the phone calls to harass the sorority girls. Interestingly, Billy pines for Barbara as he watches the girls from the outside of the house, whilst saying to himself that it is bad and he needed to be punished.

After the phone calls begin, Claire is attacked in her closet by Billy and suffocated with a piece of plastic. Once she is moved to the attic, Billy begins to comprehend his actions and begins to feel sick and in turn, the urge to call the girls again. His frantic behaviour feels placated by frightening these girls to death. One missed opportunity of the novelisation is the discovery of murdered 13-year old Janice Quaith in the park near the sorority house. It is never hinted in the film that Billy murdered the girl, but fans have theorised over the years that this was his first kill, on the way to the sorority house at the start of the story.

After Billy attacks Mrs Mac and drags her into the attic, he again shows some remorse for his actions and states that he wants to stop (a call back to one of the original script titles 'Stop Me', which Hays was working from, it's believed). Following Barb's murder in the bedroom, Billy again calls Jess, but this time his 'act' goes one step further as he vomits whilst on the phone. We also discover, just like in the film, that Billy between the phone calls later in the story had murdered the police watchmen who were stationed outside the sorority house. This could have been another added scene to the novelisation that Hays chose to omit but would certainly have been fascinating to see Billy commit murder outside of the house.

In December 2020, Bloody Disgusting Writer Paul Le reviewed the book, noting that while it is an added bonus to fans and delves into the backstories of certain characters and the narrative further, it offers little more than this. He summarised the adaptation noting that - "Something readers appreciate about these novelizations is the potential inclusion of 'new' material that isn't in the movie. This is standard practice for these books, but some writers go beyond the call of duty when padding out or expanding the story. *Black Christmas* is regretfully not one of those cases as it follows the course of the film rather faithfully; it doesn't even break 200 pages. At the very least, it's a breezy read that neatly sums up everything without straying too far from its cinematic counterpart".

Much like the movie it supplements, Hays' novelisation follows a sorority house coming under attack by an unseen intruder around the holidays. Because it follows Moore's screenplay as opposed to what unfolds on screen, there are minor yet notable differences between the movie and the book.

Some other differences between the book and the film recall the argument between Jess and Peter being a lot more heated and fiercer. While another of the deaths (and again, showing that Hays was working from the original drafts), has Barbara being stabbed by a knife (rather than the unicorn that was suggested by Sandy the AD as a much more inventive tool and thus visual on the day they shot the scene).

Additionally, while Phyl runs into Billy as she enters Barb's room, later on, her fate is more ambiguous in the final film as the door slams shut, trapping her with the killer. Moreover, the iconic shot of Billy/Clark's eye in the film is not presented, rather Billy stares at Jess from a closet, while Le also notes how "there is no startling yank of Jess' hair".

Ultimately, Le describes the book as "like any novelization, Hays' *Black Christmas* doesn't replace the movie in spite of convincing writing and sporadically clever descriptions. The book restores missing bits and pieces of the screenplay, fattens up characterization, and gives some indication of the madman's history". In the end, it is a rather intriguing piece of the *Black Christmas* legacy, one that shows up from time to time on sites such as eBay, and usually with a very expensive price tag.

xi) The other *Black Christmas*

Nine years after the release of Clark's film, a novel of the same name was to be released by Author Thomas Altman in 1983. Altman was in fact a pseudonym of Scottish Writer Campbell Armstrong, who had previously released thrillers *The True Bride* (1983) and *Kiss Daddy Goodbye* (1980), as well as being the one who turned out the novelisations of *Dressed to Kill* and *Raiders of the Lost Ark* He lived in upstate New York, where *Black Christmas* is set, but returned to Glasgow in 1990 because he didn't want his tax money to support American gun culture.

His version of *Black Christmas*, although involving a serial killer around Christmas, is much more of a Giallo-style thriller than a straight-up slasher.

We open in the small, snowy town of Murdock where a teenager named Jennifer is going to meet her boyfriend Rick. As she walks through the local park she is then attacked and killed by a mysterious assailant carrying an axe. Cutting between her murder, we meet her soon to be ex-boyfriend Rick who it is revealed, is planning to break up with her which paints him as a red herring for her death.

The 'other' *Black Christmas* novel by Thomas Altman

From here we meet Sheriff Bud Dunsmore, who along with his small team begins investigating the murder. Dunsmore discovers the girl who has been murdered is a friend of his daughter, Nancy. Bud has problems of his own too, as he tries to juggle a loveless marriage with his wife Eleanor and an affair with 20-year old Alice. In the final moments of the attack, local photographer Mitchell McCartney is walking through the woods nearby and captures some images of the attacker which he shares with Dunsmore.

Dunsmore is now analysing the murder scene and his team discovers a note on Jennifer body, which is signed by Rick. Soon after this, we meet a local drunk and former one-hit-wonder boxer Frank Tucker, who runs the local coffee shop in town. Frank finds the mentally challenged Billy Cole in the shed behind the store, the third time in the past few weeks but this time his interest is piqued when he sees a bloody axe in tow.

Dunsmore has to go tell Jennifer's parents about her murder which makes for a very uncomfortable chapter before he sets off to go find Rick and question him. Word is spreading quickly about the murder across the Murdock townsfolk and Bud is confronted by Mayor Kontakis, who despite cutting police numbers and budgets, is expecting a quick resolution to the murder. Jennifer's body undergoes an autopsy and it is revealed that she has thirteen stab wounds, which although thrown away at the time becomes quite important later on.

Billy Cole is then seen watching Dunsmore's daughter as she returns home and we find out he cannot speak or write, making him quite an unreliable witness or potential suspect for the Sheriff. Rick is found by Dunsmore hiding in his car outside his house and is taken to the station for questioning. To further complicate matters we meet Alice next whose ex-husband Dan Hamilton has mysteriously arrived back in Murdock after a long absence. He left under shady circumstances and also has a glass eye with the insinuation that he is here to raise some hell.

Frank Tucker is also having drunk fever dreams about Billy and the bloody axe, and also recalls a mysterious man in the local bar earlier in the night. The killer soon strikes again, dispatching Maryjo, another friend of Nancy's, but this time leaves the body in plain sight on the doorsteps of the Sheriff's home. Meanwhile, Dunsmore has gone to visit Alice and they discuss the return of her ex-husband, painting him as a serious suspect for Jennifer's murder. Hamilton is in fact revealed as the mysterious man at the bar as he meets Tucker again later in the night.

Tucker decides to go to the Police after his discussion with Dan and finds the axe in his shed with Billy Cole. Given his tarnished reputation in the town, Tucker isn't taken very seriously by Dunsmore. The Sheriff is also visited by a journalist from Murdock's local newspaper who probes him for answers about Jennifer's murder. It is clear that this sort of incident has never happened in the town and no one knows what to do; most of all Dunsmore.

Dunsmore discovers the body of Maryjo at his home and soon after it is revealed she also has 13 stab wounds to her body; before being laid out like a scarecrow. Strangely after the body is discovered and the second investigation commences, Eleanor decides to take a walk down to the lake near where the first murder took place. She is met by an unnamed man at the lake, who again is revealed as Hamilton who confirms her husband's infidelity to his wife.

Dan then returns to harassing his ex-wife Alice with a threatening phone call. In the aftermath of Maryjo's body being discovered, Nancy is ordered to drive to Bud's brother's home until the killer is apprehended. Murdock is now descending into chaos two days before Christmas as the local journalist musters up a mini-mob to harass Duns more about the investigation. Tucker is then questioned about the murders given his hazy account of things and plus the fact he found the bloody axe at his coffee shop following the slaying of Jennifer. He is cleared pretty much straight away and instead points the finger at Hamilton after Tucker reveals their conversation in the local bar.

Before setting out to arrest Hamilton, Alice and Bud declare their love for each other and the Sheriff now starts to plan how he will leave Eleanor for good. Once he arrives back at the Police Station, Eleanor confronts Bud about the affair, which he flat out denies. Eleanor's behaviour is becoming increasingly erratic as after discovering the affair from Hamilton, vandalises their old wedding photos before going for another of her long walks in a snow blizzard. The pace has increased considerably now, and Alice, home alone, is attacked by the killer and her fate is left on a knife-edge (excuse the pun) after she is stabbed with a piece of wood but not confirmed dead.

We are now at Christmas Eve and Murdock is still holding its annual carol service at the local church which Bud and Eleanor will still attend together to keep up the charade that they are a happy couple. It is here we learn of Alice's fate, as we discover her pinned to a cross in a dark corner of the church having been snuck in earlier by the killer. This ritualistic type of killing is one way *Black Christmas* tries to revert a Christmas and Christian trope, with a young girl strung up to look like the crucified Jesus Christ in a holy place.

Heartbroken, Bud prepares to question Hamilton at the local Police Station, and he begins to put the pieces together about who the real killer is. We discover that before leaving for the church, Eleanor called Bud's brother to ask Nancy to return home for a special meeting. Nancy is told to meet her parents at a restaurant near the local woods and lake. On arrival, she discovers quite quickly that her mother is behind all the killings, as she suspected Jennifer, Maryjo and Alice of all sleeping with her husband. She now plans to murder her own daughter who she thinks has come between her and her husband too.

Eleanor attempts to drown Nancy in the lake before Bud shows up to try to save the day. He shoves his wife away and attempts to resuscitate her on the shoreside, before carrying her lifeless body to the restaurant. Here he manages to get Nancy breathing again just as Eleanor shows up with revenge on her mind.

Although considerably different from Bob Clark's *Black Christmas*, it does have some similarities to the film such as, the mysterious identity of the killer (for the most part), a character called Billy who may or may not be the killer, harassing phone calls plus some ideas not completely realised about being an anti-Christmas story. The book was also released at the tail end of the slasher film boom of the early 1980s, making it an essential read for fans of this new breed of horror. *Black Christmas* is also featured in the smash-hit collection, *Paperbacks from Hell* by Grady Hendrix.

Hendrix had this to say about the book – "It's the night before Christmas and all through the town, someone is chopping up pregnant coeds with an axe, stabbing babysitters in the brain with a knife, and decapitating divorced ladies on broken windows. Sheriff Bud Dunsmore is dealing with a disintegrating marriage, falling in love with a much younger woman, and now he's got to handle this growing body count. He hasn't even bought his daughter a present yet!

"Less of a slasher, *Black Christmas* is actually an American Giallo, featuring all the hallmarks of the Italian horror genre: a faceless black-gloved killer, a series of elaborate stalk-n-slash set pieces, and a twist ending where the killer is revealed to be the least likely candidate, driven by psychosexual yearnings.

"It even features that most distinctive hallmark of the Giallo, a gallery of grotesques, any one of whom could be the murderer. Is it the mute man-child, Billy Cole? Is it the alcoholic ex-boxer who owns the local diner and chases underage girls? Is it a prissy, liberal college student? The bearded alcoholic ex-husband with one glass eye who is back in town to bounce his former spouse off the walls some more?"

Despite all these novelisations, and semi spin-off stories under the same title, it may have seemed like the *Black Christmas* legacy and the legend of Billy, the sorority house and the chilling ending would remain in the confines of 1974, forever immortalised and loved by fans. But a new fad was emerging, and this was the realm of the remake, an avenue that the horror genre was ripe for experimenting with by studios who had properties that they could potentially reinvest in for financial gain. And with audiences seemingly coming out in high numbers to the likes of *the Texas Chainsaw Massacre* remake and with news of *Halloween* being reimagined, modern filmmakers began to entertain plans of their own, and with major studio backing, it wouldn't be too long before Billy would be coming home for Christmas once more.

Chapter 3: Remaking Black Christmas

xii)   Origins of a new *Black Christmas*

THE origin of the 2006 remake of *Black Christmas* can be dated back to 2002 when New Line Cinema acquired the rights to the *Texas Chainsaw Massacre* franchise. The wheels were then set in motion for a modern-day remake that would kickstart a slew of reboots of older horror franchises such as *Halloween*, *A Nightmare on Elm Street*, *Friday the 13th* and of course, *Black Christmas*. At the time, Bob Weinstein was reportedly furious about not securing the rights to the Leatherface series and thus began buying up properties to start his own slew of remakes at Dimension Films.

Fast forward to March 2005 and Variety reported that 2929 Productions had acquired the rights to *Black Christmas* and hired filmmaking duo Glen Morgan and James Wong as director and producer respectively. Morgan and Wong had a long-standing working relationship dating back to work on early seasons of *The X*

Files, and at the time had more recently worked on *Willard* (directed by Morgan) and *The One* (directed by Wong).

Producer Steve Hoban from Copperheart Entertainment helped to negotiate a deal with Victor Solnicki Productions and Memento Pictures of Toronto and Adelstein-Parouse Productions of Los Angeles. The announcement also stated that Marc Butan had joined the project plus Marty Adelstein and Dawn Parouse of Adelstein/Parouse Productions and long-standing *Black Christmas* rights gatekeeper Victor Solnicki.

Billy looms large over the sorority house in the teaser image for *Black Xmas* (2006)

At the time, Copperheart Entertainment's Steve Hoban, another Producer of the film, commented to assure fans that "It's going to be a classic horror film, but it won't be a gorefest. This is an era of paranoia, so I think the timing could be really good because this is a film all about paranoia. By working with Morgan and Wong, Marc Butan, 2929 Productions, and Adelstein-Parouse in addition to our Canadian co-producers, Copperheart is continuing to play to its strengths of developing and producing theatrical genre films but is now stepping up to studio-level pictures and working with the best talent in the industry".

On 31st October 2005, Pamela McClintock reported for Variety that Dimen-sion Films had purchased the distribution rights for *Black Christmas* (2006), with a January 2006 date mooted for the start of production. Michelle Trachtenberg was the first actor to be attached to the project according to Variety, on the 25th January 2006, playing sorority sister Melissa Kitt. On 5th February, a dual cast announcement was also reported by the same publication with Lacey Chabert and Mary Elizabeth Winstead joining the cast as Dana Mathis and Heather Fitzgerald.

Later that month, on 20th February Katie Cassidy, was also announced to be joining *Black Christmas* as Kelli Presley. Stacy Dodd reported for Variety on 23rd March that Oliver Hudson had also joined the cast as Kyle Autry, with filming now underway in Vancouver.

The 258th and 259th editions of Fangoria featured an in-depth feature for *Black Christmas*, featuring interviews with Glen Morgan, James Wong, Bob Clark plus other members of the cast. During his interview, Wong stated to Reporter Dayna Van Buskirk that "We had a meeting with Bob Clark and his producing partners. Glen had done another script that dealt with a guy who was in a house. I believe the idea of that story was a kid who...I don't know if he started as a voyeur or became a voyeur, but anyway, he committed murder or something and his mom hid him from everybody in the house, in a secret room. His mom passes away and another family moves on, and this kid is, unbeknownst to anybody still living in the house. And Glen's idea for *Black Christmas* sort of stemmed from that, in that the killer could be anywhere in the house, behind the walls and looking. There's a sort of voyeuristic quality to it. So, when we talked with Bob Clark, Glen told him about those ideas and Bob was very supportive, so here we are".

With remakes generally attempting to honour their original counterparts, but also expanding on them to provide something new to an audience as well in the process, Wong revealed his intentions at the time, stating; "I guess the biggest difference is that you get to see what happened to Billy and how he came to be. But there's still a twist within that - you get a sense of him really being within the house. It's not just a killer outside. The girls are stuck. It's a snowstorm, they can't go anywhere, and when they think they're safer outside, they're not; and when they think they're safer inside, they're not. The scare levels are going to be big. The gore level will be...it will be an R-rated movie.

"There aren't as many giant casualties as *Final Destination* has; set pieces are not as big, but the ideas that we present on screen are. Fans of the genre are going to get their money's worth, that's for sure". He noted further that at Christmastime, "people are not expecting (horror). Between Thanksgiving and Christmas, there will probably not be a big deluge of horror movies, and Christmas itself is sort of a creepy holiday if you look at it in the right way. We're hoping to tap into that".

However, still acknowledging and paying tribute to the original film was always at the forefront of Wong in mind, who spoke of his great admiration for the 1974 original; "You have to go back to '74, and I think that movie was to horror what something like *Animal House* was to the teen comedy. If you look at *Animal House*, it wasn't that (extreme) and then they kept trying to top it. So as a kid I remember when Margot Kidder died; it seemed much more intense than what you actually saw. If Bob Clark hadn't wanted it (the remake), or if I heard he was annoyed, I wouldn't do it. He has been here for the last four days and has been incredibly supportive and yet non-intrusive. I asked him certain things about the first one. He could feel that we have the utmost respect for the first one and for him and what they did. I'm really trying to keep true to the tone of the original. He's been great. He's been great. He's been like a consigliere.

Mrs Mac and the sorority girls in *Black Xmas* (2006)

"I knew Ms Mac would be either Andrea Martin or Margot Kidder. My brother and I worshipped SCTV, so to have her here is just...Every day I'm blown away".

Bob Clark was also very enthusiastic about the remake and how it was treading its own path whilst respecting his film. "Basically, it's their call all the way. I met with Glen and James and was totally taken with them. I knew about *Final Destination*, which was extraordinarily clever and original. It's tough to do something fresh in this field. Glen at that time gave me a copy of *Willard*, and more importantly, I had met them and knew what they wanted to do. The clarity of their work and its intelligence is very clear and that's what I wanted to see applied", Clark said.

"It does exactly what I believe a remake does; stays true. It has the spirit of the first, but it's got its own fresh little ideas coming in. When a remake strays too far from the original, then it becomes kind of senseless unless they make a great movie. But this has the advantage of being fresh while still carrying the spirit of the first one".

Andrea Martin was looking for a slightly different take on the character of Mrs Mac, with the support of Morgan behind the camera. "I knew I didn't want it to be clichéd. I didn't know what Glen was thinking but I certainly knew that's what I didn't want to do" she said. "He's such a respectful director (Glen Morgan) and a gentleman. We had a brief conversation and I said, 'I've done a lot of housemothers, and they seem to be people who are warm and nurturing and love the opportunity to relive their youth and they're really embraced by the girls and loved like a second mother, and I'd prefer to do it that way rather than as a typical kind of clichéd performance".

Mary Elizabeth Winstead, who had previously worked with Morgan and Wong on *Final Destination 3* before joining *Black Christmas*, was more philosophical regarding how the female-led cast was approaching the film. "We all work pretty similarly. Our portrayals are very natural. We have a certain instinct in our roles. So we're kind of laid back between takes and can goof around, but when it comes to rolling the camera, we can get into it and be professional about it". Winstead was also initially hesitant to sign onto another horror film straight after the third *Final Destination* film.

"At first, when they started talking about *(Black) Christmas*, they weren't sure if it would be best for me to do another horror film. We kind of discussed that, and then Glen came to me - I believe we were at the airport doing reshoots for *FD3* and said that he thought this would be a really good thing for me, and very different from *Final Destination 3*. He told me that the character would be distinct, so I should take a look at it. I did, and I agreed. It was fresh enough for me to look into it", she commented.

"I read the script first and had some hesitation because I had just done a horror movie. Even though I was grateful to be part of it, and I love horror films, I wasn't sure if that should be my next project. So, I took a few weeks to think it over and finally settled on it".

Michelle Trachtenberg spoke about living out a college experience on-set plus finally succumbing to the horror genre, post-*Buffy*. "I'm the person who's hysterically laughing right before action is called. Then I'm like 'OK ready to work'. I didn't go to college, but a couple of my friends were in sororities, so I was like, 'This can be my college experience'. I've been avoiding doing a horror movie for a while because I didn't want to follow up *Buffy* too closely with another genre-type thing. But the original *(Black Christmas)* left a lasting impression on a lot of creative people I know; directors are like 'Yeah that was such a cool movie'", she said.

Katie Cassidy turned off the original *Black Christmas* whilst researching the role and decided to carve her own path for the character of Kelli. "I ended up turning it off because I decided I didn't want to watch it. I was just like 'No I'm going to do what I would do. I don't want to act a certain way because they did. I just wanted it to be more real and modern and cool. I read the script, Glen's version, and for the first 20 pages I was sitting at home by myself reading this, and I seriously was so freaked out. I had to put it down. I was like, 'I can't read this.' It was so scary. I was definitely into it. And then it just gets better, and I couldn't wait to see what happened", Cassidy commented.

Cassidy was almost not considered for the role of Kelli in *Black Christmas*, due to her role in the reboot of *When a Stranger Calls*. Glen Morgan saw the original *When a Stranger...* as a ripoff of *Black Christmas* and didn't want to tread too close to familiar ground with the casting on Cassidy, but her audition secured the role.

Kelli and Leigh avoid the rage of Billy and Agnes in *Black Xmas* (2006)

Ironically Cassidy was one of the cast members who stated that this would be her last horror film, and she would go on to play a major role in the short-lived horror series *Harper's Island* in 2009, *Supernatural* plus the ill-fated reboot of *A Nightmare on Elm Street* a year later.

Crystal Lowe gave away potential spoilers when discussing the work behind the scenes creating a head mould by the special effects team. "We didn't have to do face casting and stuff like that. I'm extremely claustrophobic so...if you've ever seen anyone get their face cast or if you've done it yourself...Yeah, I was freaking out, but the poor special effects guy was fabulous. I was like 'I promise I won't punch you in the face, but you can't stand close to me because I'm freaking out right now.' Because they cover your whole face, your nostrils are the only thing left, and when he was touching me, I was like 'Oh my God, get away from my face.' That was the only really intense special effect I've had to do, `` she said.

Lowe also revealed that she was originally cast in *Black Christmas* as Dana, but that role eventually went to Lacey Chabert instead. "I was originally cast as Dana, then they approached me and asked if I'd be interested in playing Lauren. Yeah, definitely. And you know what, Lacey's perfect for Dana. I read the script and had my own idea of who Lauren was, and she's very close to my own personality, so that worked".

Lowe also looked at the 1974 film and analysed the performance of Margot Kidder's Barb. "I rented the old *Black Christmas* and watched Margot Kidder do it. That was a good idea because it gave me a little bit of a different spin, and I could see where she was coming from and mix the two together, and hopefully what I've created is right", she concluded.

Morgan's real-life wife Kristen Cloke also stars in *Black Christmas* as Leigh, the older sister of one of the sorority girls. Cloke was originally meant to have a larger role in Morgan's *Willard* in 2003 but was heavily pregnant at the time, so ended up with a minor role as a psychiatrist. Cloke was initially hesitant about taking the part due to her family commitments but was talked around by Morgan.

"I have two small children now, but Glen really, really wanted me to do (*Black Christmas*), and I always love the opportunity to work with him, and my mom said she would watch our kids. But it's hard being away from them. I'm not acting that much right now, because the kids are really young. It's difficult for me to leave them, but you never know when you're going to work again and, in my case, when we'll get the opportunity to work together again. Glen and I have collaborated in a lot of capacities, but he has never directed me before".

Cloke also praised the work of Andrea Martin and was delighted to work with her, saying; "I had a number of scenes with Andrea Martin, and she is a dream, so talented, so professional, so much fun. I ran a theatre company for years and that's all about working - being an actor and focusing on the product - so it was great to have scenes with her, because she's had that experience also, and she's right there with you. I'm a major fan of hers and it was truly an honour to work with her".

Visual Effects Supervisor James Tichenor also talked about the battle between the crew regarding the use of practical or computer-generated effects for some sequences; "It's a relatively small well-contained feature. When they first started, they wanted to keep it very much in-camera, because although they did the *Final Destination* movies, and there were tonnes of effects in those, I believe that Glen does take a lot of pride in what he does in-camera. There'll be situations where we're on set and something may not be going quite perfectly right, and I'll say 'we can do this with a visual effect and I guarantee it will go really fast'. And it's almost like a challenge for him not to do it that way, which is cool", he commented.

"We're doing, for sure, the icicle that goes through (a character's) head. We also have a fork that goes into an eye and pops it out; so we're going to put a CG eyeball on the fork as he removes it. Toby Lindala has one effect where an ornament gets smashed through somebody's eye and drives it into the back of the head and through the back of the skull. We're going to enhance that with some spurting blood. But most of what Glen has picked is maintenance and invisible clean-up stuff; wire removals, possibly adding snow to a few scenes and enhancing atmosphere that way; the more practical things".

xiii) Dimension's *Black Christmas*

We open in a brightly lit sorority house clearly ready for the festive season with a focus on two girls and a big emphasis on a corkscrew and scissors. Both of these items are heavily foreshadowed as potential weapons. In a direct reference to the 1974 original, Claire hears a disturbance in her closet, and we get our first look at the venting system of the house (which will play a large part later). She had previously had a pen on her desk, which she notices is now gone and we cut to a low angle shot as a plastic bag is wrapped around her head and she is suffocated, giving her the same fate as Lynne Griffin's Clare Harrison in the original. Roll credits.

The action now switches to the Clark Sanatorium (a homage to director Bob Clark) for the criminally insane, with an orderly delivering Christmas-themed meals to the inmates. A person wearing black gloves enters the frame, which turns out to be Santa Claus who had taken a wrong turn from the Children's Ward. Who would put the children's ward so close to these clearly deranged inmates?

Again, director Glen Morgan switches to low angle shots as we get our first exposition dump, as the orderly and Santa approach the cell of Billy Lenz (Robert Mann). This is the first major difference to the original film, as Billy is named and physically revealed during the first 10 minutes, giving us an entirely different (to an extent), psychopath to contend with. You could say that this instantly demystifies the character, but the counterargument is that this is an attempt to break new ground with the character. We see Billy's room has been adorned with Christmas lights that flash on and off intermittently and he sits facing away from view in a rocking chair (which again recalls Clare's fate in the original film).

The orderly tells us and Santa that Billy has attempted to escape every year around Christmas time since his incarceration. Billy was sent to Clark Sanatorium after murdering his entire family and also ate parts of them. This is when we see Billy's Christmas dish which the orderly states "tastes just like chicken". While this incarnation of Billy is already vastly different from the mysterious figure in Clark's film, we now see that he also has a rare skin disease that has turned it yellow, as he grabs his Christmas meal through the cell door's meal hole.

In what feels like a jarring cut, we return to the sorority house from the opening scene and meet Kyle and Kelli, who are discussing their Christmas plans in the car outside. Kelli, played by Katie Cassidy has a Christmas ringtone, which looking back is such as a mid-2000s device which would help any first-time watcher guess the era this is filmed in.

Kelli does end up being our final girl of sorts, but here she is played as quite naive as we get very non-subtle hints that Kyle has been cheating on her with another sorority girl from her house. Now entering the house, we meet Mrs Mac (played by *Black Christmas* alumni Andrea Martin), who tells us about the festive tradition of Secret Santa, with even soon-to-be-revealed former resident Billy Lenz, being left a gift under the tree.

Black Christmas 2006 cannot be accused of being a slow film, as we rapidly cut back to the Clark Sanatorium with Billy leaving a note to the orderly on his empty meal plate stating "I'll be home for Xmas". The bold written statement leads the orderly to come to investigate Billy's cell, where he is promptly dispatched using a sharpened candy cane by Billy. Morgan again employs a low angle shot for this kill, which becomes constant throughout the film.

We return to the sorority house where we spend some more time with the other dysfunctional sorority sisters. Megan (Jessica Harmon), who is upstairs in her room, hears above her in the attic a noise (where Claire's body is rocking in a chair near the window) and we discover that she is the mystery sorority sister who has been sleeping with Kell, now watching a video that he has taped of them intimately available on the internet.

While this is meant to be a shocking revelation, it feels oddly flat before it is revisited later on for dramatic effect. Megan goes out into the corridor which also employs flashing Christmas lights much the same as Billy's cell at Clark Sanatorium. She gets curious about the strange noises from the attic and goes up to investigate. To Megan's horror, she discovers Claire, much the same as Mrs Mac discovers the original 1974's Clare before a bag is wrapped around her head in what is fast becoming the mysterious killer's calling card. Whilst being suffocated Megan is also stabbed with a blade in the eye, with blood flying onto a light-up

Santa statue based in the attic. This death scene is the first instance where the victim also has their eye gouged out, which like the bag suffocation technique, is used multiple times later on. While *Black Christmas* (1974) may be subtle about its anti-Christmas messages, the remake is more nonchalant in its approach.

Having already switched twice in quick succession from the sorority house to the sanatorium, it is quite clear that Billy cannot be committing the murders in the house, leaving us with a mystery killer; I wonder who it could be? Speaking of Billy, we return again to the sanatorium where Santa is walking the halls and is propositioned by a horny nurse, little does she know this is Billy, who is now successfully escaping incarceration and heading home.

Billy takes off the Santa costume and dumps his Santa sack in a large bin with a limb hanging out, signifying he has chopped up the Santa to fit him into the bag. Although this is a clever escape and genre trope, surely it would have been easier for Billy to avoid detection by keeping the Santa outfit on until he is near his old home? Mrs Mac reveals that Billy's present has become part of the lore of the sorority house, which has lasted 15 years. Melissa (Michelle Trachtenberg) now offers more background on Billy, stating that he is a spree killer rather than a full-blown serial killer. From outside we can see the silhouette of someone watching the group through the window, which is clearly love-cheat Kyle.

In the first of many, many flashbacks, we are taken back to 1970, with Mrs Mac explaining Billy's skin deformity which made him a victim of abuse from his mother, although his dad was oddly sympathetic. Billy's mother's disdain for her first-born is clear from the outset, as she sees a bauble on their Christmas tree reading 'Billy's First Xmas', and promptly crushes it in her hand before sprinkling the broken pieces in the baby's cot. Billy's mother feels like the antithesis of *Friday the 13th's* Mrs Voorhees, showing a vivid hatred for her deformed son.

Flashing forward to 1975, Billy, now five years old, is writing a letter to Santa, but his mother continues to taunt, stating, to the great comic effect, that the Russians had shot down Santa's sleigh, so he won't be visiting this year. Billy's father again shows sympathy for Billy, telling him there is a present for him after all and it is hidden in his closet, far away from the grasp of his spiteful mother. Billy goes upstairs gleefully to find his present when he hears an argument break out between his parents. He peaks under the door, only to hear a weapon strike his father in the head before he falls to the ground. Clearly, Billy's parents did not have a happy marriage and could have been driven apart due to their conflicting treatment of Billy and his skin condition.

The vents which were hinted at during the opening sequence come into place as a major plot device for the first time as Billy uses them to follow his mother and what turns out to be her secret lover, who is burying his dead father under the house. His mum spots him and hears Billy between the walls heading towards the attic.

Cutting back to the present day, the Alpha Kapa sorority house receives an obscene phone, with multiple voices asking where Agnes is. The harassing phone calls are one of the main calling cards of *Black Christmas* lore, but here it feels oddly flat and out of place whereas in the original we did get hints that these calls had been happening for some time before the night the film took place.

After another spat between the sorority sisters, Heather (Mary Elizabeth Winstead), who is clearly channelling her inner Margot Kidder, goes to leave the house before bumping into quiet loner Eve (Kathleen Kole). From her first appearance Eve is painted as a red herring for the murders taking place as she compares the sorority sisters to a family, which is another call-back to Billy's line from the 1974 film, "You're my family now", which again will pop up later.

Eve presents Heather with a Christmas gift which turns out to be a glass unicorn, much the same as the weapon used by Billy in the original film to stab Barb. Subtlety and *Black Christmas* (2006) clearly don't go together. Eve then leaves the house, as we see a person with black gloves (could it be Billy?) again watching from outside.

The long-winded backstory of Billy continues in 1992, as we witness Billy's mother and her new lover (Howard Siegel) having sex in plain view at the top of the stairs. In the intervening years since Mr Lenz's murder, Billy has retreated to the attic, where he keeps his toy telescope, which would end up being his final Christmas gift from her father. Given Billy's deformity, Mrs Lenz appears to be desperate to have another child and erase the memory of Billy for good. Her new lover, while clearly, an exhibitionist is not up to the task, so she enters the attic where she proceeds to rape Billy to try to get what she wants.

Nine months later Agnes is born, with Billy's mother stating, "She's my family now" while forming over her newborn whilst showing abject disdain for Billy. Cutting back to the present day, we see the person with black gloves enter the house. The Secret Santa charade continues as the snowstorm gets worse outside, which is a seasonal trope that this film cleverly uses to isolate the group. The group now receives another harassing phone call, but this time it is from Megan's mobile phone which noticeably spooks the group. Going upstairs to Megan's room to investigate they catch Kyle in her room, as he is trying to erase the video of them sleeping together so Kelli does not find out.

Kyle fends off the group's accusations about the missing Megan, and the subject returns to Billy Lenz as he continues the twisted backstory. The year is now 1991 (a year before he was raped by his mother), Billy uses his prized telescope to spy on happier households enjoying the festive season. We see Agnes downstairs, clearly, the apple of her mother's eye, opening Christmas gifts as her nervous parent looks on whilst chain-smoking. The Lenz household is clearly not a happy one, with the mother a twitchy mess and Agnes' father passed out drunk on the sofa.

Agnes opens one of her gifts, which turns out to be a baby doll with no eyes, which is a foreshadow, partially for her fate later. In a flash, Agnes has disappeared, and Mrs Lenz receives a phone call from Billy coining her previous phrase; "She's my family now", which leads her and her lover to the attic (where Billy now lives), not knowing their son has escaped downstairs and is heading for the living room. After not finding Billy, they rush back downstairs and find him eating one of Agnes' eyes whilst trying to suffocate her with a bag over her head. As the step-father charges over to help Agnes he is promptly dispatched with a sharpened Christmas candy cane to the eye. Billy now grabs the Christmas lights from the tree and strangles his mother to death before dragging her to the kitchen.

This part of the film was allegedly one of the ideas of Bob Weinstein, who thought the film needed to be gorier. Billy starts to beat his dead mother with a rolling pin before cutting out shapes from her back using a Christmas cookie cutter. As the police arrive at the scene young Billy is seen eating Christmas cookies of his mum's skin. We find out that Agnes survived the ordeal, losing sight in her right eye before being institutionalised and discovering her true incestuous parentage. Was she at the same facility as Billy? Surely not? Although in a film as straightforward as *Black Christmas* (2006) who knows? She has since disappeared into the ether after being released from the unnamed mental facility.

Now we finally have most of the exposition out of the way, we finally start to move forward as Clare's sister Leigh arrives unannounced in the house. Was it her with the black gloves who entered earlier? Mrs Mac does not recognise Leigh, who reveals she was a former sorority sister of Alpha Kapa, which paints her ever so slightly as a potential Agnes.

The group returns downstairs to find a present from Billy under the tree which is opened and revealed to be Agnes' eyeless baby doll in his telescope box. Leigh, after more quizzing from Mrs Mac, reveals she is actually Claire's half-sister, which again tries to press on the audience that she could be Agnes. We now discover Eve was staying in Billy's old room (despite the fact he was apparently living in the attic) to attempt to sway us back to that forgotten red herring.

The power is cut inside the house and Megan's laptop returns to manual battery power, revealing her having sex with Kyle, which Kelli conveniently sees. Kyle, it turns out is not a very decent guy, as he casually states how he regularly films sex with his (I'm guessing) multiple partners. He, after arguing with Kelli, is kicked out of the house. With Eve missing, the group raided her room and found newspaper clippings of the Billy Lenz murders, with heavily intoxicated Heather throwing up on herself randomly. She is taken to the bathroom, where we see someone watching her and Melissa through missing bathroom tiles on the floor. The power can be restored by switching back on the mains underneath the house, but the girls need to choose who will go outside in the blaring snowstorm.

Heather is put into the shower by Melissa as the eye through the floor continues to watch (another reference to *Black Christmas* 1974), as she dries off and is put to bed. Outside we see that icicles have formed all around the house in a clear foreshadowing of something untoward coming soon. Back in Eve's room, we discover a number of eyeballs of dolls amongst her newspaper clippings. Looking back this appears to have been a secret stash by Agnes, returning to the house. Eve was clearly not that bright and didn't notice the newfound items in her closet which have led to her being framed for these crimes.

Sorority sister Dana has decided to take one for the team and go and fix the power but first, she needs a cigarette. She is led to space underneath the house where she is dragged and stabbed by a person wearing pyjamas very similar to Billy's asylum outfit…

The remaining sisters receive another phone call, this time from Dana's cell, signifying her demise with the caller using the now-common phrase "She's my family now". The sisters run outside with Mrs Mac, discovering the severed head of Eve in one of their cars and a blood trail leading underneath the house.

Kelli in her infinite wisdom tries to call the police but they are unable to reach them for a number of hours due to the snowstorm. The girls begin to panic, which seems slightly delayed given that at least one of their sisters is dead and three are missing.

Mrs Mac as the head of the property tells the girls to leave the house while Kelli (much the same as Jess in the original film), refuses to leave the house without her fellow sisters. Leigh agrees with Kelli and agrees to stay and look for Claire. Mrs Mac and the fairly anonymous Lauren decide to try and leave, with Lauren trying to start the car not knowing the killer is inside. After she is killed and blood flies against the windscreen, Mrs Mac runs towards the house and slips over and is impaled through the eye with the aforementioned icicle. The double death sequence marks a noticeable change of pace in proceedings as the body count is upped considerably and the herd is thinned down to just four sorority sisters and Leigh.

While Kelli and the other girls watch Lauren try to start the car outside, we see that Eve's gift of the glass unicorn has now disappeared which cannot be a good thing. Melissa has branched off from the group having put Heather to bed, but she is now attacked by the killer with their patterned plastic bag suffocation technique. We now get a slightly better look at the killer (who is clearly Agnes) as they chase Melissa, who valiantly attempts to fight back, alas to no avail. Kelli and Leigh decided to go outside to see what is taking Lauren and Mrs Mac so long to drive for help, but they only find Mrs Mac's body impaled through the eye with the icicle. We now see that Kyle has stuck around outside watching the house, which is framed identically in some parts to Peter watching the sorority house in the 1974 film.

Clearly distressed, the girls go to get Melissa only to find she has been killed off-screen and had her eyes removed. Kyle has now re-entered the house after hearing the distressed screams of Kelli and Leigh. Kelli attempts to call Melissa but hears the phone ringing (with another trusty Christmas ringtone) upstairs in the attic.

Despite it not being the brightest idea, the trio makes their way to the attic with Kyle leading the charge with his penknife for defence. When Kyle enters the attic, he has a bag thrown over his head by Agnes (who we have now established is the main killer), who proceeds to stab him in the face with the missing glass unicorn ornament. The death of Kyle is slightly reminiscent of Mrs Mac's death in the 1974 film as he is dragged into the attic before being dispatched.

The girls break into the attic after Kyle is dragged inside and confront Agnes and attempt to subdue her. Director Morgan uses wide-angle shots here to show us that the attic is quite a large space ahead of this showdown. Kelli witnesses Agnes gauge out Kyle's eyeballs and we get our first good look at Billy's sister/daughter who is sporting a yellow eye (possibly in homage to her father's skin deformity).

Leigh and Kelli now discover the full scale of Agnes' rampage as they see a Christmas tree in the corner of the attic surrounded by bodies with eyeballs used as baubles and of the sister's heads used as a tree topper. You have to give it to Agnes; she is creative when it comes to Christmas…

Leigh suddenly falls through the attic floor, leaving Kelli alone to deal with Agnes. The killer attempts to suffocate Kelli with the plastic bag around the head but in the ensuing scuffle knocks some candles on the floor starting a fire in the attic.

Kelli finds a fork on the floor as she unwraps the bag off her head and stabs Agnes in the eye, but it turns out this is her glass eye, replacing the one Billy ate all those years ago. With violence not subduing Agnes, Kelli attempts to reason with her saying that the murdered girls are not her family and that her brother is not coming home. Agnes replies, 'No, but my daddy is'. Cue the appearance of Billy, who bursts through the attic floor towards Kelli. At this point, given we know Agnes has committed more or less all of these murders, what was Billy doing when he re-entered the house?

In a homage to Billy's murder of his mother, Agnes tries to strangle Kelli with Christmas lights from her twisted tree but falls partially through the floor herself. Agnes begins to fall as the fire rages and tries to drag Kelli with her. Despite her attempts to cling on, Agnes falls, conveniently down wall space, we suspect to her doom.

Kelli has fallen between the attic and the bedroom below but Leigh, who has recovered from falling through the floor, finds Kelli's screams and tries to drag her through the wall after breaking a hole in it. Things have become quite frantic now, with the still alive Agnes approaching Kelli from below and Billy descending from above on her. Just as Kelli is pulled to safety by Leigh, the ablaze Christmas tree in the attic catches onto the wires in the wall space and knocks Billy down and onto Agnes as the flames rage in the attic and the wall space.

We finally leave the Alpha Kapa house and head to the local hospital with a news reporter relaying tonight's bloody events for their viewers. The coroner has the bodies of all the deceased, but while drinking on the job he receives a phone call from his wife. Distracted, he then unzips the body of Agnes which appears unharmed by the flaming Christmas tree which fell on her. Agnes appears quite dead but Billy, now slightly facially disfigured from the fire, comes back to life and kills the coroner off-screen with a buzzsaw. Kelli is convalescing in her hospital bed trying to process the night's events, as she and Leigh share a tender moment despite Claire and the other girls' deaths.

Agnes is revealed to also be still alive (did the police not check for a pulse?), as she watches the girls discuss family - the overarching theme of this film. Billy on the other hand, clearly feeling outdone by his sister/daughter is seen climbing through the vents of the hospital. Kelli nips out of her room unannounced and Leigh leaves for a drink before returning to find Agnes has replaced Kelli in the bed. Agnes attacks Leigh, snapping her neck, leaving Kelli alone against the twisted Lenz family. Leigh's fate is quite a tragic one, leaving her family with two daughters to bury this Christmas with Clare also dead.

Kelli returns to her room not knowing Leigh has been killed, but she discovers blood on the bed and notices briefly, the defibrillator nearby. She now sees the blood coming from the ceiling vent and presses the emergency button. In another sly nod to the original film, the siren cannot be heard by the staff because of carol singers in the reception area. Resourceful Kelli goes to charge up the defibrillator as Agnes, who has climbed down from the vent approaches. Agnes is shocked to the face, killing her for good as Billy also starts to climb down from the vent. Kelli manages to break the glass in the door using an IV drip stand, and escape into the corridor with Billy in hot pursuit.

In true final girl fashion, Kelli attacks Billy with a crutch but then drops it in front of him, who picks it up and trips her up with it. Kelli gets to her feet and then falls over a drugs trolley as Billy pursues, claiming a scalpel en-route and starts to stab her in the back. The battle leads to a corridor overhanging the main reception of the hospital with a gigantic Christmas tree below. Kelli manages to overpower Billy, throwing him over the balcony and careening straight through the top of the Christmas tree. Billy's fate ultimately was to become the most macabre Christmas tree topper of all time.

In the first script from Morgan, the film concluded with Kelli and Leigh at the hospital receiving a phone call from Billy, as another homage to the original film. Bob Weinstein vetoed this ending and demanded something more dramatic to be shot, leading to the "tree-topper" conclusion.

xiv) On-Set of *Black Christmas* (2006)

ItsMeBilly.com Webmaster Dan Duffin was given a fantastic opportunity to visit the set of the 2006 Black Christmas while it was in production. He has exclusively written for this book, an account of his time while being there during production, and provided us with a chance to hear his thoughts and experiences from such a magical memory.

Dan Duffin on-set of *Black Xmas* (2006) with Robert Mann aka
Billy Lenz (credit to Dan Duffin)

William Alexander was the original guy who acquired the rights to *Black Christmas* after it being in legal hell for between 15 and 17 years where it wasn't available on home video or any other platform. In 2001, he finally got the DVD released for the first time, and due to my Itsmebilly.com website, he eventually invited me out to Canada to do that work on the special features for this release. I wrote and produced a small low budget documentary in a matter of hours after landing in Canada. It was lots of fun meeting the 74 Cast and crew.

I started calling and emailing 2929 Productions when I first heard about the *Black Christmas* remake. I had found out after doing some digging, where they were going to shoot the film in Vancouver, so I posted some Google Maps on its-mebilly.com and this seemed to get their attention. I got a call from producer Scott Nemes, later that night and he basically arranged for me to be flown out to the set.

Billy exits the frozen car in *Black Xmas* (2006) (credit to Dan Duffin)

They did not pay for it (in fact they said "Dan we are not adding your flight to the budget of this movie"), but they said I could come along and spend time on set covering the movie on the fansite.

I flew into Vancouver one Sunday night and went to Bridge Studios the next morning, where the film was being shot and they took me into this big studio office where all the production drawings were. I got the feeling then that this had been going on for months before I arrived as Glen had loads of pictures from films that influenced him. The crew then took me across to the warehouse where they were shooting, with the sorority house fully built inside by Marc Freeborn who had designed the *Bates Motel* house and who eventually worked on *Breaking Bad*.

They were about 3-4 weeks into production when I arrived, with most of the scenes I saw filmed being based in the living room of the house with the girls. I spent a lot of time in the video village and watched a lot of the scenes being filmed there and sat with the playback guy watching scenes that were filmed weeks before. The Editor, Robert McLachlan, was also very welcoming and talked me through the process and even made up some stills for me.

It was slightly awkward just being on-set at first, as it felt like I was pushing my boundaries a little bit here as I basically turned up every day for a week to the shoot. It was a wonderful experience to be there on-set though and experience, what I consider to be, almost a stage-show version of *Black Christmas* play out. I asked Glen and the First AD Jack Hardy if I was able to take some pictures while I was on-set and they got the studio to approve it and I spent loads of time snapping behind the scenes photos. I got to meet Andrea Martin and she was absolutely lovely and professional, and she would often give Glen the choice of a number of different takes on the same scene; a true actress, extremely funny and very welcoming to me. At the time I had a Sony PSP and had *Black Christmas* loaded on it, so I and Andrea watched parts of it on the steps of the new sorority house, a surreal experience.

Director Glen Morgan instructs Andrea Martin on *Black Xmas* (2006) (credit to Dan Duffin)

In my opinion, Glen did not have a good experience with this movie, and the production was essentially steamrolled in another direction by Harvey Weinstein backed by Marc Butan, one of the producers. When all that went down, I think that was what really led to the split between Glen and James Wong. Too many people are trying to steer the movie.

I remember being next to Glen on-set and I had the script to hand, and I had just read the scene where the girl's severed head falls out of the car outside the house. I looked at Glen and was mortified and asked him about it, and he said something like "I'm sorry but I don't have any choice". And he looked at me as if to apologise directly to me. From that moment on I did not feel like I could criticize anything, I felt bad for Glen. He had directed *Willard* just before this film, and he and Jim would alternate between directing and producing.

Glen Morgan instructs the sorority sisters on *Black Xmas* (2006) (credit to Dan Duffin)

I heard afterwards that Glen had strongly defended his vision for this movie and had disputes with other producers over the direction. Glen famously told them "I might as well go home and throw my script to *Rosemary's Baby* into the swim-

182

ming pool". They were arguing about the lack of subtlety in the film, with eyeballs being gouged out left, right and centre and icicles going through heads. He was told to up the gore in the film because what was shot was not his first script. To get the vibe of the 1974 film, Glen said he would sit down in his basement, listening to Christmas music on an old tape recorder while writing.

I think he put it like "everyone ran for the hills when Harvey Weinstein showed up on-set". Weinstein basically arrived and demanded all these changes, as it was him who planned all of those reshoots without Glen being involved. They brought a lot of the actresses back to shoot some scenes specifically for the trailers and Glen was not even aware of this. Afterwards, he emailed me the trailer and I could tell this was something else entirely from what he wanted the film to be. I emailed him after the release and told him how I thought he acted with so much dignity on set given the challenges that he faced. He seemed to appreciate this. I looked up to Glen Morgan in a big way on that film set, it opened my eyes to a lot of things. I hope he was ok with me being there.

I did get to meet Bob Clark on the set too, which was such a surreal experience for me. At this point, I knew Bob and had worked with him on the Tartan release

Original director Bob Clark is greeted on-set of Black Xmas
(2006) by Glen Morgan (credit to Dan Duffin)

previously of 1974. Around 2001, I got in touch with Bob through his agent and had a conversation with him and then in 2004, we got to meet at the 30th-anniversary screening with a lot of the cast and crew. I arrived at the hotel when I was covering the 2006 film, I opened the doors and there was Bob Clark and we got to chat again. At the end of the week, I was standing in line at the food truck and someone patted me on the shoulder and it was Bob just wishing me a good morning, which was so surreal. Bob arrived on the set one day and Glen Morgan halted the entire production and he introduced Bob, and everyone gave him a round of applause.

The cast of sorority girls was nice and welcoming to me on set. Crystal, Katie Cassidy, Lacey Chabert and Jessica Harmon were all great, Mary Elizabeth Winstead was quite stoic and distant. I rode from the set in the car with her once but spent the ride talking to her lovely mother in the backseat while Mary chatted on the phone. I did not get to know Michelle Trachtenberg at all. Dean Friss (who played Agnes) was quite the colourfully eccentric guy on-set. The Agnes character is basically him with a fake eye. He really knows his stuff on a film set though. Anyone could learn a lot from him. About a month after I got back from the set the crew sent me some items from the film, including the glass unicorn and a prosthetic eyeball. It's quite sad that this group of filmmakers were not allowed to make the film they had intended to make by the Weinsteins.

xv) *Black Christmas* 2006 Memories

The following are a series of interviews that were carried out with members of the cast and crew from *Black Christmas* (2006).

INTERVIEW

Robert Mann

'Billy Lenz at 20 & 35 Years Old'

Tell us about the audition for *Black Christmas*?

My audition for Black Christmas involved two short auditions. They wanted a video of my height and size and asked if I was okay with confined spaces, wearing prosthetic makeup etcetera and I answered yes to all of that. Then, they wanted to see the character brooding, menacing, raging. Then, it was a killing scene that they wanted to see, and I forget which one.

Did you have any discussions with Bob Clark about the character?

I never met or spoke with Bob Clark.

Once you got the role, did you revisit the 1974 original?

I didn't revisit the original film because I knew Glen Morgan had his own vision and to try to keep that fresh and unique.

Tell us about your most memorable day on set?

There are a lot of memorable days and scenes, but for sure one is the baked 'meat cookie' cannibal scene where Billy ate them with a glass of milk. We had done the very dark, scene of matricide in the kitchen with the super talented Karin Konoval and then came to this sick, surreal cannibal scene of this jaundiced maniac in pyjamas calmly cannibalizing his mom a la Christmas cookies and milk. There were laughs on set and many takes.

The cinematography and camera crew, the art department and the director really made the old house look and feel so creepy and depressing. Other memorable days were contorting myself inside an old station wagon (and I don't consider myself very flexible) - in order to get split-second shots of Billy's watching eye also for under the floorboards of the house and deck. Another funny and surreal scene was the Christmas tree impalement. I had to lay upon an elevated back brace, my legs and arms free, while they poured and set fake guts over me and then reattached the rest of the Christmas tree over me. It was darn cold where we were filming and so was the fake guts goop.

What can you recall about the scenes in the asylum?

The asylum scenes had a great look and mood to them. These were some rewrites, but us actors enjoyed the work, and it did serve for some creepy backstory as well as some good horror camp, like a candy cane shiv and Santa going down and Billy escaping as Santa Claus! The whole scene with the security guard, played by Ron Seymour and the orderly, Peter New, stands out the most.

What did you make of the yellow skin deformity of Billy?

The yellow skin, the jaundiced look of Billy, well kind of seemed comical to me, until they would put the contact lenses in and I just trusted the DOP and Glen because I could see the takes and of course with the lighting, it worked, but it was funny going to set every day and being painted yellow.

What were the differences you added to Billy from the 20-year-old version to 35?

I think the main difference in the performance of the character at different ages, is that the older Billy is more methodical and confident.

Did you discuss Billy and Agnes relationship with Dean Friss?

Dean and I talked about the character relationship, yes and I think having the two killers in the film worked as a red herring and added suspense.

What instructions were you given by Glen Morgan about how Billy should be portrayed?

Glen wanted Billy to be pent up vengeance and hate. He didn't want him over the top, but sinister as in a person badly wronged in childhood and youth and psychotic.

What can you recall about the alternative endings filmed?

I remember that the additional hospital stuff with Billy Lenz surviving the fire and hiding in the hospital walls - that was supposed to be for the U.K. and maybe Europe audience, I was told.

For two of the unused endings, you had to undergo heavy prosthetic works, how long did this take to apply?

The prosthetics/make up for the whole burn victim scene was over four hours! The special FX makeup guys did a gruesomely realistic job. I had to walk around set like that and couldn't wear anything over it to cover up so I wouldn't mess up all the hard work.

It was horrifically realistic and surreal to be 'wearing' that and walk around in that makeup on set, grossing people out, myself included.

Those scenes, Billy Lenz in the hospital bed and then behind the wall grate were all about the eyes. Good thing I'm not claustrophobic.

But the impalement scene where Billy Lenz is pushed over the ledge by the heroine and the Christmas tree gets him, that was a whole lot of fake blood and guts literally poured on me as I lay on a small square stand under my back with a hidden harness so that my arms and legs were outstretched and hanging. And that gory goop was quite cold as was the old building of Riverview Hospital and I was barefoot laying there suspended for a good while for close-ups and all!

That Christmas tree impalement stuff was again, I believe if I recall correctly, Glen's answer to Dimension's demands for more blood, more gore.

Do you recall any interference from Dimension Films during the production?

I remember some Dimension producers frequently around. I don't recall doing scenes when Glen wasn't around, but I do recall Glen being disappointed and quite frustrated with all their badgering and demands.

Glen wasn't impressed with the push for this extra stuff. He wasn't thrilled as his vision of the film was getting muddled with rewrite demands.

INTERVIEW

Christina Crivici

'Young Agnes'

What can you recall about filming *Black Christmas*?

Thinking about this film is such a wonderful memory, as it was my first break into the film world. One of the highlights I remember clearly was walking onto the set for the first time. I remember having no idea what to expect, and I was welcomed into the wonderful arms of the cast and crew - everyone was so professional and really into crafting the vision for the film to perfection. I surprisingly remember quite a bit of it all, but that's what stands out most.

Tell us about working with Glen Morgan?

Working with Glen Morgan was incredible! He's a master at what he does and was extremely accepting of my age and experience at the time. He knew how to get what he needed from me, and how to communicate his thoughts into attainable action, which is a wonderful quality when working with a director. The story I remember him telling me after we wrapped, was that I had the look they were going for, I just had to speak, and that's what sealed the deal! His willingness to share was eye-opening for me at such a young, impressionable age.

How long were you on set for?

I don't remember how long exactly, it felt like a lifetime when I think back to it... but I presume it was a few days!

***Black Christmas* is a very dark film for a child to be involved in, how did the crew keep the tone light-hearted for the younger members of the crew?**

Yes, it is definitely not the twinkliest of movies! The crew did a great job by giving us the context of the scene and the strict action we were to perform. Had I known exactly what was going on in the overall picture, things would have been different, but their consideration to give us young ones the only information we needed, was key I think.

Did you film any other scenes that never made it into the film?

From what I remember there may have been a couple of other shots here and there that didn't get put in, but the team was really efficient in knowing what they wanted, so no!

Did you work with Dean Friss so the character of Agnes had similar characteristics in both the flashbacks and present-day?

Dean and I didn't do much to work together aside from when we were filming, but I got to spend time around/with him so we were able to bond and understand each other - I think this is an ode to Casting as well - it's hard work matching present-day and flashbacks, and I think they hit the mark.

Have you ever seen the 1974 original film?

I have!

Tell us about working with Karin Konoval as Agnes mother?

Working with Karen was an experience I will never forget. Sitting in front of her while we were working gave me a peek into the way experienced actors work, and I remember being enthralled by how she was able to take notes and critique and digest them so that she as the actor was able to bring them to life what Glen was looking for. I remember being in absolute awe of her and experiencing her work first-hand when all I had to do was admire her, which was such a gift.

What was your first reaction to seeing the film?

Considering I had to wait years later to watch it... there was a whole lot of suspense leading up to it. I had NO idea what the full project entailed, and it provided all the shock value one could expect.

***Black Christmas* (2006) has quite a cult following today, does this make you proud?**

It's so nice to hear that! Yes, it definitely makes me proud.

Did you and Cainan Wiebe (Billy) strike up a friendship on set?

Cainan and I didn't actually get the opportunity to see each other very often because we were always working at different times. When we did cross paths though, it was always pleasant! We were so young that any friend to play with was good to have around!

INTERVIEW

Howard Siegel

'Mrs. Lenz's Lover/Stepfather'

When did you first hear about the *Black Christmas* reboot?

I first heard about the reboot when my agent sent me the audition sides.

What were your first discussions like with Glen Morgan?

I met Glen at the audition. He later told me that the part was mine the moment I walked into the room.

There have been rumours that the Weinstein's were an overbearing influence on production, did you notice any of this?

We had no discussions about the Weinstein's.

How long did you spend on-set?

I was on set for several days.

Stepfathers in horror films can be quite despicable characters, was there any research process for you or was it simply following the script?

I have some experience playing despicable characters and have for good or ill, embraced the box the casting directors have put me in.

What was it like working with Karin Konoval?

Karin and I go back a number of years. I first met her when I directed a production of Dads in Bondage at the Arts Club Theatre in Vancouver where she played 3 different women married to 3 men who were staying at home with the kids. She was marvellous. It was great fun working with her again after all those years.

Your character also gets one of Billy's lines from the 1974 original as you are chasing Billy around the house, how much fun was that scene to film?

I was unaware that I was using any lines from the original film.

Talk us through your death scene; was there much prosthetics work involved?

The death scene was a gas to shoot. I spent a couple of days working with the LIndala group who created the prosthetics and was truly amazed at how well it worked and looked in the finished scene.

Did you get a chance to see the finished film?

I saw the film on Christmas Day the first time it was released. There were maybe 20 people in the cinema. I sat with a couple of the crew (costumes and makeup) and we laughed all the way through. Most of the other patrons were Asian who along with us had a great afternoon.

INTERVIEW

June Reudinger
'Morgue Attendant'

Can you recall how you got involved in *Black Christmas*?

Working on Black Christmas feels like a lifetime ago -- I don't think I actually auditioned for the film. I think I was lucky enough to be offered the part, and it may have been the first time I landed a role that way since this was very early in my acting career. It was a great experience.

Was your scene as the mortician part of any reshoots or was it part of the original shoot?

I came on for the reshoots, and my scene was probably one of the last ones they shot for the film.

What instructions were you given by director Glen Morgan?

Glen let me have fun with the role. I was given a lot of freedom to play on the day. Can't remember if it was my idea or Glen's for my character to try to unwrap the candy cane with the surgical tool, but I'm glad that moment made the cut.

Was it creepy to be on a morgue set?

Yes. That was probably my first time shooting at the Riverview Hospital in Vancouver, which has since become one of Vancouver's most popular shooting locations, and which many people believe is actually haunted. It definitely has creepy energy, which is why it's such a great location for a film set.

How much time had you spent on-set before your scene?

Not much. I think we started shooting the scene soon after I showed up.

There were other scenes filmed with a more disfigured Billy with yourself?

No, this was the only scene I shot for the film.

Your character meets a very gruesome demise with a drill, this wasn't shown on screen, was the death scene filmed in all its gory glory?

No, I think my character's death was always meant to be off camera. Let the blood and screams do the talking.

Did you know about the original Black Christmas before signing up to the 2006 movie?

No, sadly I wasn't aware of the original until after the fact.

INTERVIEW

Robert McLachlan

'Cinematographer'

Tell us how you got the job on *Black Christmas*?

I had made the series Millennium with James Wong and Glen Morgan as well as the movies Final Destination, Final Destination 3, The One and Willard with Morgan and Wong.

At that point in your career, you had a unique mix of TV and film work but an interesting mix of horror projects; are you a fan of the genre or is it just considered another job?

I'm not so much a fan of horror as much as a fan of just good film making. A lot of horror films are made by inept filmmakers often just starting out, but Glen Morgan is a terrific filmmaker and storyteller.

When did you first start location scouting for *Black Christmas*?

I think we began scouting very early on in Vancouver BC - knowing we wanted to shoot in winter or early spring.

You had worked with Glen Morgan on the series *Millennium* previously, did this help with your working relationship on-set?

Glen and I from Millennium as well as Willard which he directed and the Final Destination movies which he produced and co-wrote gave us a very comfortable working relationship.

Were there are any aspects that you and Glen disagreed on for *Black Christmas*?

Glen and I were really on the same page all the time, so it went very smoothly. There is lots of give and take. He's very specific about his shots which makes my job very easy

The colours really pop in *Black Christmas* with the theme overtly Christmas, was your aim, in terms of set design to make it look like a stereotypical seasonal feel?

The running theme was when red appeared someone would soon be dead.

There were rumours after the film's release of interference by the studio regarding the supposed lack of gore, was this the case and did it make your job harder?

I don't know about gore but what happened was that Harvey Weinstein got distribution rights sometime in post-production and became super meddlesome - making us change the opening and ending and severely damaging what could have been a great scary mystery by dumbing it down. When the reshoots were done I was in the UK shooting Golden Compass and wasn't there, but I believe it was not pleasant.

It was about the same time when I did Cursed with Wes Craven who also got jerked around a lot by Weinstein. Both Wes and Glen despised the man. I heard later that he was on some kind of medication that made him nuts basically.

How much input, if any, did Bob Clark have on the film?

He came by set once but I don't think Bob had any input but was very nice.

Was the Agnes character always part of the story or was this added later into production?

Agnes was always in the script and was always going to be played by my Focus Puller/ 1st AC Dean Friss who had worked with Jim and Glen several times. Glen wrote the character with Dean in mind.

Did you have a hand in any of the promotional material for the film and if so what did you want to capture with the trailers and posters?

DPs have no hand in anything other than the colour timing once it's shot and in this case my Millennium Colourist Phillip Azenzer and Glen did it.

Olivia Hussey previously stated she was approached about being part of the PR campaign for the film, were any other original cast members (other than Andrea Martin) approached about being part of *Black Christmas* 2006?

I don't think so.

Did you get the chance to go to the premiere or see the film after its release?

Unfortunately, I was in London at the time and watched it in a half-empty theatre in Leicester Square. It was a pretty disappointing experience after all that hard work - especially the butchery by Weinstein.

INTERVIEW

Geoff Redknap

'Special Effects Make-Up Artist'

Tell us how you got involved with *Black Christmas* (2006)?

My first professional special makeup effects work was on the original run of The X-Files. I was working for Toby Lindala on that series. When he got the job to design the makeup effects for Black Christmas, he contacted me. Perhaps it had something to do with the fact that I had worked with Glen Morgan before on The X-Files and Millennium. To be honest, I don't think I ever saw the original, but I did know that it was a Canadian classic, and I figured I should be a part of this film.

How different was this from your work on *Final Destination* six years previous?

Final Destination was one of the first times I had worked for a different shop. Vancouver only had a few at the time, but I had started at Toby's shop and then moved on to working on set for various productions.

When a colleague of mine started a new shop called Flesh & Fantasy, he asked if I'd like to come to work there. Final Destination was their first big show, as I recall, and that fact encouraged me to sign up. As you know the Final Destination series is very much about bizarre deaths, so from a makeup effects perspective, that means gags rather than character makeups.

My main role on Final Destination was building a life-sized replica of an actress that was to be hit by a bus. On Black Christmas, there were gags, but mostly I was handling Agnes' makeup after she gets stabbed in the eye. That involved a prosthetic over the actor's eye and matching the disturbing 'beauty2 makeup which was established by the makeup department.

Black Christmas is extremely gory, with some creative kills, tell us about some of the challenges this presented to you and your team?

It has been a few years, so I'm not sure I remember all the kills. I do remember rolling a severed head out of a car. Bowling a severed head is never easy. I mean, maybe once or twice it lands right on the first take, but usually it's a lot of takes until it lands the way they want it. I mean, even if you manage to get it to stop on the mark they want for the shot, there's a good chance it will be facing the wrong way. Sometimes it lands perfectly, but it picks up dirt or blood. Every take, you have to clean the head, redress the blood and try again. Eventually, you get a take that everyone is happy with.

There are a lot of gruesome scenes with eyeballs in this film, how hard were they to create?

I didn't personally make any of the eyeballs. At that point in my career, I had opted to spend my time on set, rather than in the shop building the makeups or gags. To be honest, my strength is on set. I'm a problem solver. I have a thorough understanding of how sets work. Who is responsible for what? How to work with directors, actors, DPs and ADs. I'm also a director, so I have a good idea of what directors need from both a story sense and an editorial sense. That said, I did handle the eyeballs on set. From what I recall they were pretty basic builds.

Eyeballs are fairly easy to build unless they are going to be featured in close-ups. In that case, they need to be extremely detailed. That involves a skilled painter to capture realism in the iris and blood vessels. Sometimes the iris will be printed on photographic paper and built into the eye. It involves a lot of layers. Generally speaking, eyes are made by makeup effects artists that specialize in eyes. When it gets to set, it's about dressing blood on it and keeping it safe. You don't want anyone stepping on them unless that's the gag.

How closely did you work with Director Glen Morgan?

I don't recall having a lot of direct involvement with Glen, but I had worked with him before, and since for that matter, on the new Twilight Zone. Black Christmas was an interesting experience for a lot of reasons, but one, in particular, stands out. The character of Agnes was played by an actor named Dean Friss. Dean had been a focus puller and Glen knew him from previous projects.

As I understood it, Glen had for years wanted to cast Dean in something, due to his unique look and personality. Black Christmas gave him the opportunity to put Dean in front of the camera. I knew Dean from working on sets with him over the years. As I was responsible for his makeup much of the time, I was often nearby when Glen gave Dean direction or just chatted with him. So, by association, I was around Glen quite a bit.

Can you recall any problems on-set?

Nothing comes to mind. The aforementioned severed head bowling, but other than that, working in snow and fake snow, is always a challenge.

Were there any scenes you filmed that hit the cutting room floor?

I think some of the gore gags were trimmed a bit. I don't recall any scenes that were cut entirely, but from reviewing the film, it feels like Glen was going for shock value. His approach of combining hits and stabs with hard cuts seems to have prevented too much lingering on the gore.

Did you ever get a chance to see the finished film?

I saw the film at a cast and crew screening just before it opened with most of the makeup effects team in attendance. Glen has done a lot of work in Vancouver, so they were good to the crew and made sure we had a private screening.

How did you get involved in special effects?

That's a cool story. I was living in a small northern town in Canada. The town was so small that my school library was really basic, but somehow a book found its way there. At the time, there were only a few books on the subject of special makeup effects, but somehow, even though it had no earthly reason for being there, Lee Baygan's Techniques of Three-Dimensional Makeup found me.

This book fuelled a hobby that turned into a passion which turned into a career. The last part, the career, started shortly after I finished university and became aware that The X-Files was being filmed in Vancouver. I got a phone number from a friend of a friend and a few weeks later I was working on a little show that would go on to define an era.

Were there any films or people that inspired you to pursue this career?

I fell in love with films at a young age and like many makeup effects artists of my generation, the film that really hooked me was Jaws. Not long after that came Star Wars, ET and Raiders of the Lost Ark. All these films showed me that practical effects and great storytelling could come together and produce inspirational films. John Carpenter's films: Halloween, Escape From New York and The Thing also made a big impression on my growing mind.

As for people, the first big influence from the world of special makeup effects was Tom Savini. His early films and his book Grande Illusions taught me that there was so much more to makeup effect than gluing rubber to faces. It showed me behind the scenes of gags and puppets. He taught me to think of makeup effects as illusions in the same way that magicians work. Along with Tom Savini, Dick Smith, Rick Baker, Stan Winston and Rob Bottin were the biggest influences when I started.

Are you a fan of horror films?

I am a cinephile. When people ask me what sort of films I like, I answer "Good films". When I was younger, I was more into horror films than I am now. I would watch every horror film I could find. As I got older my palette expanded. That's not to say I'm not a fan of horror films, but I'm more particular than I used to be. Of course, I do still revisit the classic horror films I grew up with.

How did *Black Christmas* compare to working on the Masters of Horror series?

Black Christmas was made by a lot of the same crew as Millennium, so it was a bit of a reunion. There was a familiarity with Glen and the crew and even several of the actors. Masters of Horror was very different. It was a different director every episode. Some episodes were better than others. Some were a lot of fun, but some were extremely challenging. Without a doubt, the best part of Masters of Horror was working with the legendary directors: John Carpenter, John Landis, Joe Dante, etc.

INTERVIEW

Christopher Dusendschon

Digital Imaging Supervisor

How did you get into digital imaging work?

I started my career in Hollywood working in special effects, motion control and optical printer effects.

I was brought to Hollywood by effects guru Robert Abel to work on Tron, designing and building numerous Mitchell cameras with animation motors for individual animation rigs as well as working on the gigantic track cameras complete with rear projection systems. This was in the early 80's so there really wasn't much off the shelf gear for any of those applications at the time. Everything was designed and built from scratch.

Abel was an early adopter of digital technology starting with motion control and shooting film of computer images on Huge Evans and Sutherland monitors to eventually using the VAX Mainframe computer to generate some of the first commercial raster graphics in the computer. It was during this time that I met John Whitney Sr., long considered the 'father' of Computer Animation.

I also met Linwood Dunn, one of the 'fathers' of the optical printer. I was lucky to work and learn from Abel's amazing array of artists and technicians; Con Pederson of 2001 fame, Ray Feeney the mastermind of digital image processing, writing motion control code at first in FORTRAN and later he created CHALLIS software which was node-based and is very much like today's FUSION software. As for digital, I was privileged to work on one of the First film recorders utilizing a Xytron scanning oscilloscope and an Oxberry animation camera to capture the computer-generated images.

Were you a fan of horror films growing up?

Yes, from a very early age. I used to write to Forest J. Ackerman back when he was publishing Famous Monsters of Filmland Magazine with all sorts of questions about various productions, etc. I was also really into the Aurora Plastic Monster Models - I had them all.

Tell us how you got involved with the 2006 version of *Black Christmas*?

I helped found a Digital Film Company called iO Film and this was one of the jobs awarded to us.

What did your work entail on *Black Christmas*?

Working in the Film to computer then back to film process called the Digital Intermediate Process. This entailed shooting film then ingesting it into the computer where it was assembled and effects and other enhancements, including digital VFX, Title Sequence and end credits were added.

Then the final movie was edited into lengths of traditional film rolls and the images were painted onto new raw stock using the Arriflex Laser film Recorder. This created the final printing master negative for the laboratory to print traditional release prints for theatrical projection.

Did you spend much time on-set, if so what was the atmosphere like?

No, I worked in Post-Production on the film, and I did meet the Director and Post Supervisor.

We have heard that there were clashes between Glen Morgan and the Weinsteins over the production; did you hear about any of this?

I worked on the film after the editorial process was completed, so we lowly technicians rarely hear about gossip like in-fighting during production.

Did you get a chance to see the finished film?

Yes, I enjoyed it for all the right reasons.

You have worked on hundreds of productions, what is your best work to date?

Scanning and Film Recording Work: Crash, Yellow Submarine, Magical Mystery Tour, Pulp Fiction (2019 4K DolbyVision HDR Remastering)

Animation/Optical Effects: Tron, 2010, A-ha: Take on Me Music Video, Yello: Lightmaker Music Feature Film

INTERVIEW

Matthias Mazetti

Graphic Poster Designer

Tell us how you got the role of designing one of the posters for *Black Christmas* 2006?

I worked for several years for a company that dealt with film distribution in the role of Graphic Designer. Among the various titles, I was very happy with the acquisition of the rights to Black Christmas!

I take it your role involves working more with Dimension Films marketing department rather than the filmmakers themselves?

The contacts were held directly by the Marketing Director, I worked with some autonomy on this project.

Do you get the chance to see the film before starting to work on the poster?

This is a classic problem that we have in the creative project phase: it often happens that we cannot see the finished film before starting to work! Which makes everything more difficult. Fortunately, with the script, the trailer or some materials provided by the producers you can overcome this problem.

What sort of guidance were you given in terms of the design?

The idea of the marketing team (and I agreed) was not to push too hard on violence, but to leave more space for a thriller side of the film, to widen the possible audience. The original teaser poster was not touched, while the idea was to make the main poster clearer, playing more on the face of the actress.

Was one of the themes given, to sort of portray an anti-Christmas?

Giving a thrill on such a special evening was an opportunity not to be missed.

Interestingly your poster shows Michelle Trachtenberg's character with blood around the eyes, whereas in other promotional work her eyeballs were removed, were you instructed to keep her eyes in?

No, it was a precise choice. We didn't want to make a poster that was too splattery. It was supposed to be recognized that it was a blood horror movie, but we didn't want to make it too extreme, playing more with tension and mystery (the creepy figure in the Christmas ball)

Was there any initial feedback from Dimension Films about your design or anything that drastically changed?

This should be asked of the marketing department at the time: I was simply told: let's go full speed, here we are!

Were you surprised that given Michelle's character featured heavily in promotional artwork that her role was fairly minimal in the film?

It didn't surprise me, a girl on a horror poster is a great classic, an irresistible mix. The poster does not always represent what will happen in the film, but it is part of the game ... Michelle's expressiveness could not be excluded.

How long did it take for you to finish this design?

As often happens, you have to rush, create a definitive poster in a short time or with few materials. The problems are innumerable. The lead time is difficult to quantify precisely. I believe this project was closed in two weeks.

xvi) *Black Christmas* (2006) Reviews and Reactions

UK cinemagoers were the first to see the remake of *Black Christmas* on 15th December 2006, with US audiences having to wait another ten days for their scheduled Christmas day release. Ironically, the premiere of the film took place on 19th December 2006 in Los Angeles. Dimension Films' reasoning for the Christmas Day release was linked to the box office success the prior year of *Wolf Creek*. The film was not screened for critics and given the film's challenging production which included secret reshoots without director Glen Morgan, it certainly feels like Dimension wanted this film released and quickly forgotten about.

Billy stares through the floorboards in *Black Xmas* (2006)

The US Christmas Day release drew criticism from Christian groups including Liberty Counsel and Operation 'Just Say Merry Christmas' who described the film as "insensitive" and "ill-founded". This type of protest echoes a similar movement in November 1984 for the slasher film *Silent Night Deadly Night*, which was criticised for its portrayal of a killer dressed as Santa Claus. Dimension Films did respond with a press release which stated, "There is a long tradition of releasing horror movies during the holiday season as counter-programming to the more regular yuletide fare".

Once critics did get the chance to see *Black Christmas* (2006), the reviews were mixed, to say the least. Randy Cordova from The Arizona Republic wrote in the 29th December edition,

> *"The new version features more gore than the original and gruesome nastiness. The murders are gruesomely depicted, but they're not particularly clever as far as these things go. Ultimately, the whole thing is a bloody bore. Black Christmas? Try Blah Christmas".*

Elizabeth Weitzman was equally as scathing in The New York Daily News on 28th December, saying;

> *"Despite its considerable potential, this 'Christmas' feels drained of life long before the killer gets his slash on. Even a decent gift is useless if you forget to include the batteries".*

John Monaghan from The Detroit Free Press was slightly more complimentary in the 29th December edition of the Lexington Herald Leader;

> *"Black Christmas is a gore-filled present wrapped with a blood-red bow for fans of old-school horror. For me, this was one of the best horror movies of the year, which sounds glowing until you consider the competition", he said.*

Andrea Martin as Mrs. Mac in *Black Xmas* (2006)

Katherine Monk at The National Post (22nd December edition) was also complimentary of Andrea Martin's return to *Black Christmas* plus Morgan handling of action sequences, saying;

"Andrea Martin's return to the sorority house in the remake brings an inevitable comic element to the proceedings - she was one of the gals from the original - and Director/Co-Writer Glen Morgan has a knack for finding the right beats in the action".

Journal News Wire reported that the updated cast was nowhere near on par with the 1974 film, saying;

"In the acting department, it would be hard to compete with the 1974 original, which featured Olivia Hussey, Margot Kidder and Keir Dullea. The girls here are played by vacuous young Barbies".

Desson Thompson from The Washington Post reviewed the film in The Spokesman on 29th December and was particularly scathing;

"Horror movie audiences, their sensibilities sharpened by such box office hits as 'Scream' and 'I Know What You Did Last Summer', in which horror and postmodern irony are equal partners, will be roundly disappointed by this movie's conventional tactics. The flashbacks are hokey - the kind with grainy footage and overacting. And the characters are dull even by the pass-fail standard of cheap horror flicks", he said.

Peter Bradshaw from The Guardian (15th December 2006) had minor praise for the film, saying;

"This new version creates an elaborate, and reasonably ingenious backstory for the killer: the sorority house was once his family home, where he com-

mitted yucky acts of incest and murder. For the first 20 minutes or so, Black Christmas has some smart ideas and gags: then it all just gets predictable. One for real horror-buffs only".

Horror fan site Bloody-Disgusting.com praised the work of Glen Morgan and James Wong whilst also suggesting viewers go in not expecting a complete rehash of 1974. Loomis7 commented;

"Morgan and Wong have their strengths (dark humour, over the top gore, etc), and they adapt the basic concept of a killer inside a sorority house at Christmastime to play to those strengths. In the end, it's a pretty good modern slasher. There's no self-referential humour, there are no annoying pop stars playing sassy friends, and no obvious re-editing. Instead, there's gore, a few decent creepy moments, and some well-implemented dark humour, which is more than you can say for most slashers of the past decade. If you love the original, this film's existence is not going to change that, so please let the remake bias cease and start judging a film on its own merits. You can still hate it, but hate it for being bad, not for sharing a title and concept with another film".

Despite the polarising reviews, *Black Christmas* opened to 1544 screens across the United States, debuting at number six in the Box Office with a $3.3 million opening. This would be the high point for its theatrical release as it tumbled out of the top ten the following week into relative obscurity by its final week of release in the week commencing 15th February 2007. The film's final box office gross was $21.5 million worldwide.

Black Christmas (2006) was released on DVD on 15th April 2007, with different versions made available including an unrated cut that was 2 minutes longer than the theatrical cut. In 2008 the film received a short run Region A release on Blu Ray in Canada, but as of writing, has yet to receive a Blu Ray release in either the United States or the United Kingdom. Horror collectors can get hold of a

Black Xmas (2006) unrated on DVD

region-free blu ray release from Germany, which contains both the theatrical and aforementioned unrated cut.

In a strange twist of fate, the DVD sales of *Black Christmas* proved to be more lucrative than its theatrical release, with a gross of $29.4 million to date. Given the film was made on a budget of $9 million; a gross across cinematic and home media release of $50.4 million in 2007 is not to be sniffed at. In the 15 years since its release, *Black Christmas* (2006) has gained a cult audience with many horror fans comparing it to the more splatter-filled slashers of the early 1980s than Bob Clark's masterpiece, given its excessive gore and truly bonkers narrative.

xvii) The Third Coming of *Black Christmas*

It feels quite ironic that many horror fans think that John Carpenter's *Halloween* owes a lot to *Black Christmas* but the roles would be reversed 40 years later as the latter was prepared for a second re-envisioning. Blumhouse, with John Carpenter in an advisory role and taking care of score duties alongside his son Cody and godson Daniel Davies, had teamed up with original star Jamie Lee Curtis in October 2018 and breathed new life into the ailing *Halloween* franchise. With a record series box office of over $250 million, the slasher film suddenly became a seriously marketable asset for studios again.

Meanwhile, the *Friday the 13th* series was stuck in a bitter lawsuit between original Writer Victor Miller and Director Sean S. Cunningham while the *Nightmare on Elm Street* franchise had remained dormant since a failed reboot in 2010. What other properties could be acquired and filmed on a relatively small budget ready for 2019? This is where *Black Christmas* comes into the equation.

With the fallout from the Harvey Weinstein arrest, properties owned by the Weinstein Company became available for other studios to purchase. Most notably the *Scream* franchise was purchased by Spyglass Media Group in November 2019 and development began on a fifth film in the Ghostface series.

First teaser artwork for *Black Christmas* (2019)

Independent Producer Ben Cosgrove had researched and subsequently bought the rights to *Black Christmas* in early 2019, with a view to working with Blumhouse on a new film. He had discovered that the rights had reverted back to the original creators of the first film, as neither 2929 nor The Weinstein Company had commenced with a sequel idea to their 2006 remake, within a specified amount of time. He contacted the trustee of the estate and optioned the rights out of his own pocket. Cosgrove was not an expert on the horror genre, so instead called Jason Blum to ask if he'd like to partner up on the film. Blum accepted the offer immediately to get the film made, alongside their studio release partner, Universal Studios, offering them a tentative festive release slot of Friday 13th December 2019, which meant it would be in cinemas in just nine months' time!

During an interview with Polygon in October 2018, Blumhouse CEO Jason Blum stated "There are not a lot of female directors period and even less who are inclined to do horror". This comment led to severe online criticism across social media, with many feeling that Blum was not giving female talent the top jobs in his studio's films. During the premiere of *Halloween* (2018) on 18th October 2018, Blum sought to clarify his comments via Twitter, saying "Thank you, everyone, for calling me out on my dumb comments in that interview. I made a stupid mistake".

"I spoke too quickly about a serious issue - an issue I am passionate about. Over 50 per cent of our audience is female. Over 50 percent of Blumhouse execs are women. Some of our most successful franchises are anchored by women, including the one opening today/tomorrow, led by the biggest female legend in the genre. But we have not done a good enough job working with female directors and it is not because they don't exist. I heard from many today. The way my passion came out was dumb. And for that I am sorry. I will do better".

The comments certainly did not pressure Blum or Blumhouse to look specifically for a female director for *Black Christmas* 2019, but it would be considered a smart marketing move given the origins of the narrative are deep-rooted in powerful women thwarting male oppressors. Enter Sophia Takal. The actress/filmmaker had worked with Blumhouse that same year (2018), directing an episode of the Hulu series *Into Dark*, entitled 'New Year, New You' and while Takal is not a huge horror fan, she was happy to take on what would be a very time-sensitive production.

Director Sophia Takal instructs on the set of *Black Christmas* (2019)

Takal teamed up with writer April Wolfe, to put together a very different take on *Black Christmas*, with an underlying message that would certainly resonate with the #MeToo movement, which spoke out against the sexual abuse and harassment against women. Ironically it was revelations of Harvey Weinstein's (whose company previously owned the *Black Christmas* property), abusive past which triggered many women to share their stories, including original *Scream* actress Rose McGowan.

Takal told EW.com on 26th November 2019 about the production of *Black Christmas*; "It's been a crazy, crazy timeline. There's no time to second-guess anything, which has been kind of a fun experience. I'm so used to making indie movies, where it takes years and years and years to get off the ground. But this was brought to me in February or March of this year with no script or anything. So, it's been way faster than anything I've ever done".

Riley evades the killer(s) in *Black Christmas* (2019)

Recalling the first meeting with Blum, in an interview with Vulture.com on 2nd January 2020, Takal stated rather surprisingly that "they said there's no script. You can do whatever you want. It just has to come out on December 13. They were like, 'Do you think you can handle it?' I was like, 'No, but I'm going to try'. So, I spent about a month in a frantic Adderall haze writing probably eight drafts on my own". Takal described a prior draft, involving "some crazy, like an incel school shooting, kind of like that movie *Targets* by [Peter] Bogdanovich".

The scriptwriting process was crammed into three weeks during April, once the duo had agreed to work together beforehand. During this time locations were being scouted for the shoot, with production scheduled to start in June. Locations in South America were considered, such as Argentina, due to its colder weather during this time of year but the producers decided on New Zealand, with filming set to start on 23rd June and last until 31st July. The main location for the shoot would be the University of Otago, which had aesthetics that fit with Takal and Wolfe's vision as well as the producers.

The casting was also taking place during this time, with many of the actors sourced from smaller roles coming from New Zealand casting agents. The main casting, in terms of the largely female cast, was Imogen Poots, who had previous horror credentials with *Vivarium* (2019), *Green Room* (2015) plus the *Fright Night* remake in 2011. Poots had previously worked with New Zealand-born actor Sam Neill (*Jurassic Park*), on *A Long Way Down* (2014) and had, by all accounts, enjoyed working together. A fun fact is that Neill owns a farm in New Zealand and names one of his animals after every actor he works with; so somewhere out there, there could be a pig named Imogen Poots!

Neill was being eyed for the role of Professor Gelson but given the short filming schedule, the actor was unavailable. The second name discussed for the part was British actor Cary Elwes, who was flown in for the production. Once the scenes involving Gelson were being shot, it quickly became apparent that Takal and Elwes had a difference of opinion on how the character should be portrayed. Elwes would constantly improvise lines and refuse to listen to Takal's direction which caused many arguments on-set.

Kris is trapped by one of the Hawthorne College cult.

Takal was desperate to get a good vibe on the set from the start and would frequently take the cast out to eat and unwind following long days of production; all except Elwes. He would often distance himself from the rest of the cast (including not mixing with the rest of the cast on these outings), with Takal quickly realising he was being problematic and shifting some of the shooting schedules around so that his scenes could be completed first and he would not disrupt the rest of the production.

Madeleine Adams was a talent who had a very different experience on *Black Christmas*. Initially, her role as Helena was quite brief, but after seeing her work, Takal and Wolfe quickly re-worked some of the story elements on-set to give her more to do.

Pre-production was well underway when on 13th June, Blumhouse tweeted that *Black Christmas* would be in cinemas on 13th December. At this point, details on the overall plot were not released with this being saved for the first teaser trailer which dropped on 5th September 2019. The trailer showed the students of Hawthorne College preparing for their last semester and a Christmas break. We see the usual fraternity signifiers such as plenty of alcohol, dancing and because of the season - Christmas lights adorning most rooms. These scenes are intercut with Helena being stalked by an unknown person, although this turns into a false scare which again is quickly reversed as she runs into a hooded figure with a black mask on. Knocking over a Christmas tree, she is seemingly attacked by the person using an icicle as a weapon.

Her friends, now realising she is missing, begin a search whilst not knowing they are now being targeted too. The big recall to the 1974 film is Poots' Riley receiving a harassing phone call whilst at a Christmas tree nursery. We now see the black-masked figure destroying Christmas decorations such as baubles as they stalk the sorority house that the girls are staying in. The girls manage to corner their attacker before Riley stabs them in the head, only to find that the person has become a white statue. Another call back to Bob Clark's film shows one of the girls adorned with Christmas lights and rocking in a chair in the sorority attic, much the same as Clare in 1974.

This is the point where the trailer takes a turn for many as Elwes' Gelson's voiceover talks of sacrifices and we see what looks like a hooded cult of teenage boys in a darkened room, intercut with action sequences of the girls facing off against this black-masked threat. The main criticism that was levelled at this trailer was the fact, it felt like the entire plot of the film, plus its twists, were given away. Blum has previously counteracted these types of comments by stating how hard it can be to get audiences to commit to going to the cinema, which is why some of Blumhouse's productions show more of their hand.

Black Christmas was released on 13th December 2019, with an initial taking of $10.4 million in the United States, before taking $8.1 million in other territories, leaving it with a total box office of $18.5 million.

xviii) Blumhouse's *Black Christmas* (2019)

We open the 2019 version of *Black Christmas* with a quote from the fictional character Calvin Hawthorne, founder of Hawthorne College in 1889, which reads - "Man possesses powers so formidable they can only be considered supernatural. With a proper education, men can wield these powers and go forth into the world".

By stating man/men in both sentences of this opening scrawl, you certainly get an indication of what you are about to see play out on screen. This very much feels like Sophia Takal's mission statement for *Black Christmas*. We start to hear chanting behind closed doors and see robed and hooded figures performing some sort of ritual within the college amongst candles and what we believe to be a life-size bust of Hawthorne, the aforementioned founder of the college. The statue is drowned out by the sight of flames which is a precursor to events that will unfold later in the film. Overlays of men chanting and women screaming play over the flames and the opening credits, which again within the first 2 minutes of the film, reaffirm what sort of message this film wants to send.

Cutting to the festive season, we are now present in the girls' sorority house at Hawthorne College, intercut with Lindsay Helms, the absent fraternity sister on her way home. Lindsay receives a call from Kris at the house and they discuss their plans for the Christmas break and their secret Santa gifts. Kris reveals that she has brought Lindsay a cat for Christmas, which will turn out to be the modern-day Claudette, a gender-flipped instant call back to the original film. Buying the cat, Kris jokes that Lindsay will "never need a man" with Claudette around.

Following Lindsay, we see someone behind her start to appear to follow as she receives a text message from 'Calvin Hawthorne' with pig and cat emojis. The use of mobile phones in this version of *Black Christmas* is very intriguing, with the use of texts replacing harassing phone calls. Although this is a modern-day iteration of mobile communication, it really does lack any sort of suspense like Billy's phone calls had. Lindsay starts to become quite unnerved by Calvin's text messages as the man behind her gets closer whilst also texting someone. Takal executes the tension here really well as we flip back and forth between the two as the music starts to soar and we expect some kind of confrontation.

Believing an attack is imminent, Lindsay turns around just as the man walks off in another direction. She starts to relax before turning to face a robed and hooded figure dressed in black who starts to chase her, as she calls for help at the nearest home's front door. Lindsay, now extremely alarmed, attempts to phone Kris back, who is too busy partying with the other sorority girls. The phantom now re-appears and she falls over a snowman in the front yard and starts to run away. Her ordeal could be seen as a metaphor, as her literal cries for help go unnoticed in this suburban village of, we assume, nuclear families who reject the calls of a young female in distress. Further confirmation of this theory is when someone does answer the door and it is the black mask and hooded would-be attacker.

The attacker takes an icicle from the roof of the porch before knocking Lindsay down onto the lawn, with her appearing to make snow angels as she is attacked. Is this a reference to her imminent death and thus becoming one of the angels, in a religious sense? She is promptly stabbed with the icicle through the heart as we pan up on her dying body, with her angel wings now complete.

The morning after we see Claude the cat waking Riley (Imogen Poots), who changes for the day ahead before being interrupted by Fran who asks her for a tampon which she promptly puts on whilst still in the room. Clearly, this scene is meant to show the warts and all lifestyles of living in a dorm or fraternity, where behaviour you may consider private when in a home setting, becomes the norm when amongst friends or in this case sisters. Riley and Helena then discuss the sisters' upcoming Christmas musical performance for the Orphans Dinner as they navigate the busy sorority house. There is a commentary here on sisterhood, as Riley states as Helena's big sister she is designated to take care of her.

Often at college or university (here in the UK) people often find a non-conventional 'family' in their friends or sorority or fraternity co-habits, which is perfectly conveyed by Takal during this scene. Oona (Zoe Robins) asks to borrow Riley's red dress which she had previously performed in but what we also find is attached to another more painful memory. Riley becomes the focal point here of the story as we follow her on the way to Hawthorne College, where she walks through a gateway that can be seen to be entering this more male-dominated space, as perceived by the opening quotation from its founder.

Cary Elwes as Professor Gelson in
Black Christmas (2019)

Our introduction to Professor Gelson (Cary Elwes) is again straight on the nose, as he talks about men bonding together to invent culture as a defence against female nature. He ends by reading that male civilisation has been lifted by this process and women, as a result too. Clearly re-affirming the division between the sexes does nothing to endear us to this character and it almost feels like he is reaching for a bygone time when men had almost a completely final say in how their female counterparts live their lives. Riley is surprisingly called out by Gelson to ask for an interpretation of this text, which she states is more about women thinking with their bodies and men thinking with their brains and women living in men's worlds whether they want to or not.

In a business sense, this feels like an interpretation of the 'glass ceiling' where people, a lot of the time women, are discriminated against for higher roles because of their sex. Gelson reveals that the writer of this text he has recited is in fact a woman and a doctor to try to show that the curriculum he teaches may contain older and outdated views, but they are not always what they seem. Sadly, the film does kind of move away from this interesting line of thought and become more linear as we go on.

Here we find out that there is a petition going around campus to get Gelson fired, for what is perceived to be his more misogynistic views on the world. Gelson states that there are no secret meetings and covert operations aimed at suppressing the female voice, whereas we come to find this is exactly the case. This action could be interpreted as a would-be-attacker telling his proposed victim everything they will do to them before committing the act. As the class ends we find Kris outside trying to get a male student to sign her petition against Gelson, without success. Interestingly, a white male passes her by whereas the next person she asks, a young black man happily signs the petition. Is Takal looking to make a commentary on oppressed groups such as women and the black community being more welcoming of change whereas the white male (at this as stated by Gelson expensive College) is happy to stick to the status quo?

Kris meets with Riley and Helena and celebrates getting up to 50 signatures on the petition as the girls discuss the upcoming Orphan's Dinner again and allude to Riley's previous trauma. The conversation quickly turns to college founder Calvin Hawthorne who they say owned slaves and also dabbled in black magic sacrificing women to male pagan gods. Dropping this sort of exposition feels very deliberate by Takal, especially straight after a scene showing Gelson as somewhat of a misogynist. The girls continue to discuss the petition at the coffee shop where Riley works as Landon looks on. Kris states that Gelson's syllabus featured no women, anyone of colour or who wasn't heterosexual making it a dated program to be showing teenagers in 2019.

Kris and Helena continue to discuss Riley's previous ordeal in this public setting which feels slightly disrespectful as she is just feet away from other paying customers. The flipside of this is that victims of crimes should not be silenced, but does discuss what happened in such a casual manner really help? This is debatable. Here Kris starts a tangent about the white supremacist agenda, which again feels very timely given the race riots and widespread condemnation of the Trump presidency in the US for not speaking out definitively against racism and other forms of oppression against women.

Landon overhears this entire conversation and offers to sign Kris' petition and says he feels bad for how Gelson singled out Riley in class. She responds by apologising for his late coffee order, to which he responds, "I don't mind waiting", which feels like a very deliberate line. The reading I took from this line is similar to a young couple discussing having sex for the first time and one party stating they would like to wait, a wish that is respected by the other party. For Riley, this could carry extra resonance given her previous sexual ordeals that we will find out about soon.

Immediately Riley feels a slight connection to Landon, who appears slightly shy, well-mannered and respectful of her as a person. Her smile instantly turns to a frown as Phil enters the coffee house. We find out here that fraternity brother Phil is friends with former Hawthorne College alumni Brian, the ex-boyfriend of Riley.

Riley is assaulted by one of the cult in *Black Christmas* (2019)

He makes a joke about consent, to which Kris throws a glass of water in his face. This encounter clearly unnerves Riley, who reveals the encounter that is continually alluded to took place three years ago. At this stage, it is clear that she is suffering some form of PTSD which hasn't fully been resolved.

Cut to 'The Founder's Fraternity' at one of the Fraternity houses where the Orphan's Dinner will take place. The girls are getting ready for their performance as Riley arrives. We find out that Helena has been having pre-drinks before the performance which instantly unnerves Riley. At this stage, the viewer can put the pieces together and surmise that she was the victim of a sexual assault, where she was potentially date raped. Riley leaves to go look for Helena and walks the halls of the frat house, with portraits, including that of Gelson, almost watching her as she navigates the house. She comes to the portrait of Brian who we find out was the previous Fraternity President for his three years at the College. Approaching the doors where we heard chanting throughout the opening credits, Riley opens the door to see cloaked fraternity brothers in a circle performing a ritual, with a black substance coming from the head bust of Hawthorne.

With the black substance on her hands, Riley looks to walk away, but as she goes up the corridor she sees a clearly drunk Helena in a sexual embrace with Phil. She interrupts the encounter, which angers Phil and she addresses Helena and asks her if she wants her to leave, meaning she gives consent to Phil's actions. Helena looks increasingly afraid as Phil picks up his stuff and makes a misogynistic gesture about women all being just a bunch of teases, which again feels like a trigger for survivors of sexual abuse. Phil now actively calls out Riley as a liar before leaving.

After throwing up Helena starts to feel better and gives Riley her blessing to go home as the other sorority sisters prepare for their performance with some drinks. The girl group is now one person down though, with the girls now asking Riley to join them. She strongly opposes this as her former oppressor Brian will be watching in the crowd. Kris points out that doing the performance in front of him and the other fraternity brothers will be a sign of strength and again is another example of a survivor facing up to their attacker and showing that while they may be part of their past, they will not dictate their future.

The four girls start their routine but as Riley goes towards the front of the stage she spots Brian at the back of the room conversing with Phil. He cheekily winks at her which clearly throws her off-balance slightly, but Kris encourages her to stay strong. The three other girls basically shield Riley, who has become frozen but as the lyrics of the song, detailing a sexual assault continues she takes centre stage once again, wiping the grin off Brian's face. The male Fraternity crowd starts to become annoyed at the explicit connotations of the song, with the women in attendance getting increasingly boisterous. The sisters leave, feeling empowered as Landon catches up to Riley and praises their performance before joining them.

Back at the sorority house, Helena is packing for her trip home tomorrow for Christmas, before going to throw up again. Riley and Landon start to get to know each other, with him being shown as a binary opposite of what Brian appears to be within the story. Helena now receives two text messages from 'Calvin Hawthorne' and starts to think there could be someone else in the house with her. Takal executes an excellent jump scare here as Helena closes the door and we see the black-masked figure appear behind her.

Riley has a dream flashback to her assault by Brian before being woken by text messages asking if one of the girls got home safe. The group now leaves the house, with Fran left behind looking for Claudette, which feels like a direct reference to Mrs Mac from the original film. Takal frames this scene excellently with a unique mix of light centrally and darkness in the corners. As Fran enters the darkness and searches the rooms Claudette appears before a black hooded figure springs from one of the rooms and strangles her with Christmas lights. The style of this sequence, while not quite as well executed, harks back to the classic jump scare in *Exorcist III* in the hospital.

The remaining girls and Marty's boyfriend Nate have gone to buy a Christmas tree as Riley begins to receive mysterious text messages, which she thinks are part of a fraternity prank. Isolated from the group she receives a no caller ID phone call, which features a person making strange noises that feel quite Billy-esque before the signal aligns and it is in fact Helena's mum asking about her daughter's whereabouts. While this makes sense within the narrative, this feels like a missed opportunity to have another homage to *Black Christmas*. Riley is concerned that Helena is not home yet and goes to investigate once the group arrives home. Thinking logically she suggests that they call campus security about Helena plus the still-missing Lindsay, who we know was killed in the opening reel.

As Riley leaves the sorority house we pan out to find the frozen corpse of Fran on one of the balconies. Calvin Hawthorne is now sending harassing texts to Riley, who has the first instance that something is out of place. She runs into Landon and we see that the statue of Hawthorne has been temporarily removed, no doubt for nefarious means. Riley then talks to Gil, the campus security detailing Helena's disappearance plus the harassing text messages she has been receiving. In a similar way to John Saxon's Lieutenant Fuller in the original film, Gil dismisses her claims. Given he is an employee of the college it just feels tonally right that he would wave away Riley's allegations, although at this stage there is no concrete evidence of something untoward going on.

Gil does go to the DKO Fraternity House bangs on the door once and asks Riley to come to find him tomorrow if Helena hasn't got home by then. He uses the line, "Boys will be....", which feels like an apologist line for disrespectful behaviour which again has been part of society and used as an excuse for inappropriate actions. Whilst spying on the DKO House, Riley is scared by Gelson who has finally reappeared, knocking over his sheet of papers which she notices has the names of some of the sorority girls on it. For a potential mastermind of this deception, you would think he would hide obvious evidence like that more carefully. Gelson lets Riley into the Fraternity, which is supposedly empty, with the boys going on a ski trip with the returning Brian.

In another attempt to undermine Riley and the girls, he states that the dance routine they performed the night before was "too far" and has had videos of it removed from social media since. He states that "many sacrifices have been made to uphold the traditions of Hawthorne College". Given the opportunity to enter DKO, Riley resists leaving Gelson to go into this house alone. An interpretation of this scene could be Riley resisting this patriarchal figure and choosing to make her own path to find out what happened to Helena having got no help from Gil or Gelson.

The girls are now enjoying a roast ham for dinner, as Riley enters distraught about the video posted of their performance at DKO the previous night. Kris believes that by posting the video they were highlighting fratboy rape culture whereas Riley believes they are making people angry and recalls her encounter earlier with Gelson. We find out now that a number of the girls are receiving weird messages as Jesse goes to find Christmas lights upstairs. While trying out Christmas lights in the attic, she is attacked by the black-masked figure in what is again quite a well-timed jump scare.

Downstairs Riley and Kris get into a heated argument, with Nate becoming increasingly irritated. He speaks out against Kris' views and states that not all men have power and don't all conform to the same ideals at the fraternity brothers of DKO and across the campus. Interestingly, as Nate tries to get a point across he is shouted down and promptly thrown out of the house by Marty. There is a very interesting discussion point here as Kris is seen as a 'man hater' who has lumped Nate into the same boat as Brian and company.

The relationship between Nate and Marty is questionable after this scene, as looking back he appears to be the submissive one in the couple but when he speaks out against Kris' supposed hypocrisy he is chastised and thrown out. All of the girls now receive the same text messages with threats from Calvin Hawthorne before they are attacked by the black-masked figure who is using a bow and arrow as their weapon of choice. *Black Christmas* now finally veers into slasher territory as the three sisters run and hide from their attacker upstairs. Marty is unable to walk after being slashed in the leg by an arrow, with Kris and Riley attempting to hatch a plan to escape. Kris agrees to stay with Marty, with Riley forging a weapon from a broom handle before trying to get to a phone to call the police.

Riley gets downstairs as we see the attacker stalk the halls, bow in hand ready to strike. We now cut between Riley and Kris who are both making their way around the house, in search of a phone leaving Marty alone in the room upstairs. Kris finds Jesse strung up in Christmas lights on a rocking chair in one of the spare rooms, which is another homage to the original *Black Christmas*, minus obviously the bag over her head. Hiding behind the sofa Riley is discovered by Nate who has returned, wanting to apologise to Marty. Just as he is about to take a pickaxe and hunt the attacker, he is promptly shot in the face with an arrow, leaving the girls to fend for themselves. So much for the big male saviour.

The attacker then grabs Riley and uses a blade to slash lines in both her cheeks then seeing the mistletoe above, kiss her in what feels like another sexual assault trigger. Distracted by a singing Santa ornament Riley manages to escape his clutches briefly to try and get the pickaxe, but instead, she grabs the car keys and stabs her attacker in the neck causing a black substance to spew from it. Kris and

Marty find her and Riley goes to unmask the attacker just as another person in a black mask and cape arrives at the door behind them. As they arrive at the front door, another masked figure appears blocking the door, so for anyone expecting a Billy type character at this stage, I think it's safe to say it's not going to happen.

Marty, pickaxe in hand, attempts to threaten one of the masked figures who overpowers her and stabs her in the stomach with the axe leaving Kris and Riley alone. The girls hide in the kitchen as a dying Marty makes a 911 call which is quickly referred to Gil to investigate. Kris attempts to sneak out from behind the kitchen unit only for us to see the black-masked figure above her waiting to strike. The lack of musical cues for this initial moment works well and certainly, helps to build up tension before he strikes. The girls double team the attacker with Riley stabbing him in the back before Kris stabs him in the top of the head.

In an excellent subversion, we find out that Gil has gone to another sorority house where some other sisters are dealing with more masked killers who are apparently running amok across campus. This opens up the story to a wider base and veers even further from what the traditional *Black Christmas* fan may have been expecting with this film. Riley unmasks the attacker, who she previously saw being pledged to the DKO fraternity, basically confirming the oppressive male sorority cult previously alluded to. Kris goes to the other room to unmask the other attacker before she is attacked again but is saved by Riley who chokes them with a plastic bag over the head (sound familiar?).

Taking a pink shovel Riley and Kris try to escape in their car as the third attacker approaches, bow and arrow in hand. They manage to escape, with Riley telling Kris about her theory of the supernatural frat boy cult which at this point feels moderately believable. Kris points out that they should go to the police with Riley, counteracting that the police may not believe that these actions were done in self-defence. This could be a commentary on the authorities siding with attackers instead of victims.

Riley makes Kris stop the car before running into Landon again on the street with Kris left to go get help. She finds some of the other sisters from the campus, who have also been attacked and are asking for help. Landon and Riley make it to DKO, aiming to destroy the statue of Hawthorne, which she believes will end this murder spree. He creates a distraction in the main hall as Riley sneaks into the house. Hearing a scream from another room, Riley finds Helena alive and tied up in another room. We discover that this is a ruse and Helena has joined the fraternity as Riley is knocked out from behind. Waking up, Riley sees the fraternity ritual taking place on Landon in the main hall with Gelson revealed as the mastermind behind it all. Gelson gives another exposition dump about the statue of Hawthorne carrying supernatural powers to stop the "threat of women". He states that the founder wanted to create an army to "take our control back" if they (women) ever fell out of line. Those lines feel like they are lifted from some conservative values handbook.

Gelson states that this 'army' will venture into high powered positions upon graduation, ensuring the men of this college continue to rule the world, which harks back to the previously alluded to 'glass ceiling'. The masks that they wear following the ritual inhabit the boys with the (murderous) spirit of Hawthorne, with women who have stepped out of line chosen to be eliminated and sacrificed. Brian now re-appears and tells Riley to bow to the black-masked figure, and become a "proper woman". Calling her a bitch, he again tries to re-assert his power over her by having the masked figure murder Helena. This again shows the dog eat dog nature of these men, who will attempt to eliminate or silence anyone who doesn't fit their ideals.

The sorority girls take control in *Black Christmas* (2019)

Riley gives a faux demonstration of loyalty bowing at Brian basically bouncing around the room, gloating his apparent victory but she quickly runs to grab her hairband and slashes him with it across the face. The fraternity cult is firm believers in turning their backs on victims as Gelson encourages them to see no evil as Riley is choked by the masked figure. In her moment of need though, Kris along with the other attacked sisters appear in the room equipped with weapons to down their oppressors.

As the girl's attacks, Riley goes for the statue charging Brian who slams her down in what appears to be a rehashing of their last non-consensual sexual encounter. The sisters start to lose the battle until Riley overthrows Brian and slams his head against one of the steps. She now grabs the Hawthorne statue and despite Gelson's attempts to talk her down, Riley smashes it on the floor, downing a number of the masked frat boys in the process. Not finished, Kris then throws a burning candle at Gelson, setting him ablaze. The room starts to burn as the battle rages on, with the girls managing to escape along with the now reformed Landon as DKO burns to the ground. The final moments of the film feel like a catharsis for Riley as her attacker is now gone and she can now move on with her life.

It goes without saying that this was not the film horror fans were expecting when *Black Christmas* 2019 was announced. While it has a lot of interesting points to make and some beautifully shot scenes, it so far removed from what it could have been produced, especially off the back of *Halloween* (2018), that it feels like it would have been much easier to rename the film something else because the ties to the lore it comes from are loose at best.

It is definitely more of a political message masquerading as a film, rather than vice versa.

INTERVIEW

Madeleine Adams

'Helena'

Tell us how you got the role of Helena?

The casting process for Black Christmas was pretty normal. I auditioned with Liz Mullane and Rachel Bullock (two of my favourite casting directors) and got a callback about a week later. Sophia was in the room for my callback, and we hit it off straight away. One of my favourite moments from this recall was when Sophia stood up and taught me a really handy trick of how to convincingly pull off drunk-acting. It was so funny, and is a skill I will definitely be using for the rest of my career!

Were you given any instructions by the director in terms of mannerisms or quirks of the character?

Sophia is a very generous director and had a bounty of resources and references when it came to developing our characters. To make sure I could deliver a convincing performance, it was important that I fully understood Helena's POV when it came to the issues surrounding women's rights and the gender power imbalance. Sophia sent me through some reading material of an American author and philosopher named Christina Hoff Somers, who we believed Helena would most relate to. This was very helpful in my pursuit of forming a deeper understanding of Helena; why she believes in the things she believes in, and therefore why she does the things she does.

How much time did you spend on-set?

My time on-set was spread pretty evenly over the whole shoot, so I got to witness the progression of the film over that couple of months. I flew from Wellington (where I was based at the time), down to Dunedin and back a good handful of times. I was lucky enough to be in the last scene on the last day of filming (the scene where Helena is home alone in the sorority house and gets a spooky text) -

which felt really special. It was obviously very bittersweet because, on one hand, it was over, but on the other hand, we all felt such a sense of pride and accomplishment. I'm forever grateful I got to be there and experience that moment.

What was the atmosphere like when filming, did all of the female cast bond?

I cannot fault a single second of the time I spent filming Black Christmas. Even though we were making a horror film that dealt with pretty heavy topics, the atmosphere on set was always light, friendly and fun. The majority of my scenes were with Imogen Poots, so I got to spend a good chunk of time with her. We got along so well, and she ended up feeling like just as much of a big sister to me, as Riley was to Helena.

Do you think we need more female empowerment stories in the horror genre?

I think there is more room for female empowerment stories in every genre, but in the horror genre especially. Some of my favourite horror films include Karyn Kusuma's Jennifer's Body, and Josephine Decker's Shirley - both of which are centred around the expectations and anxieties surrounding womanhood. I am so excited to witness the increase in female-focused horror films and believe Black Christmas was a great stepping stone in this movement.

What was the hardest scene to film for you?

Every scene has different challenges for different reasons. The scene I found most challenging but equally most satisfying, was the scene when Helena reveals herself to Riley as a 'traitor'. As an actor, it is so important that you never judge your characters' thoughts, opinions or decisions. So this scene really pushed me out of my comfort zone, as I had to remove 'Madeleine' entirely and focus solely on Helena's point of view (regardless of the fact that it was so opposite to my own).

However, these are the kinds of challenges I love, as it gives me an opportunity to learn more about different perspectives and opinions, and therefore increase the amount of empathy I hold for others and the world around me.

Do you have any funny stories from filming?

I have so many funny memories from my time filming Black Christmas. One of my highlights was during the last few days of filming when the art department realised they had so many leftover props and set decorations, so they decided to put on a treasure hunt. They wrapped everything up in little packages, hid them all over the set, and let the rest of the cast and crew go find them.

It was so funny watching everyone running around, scrambling over each other to claim the treasures, and just having a really good time. Nathalie Morris, who plays Fran, definitely had the best find of all - a copy of the Spice Girls movie on VCR!

Have you kept in touch with any of the cast since *Black Christmas* wrapped?

Because the New Zealand acting industry is so small, I was already mates with the majority of the kiwi cast. Ben Black, who plays Phil, was actually my flatmate for a year prior to filming! I keep in touch with the American cast mainly through social media and absolutely love keeping up to date on all the new projects they are working on. I will most definitely be catching up with them as soon as I find myself over that side of the world!

Had you seen the 1974 or 2006 *Black Christmas* movies before getting the role of Helena?

I hadn't seen either the 1974 or 2006 versions of Black Christmas before getting the role of Helena, and I still haven't! I didn't feel it was overly necessary, simply because our version was more of a 'reimagining' than a 'remake'. In the lead-up to filming, I did however watch Luca Guadagnino's Suspiria (2018), Stanley Kubrick's The Shining (1980) and Jordan Peele's Get Out (2017) as these were Sophia's references in terms of style, tone and performance. Watching these films was really helpful to my process, as I got an idea of the kind of film we were seeking to make, and therefore knew where to pitch my performance.

INTERVIEW

Mark Neilson

'Gil'

Tell us how you got the role of Gil in *Black Christmas*?

I was subbed by my agency, Auckland Actors, and was lucky enough to get to audition for Sophia personally. When she found out that I had been a professional actor for 20-odd years, but was currently working in Campus Security (auditioning in uniform no less) she cast me on the spot.

Did it surprise you that an American horror film from Blumhouse would be filming in New Zealand?

Surprise? Not really. While the South Island of NZ isn't exactly Hollywood, there is a steady film industry here, especially in nearby Queenstown. The Dunedin's University of Otago is a very beautiful campus with lots of gothic revival architecture. There are myriad locations within a couple of hours drive too. I was delighted, but not surprised.

Were you aware of the 1974 and 2006 films before signing up?

No. To be honest, I'm not much of a horror guy. I have an enormous soft spot for facets of the genre, zombie and monster flicks in particular, but seldom seek out horror films. I have watched the 1974 film since and found it to have similar themes of feminism running through it, despite being a very different beast to the 2019 version.

How much time did you spend on-set?

I only had 3 shoot days and 3 travel days.

This was one of your first experiences in a horror film, what was this like for you?

I had been involved in I Survived a Zombie Holocaust years previously, but that was definitely more horror-comedy. Black Christmas was a more developed and professional production. Honestly, the horror elements of Black Christmas didn't come through for me on set. My scenes were mostly extraordinarily mundane.

Tell us about working with director Sophia Takal?

I think Sophia is rad. As soon as I read her script, I appreciated her Moxy. I recall finishing the screenplay and saying to my wife "This film is going to piss off so many MRAs". I was right. Turns out that shining any kind of light on toxic masculinity fires up the internet no end. As a director, she certainly knew how to talk to me. Lovely, light touches of direction shifted the focus of my performance so neatly. I would love to work with her again.

What did you make of the film's messages regarding men's treatment of women?

I'm a husband and a father of 3 girls. I identify as a feminist, and I work in security/pastoral care on one of New Zealand's most infamous party campuses. The amount of vile shit I encounter weekly in regard to sexual entitlement, party-boy culture and toxic masculinity is staggering. I initially thought the screenplay was a direct response to the Brock Turner sexual assault (and it may well be). I thought a film that literally weaponised the patriarchy would be a refreshing, if controversial, addition to the genre.

Did you enjoy working with Imogen Poots and the rest of the cast?

I was on set enough to develop a great fondness for Aleyse, Caleb, Imogen, Brittany, Lily and Sophia in particular. I tried to introduce them to cricket via the heartbreaking 2019 ODI World Cup Final, which was happening during the shoot. Imogen was wonderfully generous in our scenes. A real actor's actor, if you follow me. I would love to work on some theatre with her.

Given the filming concluded in July, were you surprised the film was in cinemas for December?

Yes. I guess I shouldn't have been surprised they we're aiming for the holiday market, but it did seem very rapid for a post-production period.

Did you get a chance to see the finished film?

Yes. It's not The Exorcist, but I don't think it's as bad as many online reviews suggest. Those angry MRA internet types really went to town on this production.

INTERVIEW

Martin Bailey

Storyboard Artist

How did you start working as a storyboard artist?

I'm originally (and still) an illustrator, and my first storyboard job was a 6 month stint filling in for the storyboarder on Xena, Warrior Princess, the TV series (late '90s).

Tell us how you got involved in *Black Christmas* 2019?

I possibly got the call for Black Christmas through the New Zealand line producer and didn't ask any questions.

What were your first impressions of Sophia Takal and April Wolfe?

I didn't meet April Wolfe, only Sophia (and only once). Sophia didn't seem over-awed with the task of directing her first big feature.

How far in advance of cameras rolling do you start working on storyboards?

All briefings were online via skype and between myself, Sophia and the D.O.P. (Mark). Consequently, I spent no time on set (Dunedin/Otago), as I was working from my home in Auckland. I think we started boarding about 4-6 weeks from the relevant shoot date. The budget was reasonably tight, so they didn't go overboard with storyboards. Mainly just the action scenes. Pretty much what you see in the trailer plus a bit more.

What did you make of this new interpretation of *Black Christmas*?

I didn't watch the previous Black Christmas' before starting; Sophia did suggest I watch a particular (the 70s I think) movie though before I started if I can just remember which it was. I'll have to think about that. She was using it as inspiration for this movie.

Were there any scenes you found particularly difficult to put together?

There always seems to be some sort of change between boards and final shots, I guess storyboards for many directors are as much 'inspiration' as 'aspiration'.

How much does a scene change from script to storyboard to filming in your experience?

Sophia was pretty clear on what she wanted and with additional input from Mark, there wasn't much space for extra interpretation on my part. This is a good thing in my view, as interpretations usually result in changes!

What did you think of the finished film?

I think the final product does a good job of marrying a high-brow ideal (strident feminism) with a low-brow genre (horror). There are some good, edgy moments in the movie, and some I'd change, but overall, a good teen flick and a competent debut.

INTERVIEW

The Blair Brothers

Music

You had both worked on a number of horror productions before *Black Christmas*, tell us when you got approached about being involved?

We have, Sophia knew another director we've worked with before, so I think that was how a connection was made. The post-production process was actually very fast-paced, so if I recall correctly, we were approached in later October 2019 - and had about 6 weeks to get the score finished.

For score composers of films, is there an audition process or did you come recommended? Did you spend any time on-set?

Again, we were hired after the wrapping of the film - so we didn't get to spend any time on set - (which was also in New Zealand, and we're based on the east coast of the U.S.) Sometimes we're hired before a film shoots, or during or after. The process of making a movie has so many moving parts - our working schedule and our involvement are always very different in each movie.

What interactions did you have with Sophia Takal? What sort of tone did you want to strike with this score? This was a fast production, was there much pressure on you in turning around the score quickly?

There's always a lot of pressure to deliver the best score you can - normally a healthy amount of that pressure is self-imposed. It's a great honour to be asked to contribute to such a BIG, collaborative project as a movie - so we don't take it lightly.

But the best collaborations come from a director who trusts us and encourages us to explore what we think the score needs. Sophia was so great and so supportive, and I think we quickly developed a trust and a sound/shape of the score that we all felt pretty good about it. She always allowed us to try new things and in a lot of cases, she pushed us to go TOO far, TOO much, TOO extreme, perhaps - and we then could scale things back where they needed to be.

Did you use any films or series as inspirations for parts of the score?

We always are pulling on other sounds and performance techniques from things we hear, experiences we've had and the wonderful many musicians we work with - but in this case, nothing directly. We didn't have a literal inspiration to pull from - maybe as there wasn't time to explore such an approach. In many scenes, we worked with a cello player, a viola player, and other soloists - and we discussed what the scene needed, and we guided a LOT of improvisations to get the sounds we were looking for.

What is your favourite part of scoring a film?

Improvising with percussion or orchestral instrumentation in a non-traditional way is always very exciting. Using instruments in atypical ways that only the scene in front of you can inspire is always a lot of fun.

What did you think of the finished film? *Black Christmas* **2019 feels like a by-product of the #MeToo movement, do you think that is a fair assessment?**

I think the film is fantastic. Sophia did an amazing job paying homage to the original but creating a new work of its own. I'm not sure it's accurate to assume the film is a by-product of the MeToo movement - in that it wouldn't exist if this movement hadn't begun. I think men, privileged men pose a serious threat in general, especially in large groups - and they've never been explored as a villain in and of themselves. For men to be villains and truly scary - most movies need to make them totally insane, or very damaged, or even possessed, etc.

I think Sophia (and writer, April Wolfe) created a very REAL and very scary villain in a way that hasn't been done before. I think there's a reality that a group of frat boys emboldened by their privilege and their sheer numbers is very scary, and I don't think the MeToo movement is part of creating that - it's a reaction to it.

INTERVIEW

April Wolfe

Co-Writer

When did you first hear about *Black Christmas* 2019?

I first heard about the Black Christmas project, I think, in February 2019. Sophia and I were casually working together on a separate project I'd written that she'll now be directing shortly, but Blumhouse had given her this opportunity, and it needed to take precedence, because the stipulation was that it had to come out December 13, 2019. I think there's always going to be a lot of pressure when you try to take on a work that's beloved by a small but vocal group of people, so that's not something that bothered me much.

The issue for remakes and reboots, however, is whether or not there's a reason to tell the story again, and the original film already had so much amazing relevancy that the prospect of getting more younger people watching it through discovering our film felt pretty exciting. But that also meant we had to separate our script as much as possible from the original—making it contemporary and almost pop in its sensibility—because you also want a film to be able to stand on its own, apart from its lineage.

Jason Blum was scolded by online critics for comments leading up to *Black Christmas* regarding female filmmakers, why do you think there isn't more female creatives getting high-profile work in Hollywood?

Because Hollywood is still deeply sexist in ways I can't even describe, and if I shared specific stories with you, I probably wouldn't ever work again. But just know that they are nearly unbelievable and jaw dropping, and that every day I want to rip my hair out and set myself on fire. Like, sometimes you're just grateful when someone doesn't use the word "bitch" in a meeting. That's how low the bar is.

When you do get an opportunity, it's often because people see you as a 'woman commodity', a token they can hold up to say that they did all they could, when in reality, the opportunity is the least they could do. One also has to provide support and guidance and protection. I feel pretty grateful for Couper Samuelson specifically at Blumhouse, though.

What parts of the script were your ideas compared to Sophia's?

This is nearly impossible to explain, but Sophia had the four lead women she wanted and the character of Nate as the boyfriend. She knew she wanted to kind of riff on the modern teen classics, so that's why you get kind of a wink and nod at Mean Girls with the talent show, and that sort of thing. I came up with the mechanics to try to make that work within a horror framework.

So, like, the character of Helena turning out to be the complicit culprit was me. Though I was doing the bulk of the writing and formulating a lot of the action sequences, it really had to be about putting to script something Sophia felt comfortable with, and sometimes she was less comfortable with more overt horror themes, so I worked within that framework.

Unfortunately, I think some of the best scenes we crafted with the most creative scares ended up getting cut for budget. We were writing this script while we were already in prep in New Zealand, so there would be times when the props department might tell me, "Ok, we don't have the budget to make that prop axe, so you have to write something different," and that would mean I'd have to scrap an entire set piece that I was really proud of and strip it down to the bare minimum, and sometimes this would happen multiple times for the same set piece until you kind of forgot what it is that you wrote originally.

I look back at those drafts wistfully. The thing I was most proud of was the diversion Silence of the Lambs bit that I wrote in—and fought to keep—where Marty's dying and reaching for the cell phone, and you cut to the campus police, and you think, "Oh! He's going to save them and get added to the mix!" But then when he opens the door, you realize you're in a totally different sorority's house, and I love that 'Oh shit' moment, where the campus cop has a half-second of recognition because the assailant kills him, too. That's the sort of misdirection type of thing that I enjoy writing, playing with tropes and expectations.

Was it always the aim to provide a commentary on the frat rape culture?

Yes and no. Sophia's original idea was closer to an Elliott Rodgers commentary about an incel, but the problem with that is that it's really hard to write. And I don't mean that in terms of technicality or skill, I mean it emotionally. In 2019, neither of us were feeling great about being women moving in the world, and the process of looking at these types of men just did not feel like any fun. Maybe we could figure out a way to do it now, but not at the time.

That's when we started moving towards the bogus 'free speech' campus arguments—conservatives cannot get enough of this bullshit—and the general rape culture within the Greek system, despite the fact that many progressive Greek houses have really tried to abolish certain behaviour. That mechanism felt like we could somehow have a little more fun with it by providing almost a campy sensibility, some kind of distance, that would allow the audience to potentially laugh at how ridiculous these people were—even though the shit they're saying is like almost verbatim to real life! It's just that this movie was made at a time when real life felt like a fucking cartoon. Nothing felt real.

Everything felt like we were stuck in some ridiculous ancient evil you couldn't kill. Gelson is modelled on fucking Jordan Peterson, and he's quoting fucking Camille Paglia, just the most notorious campus trolls you could imagine. I mean, real life is fucking awful.

What was the research process like for these sort of themes; did you talk to any rape survivors?

Well, I am a rape survivor. It happened on campus in grad school. A peer of mine date raped me. And I'd say that about a good half of my female friends have gone through something similar or more horrific. So, it's something I swim in daily.

One of the things I didn't want to do was portray Riley as a rape survivor who's just destroyed and has no sense of humour or inner life or bravery, because that's such a one-dimensional portrayal you get in a lot of genre movies for that kind of character. She's not, like, sulking in a corner. She has her ups and downs, and she's sometimes scared, sometimes brave. That's all realistic.

Was there always a supernatural element to the script?

There wasn't always a supernatural element to the script, but that came around because Sophia was just having a really difficult time getting excited for making a movie where a bunch of women get murdered. It's that distance I was talking about before, the supernatural element making it slightly less real as a means to allow a sensitive audience to process the information and to have just a modicum of fun while watching a movie that deals with something so pervasive and so real.

John Carpenter did that so much, and that's something I always admired about his work. The social commentary was hitting you right in the face, but there was this supernatural element that gave everything a veneer of popcorn fun. When we were in New Zealand, we talked a lot about the 'hammer to the nose' bluntness of our movie, and sometimes that's a thing that falls out of favour, and sometimes people can see it for what it is. But John Carpenter is really the king of that.

You had to turn around that script very quickly; do you feel any elements were rushed?

The funniest thing is that I could have done with slightly less time and more budget. Because the set pieces in some of our earlier drafts, these really beautiful kills that had so much atmosphere and revealed character, those were the first we had to cut, and then you get bogged down by having to work and rework everything to fit a budget and a location, and, yeah, give me a finite amount of time and enough money to carry it out.

Shooting in New Zealand really killed us. I don't know who thought there would be snow there, but there wasn't. They also have a very different way of working there that costs way more money and isn't suited to independent projects. They work best on American fare where there's a Lord of the Rings budget and all the time in the world, whereas Sophia and I come from an independent background, and we're just pulling our hair out, being like, "Okay, can we please, please lock down a location?"

But there would be all these kinds of social norms of politesse that you couldn't cross, and if you were too aggressive or American, then ok you don't get that location, even though it was a major reason you flew halfway around the world to shoot this thing. A big chunk of our budget was blown just on lodging cast and crew, because there was NO crew in Dunedin. None. So, we had to import an entire crew for a low-budget feature and then there were zero homes that could even potentially double for American houses. The only one we could find—which I thought was actually pretty great, in the end—was located like a two-hour drive into the rural countryside, way out past the Steam Punk capital of the world, and so you're lodging everyone again, even further out than before where there are literally just not even enough places to lodge people.

That house was nearly falling apart. Birds had taken it over and so there was shit everywhere, so I think they had to do an entire weekend of like hazmat cleaning or something, you'd have to ask the producers. And then the fucking mayonnaise packets. You know those mayonnaise packets the campus cop keeps squeezing onto his sandwich, packets you could find at any food supply store or restaurant in North America? Yeah, they cost like an insane amount of money to create in New Zealand.

The dancing Santa we had to import from fucking Russia on eBay. The snow shovel had to ship from the U.S. Every single thing you'd consider easily available in America had to be manufactured or sourced internationally. The props genius, Sophie Durham, felt so bad about the cost of the shovel that she secretly paid for it out of her own pocket. I realize this is getting granular, but I feel insane thinking about how much money went into that, when I was watching my peers shoot in Georgia and Canada and getting their money's worth.

Regarding *Black Christmas* as a property, how much did you know about the 1974 film and how much did you intend to infuse into your *Black Christmas*?

I would consider myself extremely knowledgeable about the original, which is probably why I wanted to get so far away from it in the script process. I find it already to be a perfect film. There's so much inventiveness to the script, shooting, score, sound design, everything. It is the exact opposite of a studio film.

I heard that Sam Neill was originally wanted for the role of Gelson, how much would this have changed the filming process?

Sam Neill was one of the actors we originally approached, and that was partially because I was obsessed with him from Possession, In the Mouth of Madness, and Event Horizon. He has this rare ability to go big but still ground his character in the scene.

I don't know how that would have changed the filming process, but I think it probably would have been easier, since he's already living in that part of the world.

Did you get the opportunity to bond with any of the cast during the shoot?

I got to do some cast dinners before I flew back to the States. Something I'll forever be grateful for is this fantastic cast, these thoughtful, talented people. Imogen Poots can make anything fly. Sometimes we'd have to write a line of dialogue that was kind of requested that would feel really cardboard to us, but Imogen made it all natural. We were really relying on her talent. And then Aleyse Shannon is exactly the woman you want as your flawed hero. Such a quick wit. Lily Donoghue seemed such a kind, sensitive soul, and then there's Brittany O'Grady, who I wish everything good for.

I think I spoke with her the most, but that's also because she's the kind of person who will ask you a question, remember what you said, and then follow up on it the next time she sees you. That's the mark of a great actor, someone who's listening. Caleb Eberhardt, who plays Landon, I can see a big career for him, too. There isn't anyone in this cast who didn't turn out to be the best person for the role. I really admire them.

Was there anything you would have liked to have seen in *Black Christmas* 2019 that never made it into the script or finished film?

A lot. It's endless. We had some interesting editing techniques that we were baking into the script that never made it in, for instance, the tri-split screen pioneered by Lois Weber. But that's not the kind of thing mainstream audiences want to see, I guess? Either way, it didn't end up in the cuts. There was certainly a whole lot more blood, but because of budget and location restrictions, that all got stripped out.

But just in general the kill set pieces we originally had are what I miss most, particularly Jesse's death, which when Brittany O'Grady signed on for the part had her in a workout room and which—for me—was inspired by Aerobicide (Killer Workout). It was super fun, but then they said oh we don't have the money for stunts, so then you write that out and come up with something that requires no money at all.

How nerve-wracking is it for a writer to watch their own work back?

In this case, I wasn't particularly nervous. I was too drained from the process to feel anything. That Sophia was able to get this thing done and in theaters despite every hurdle that kept presenting itself, stuff that I still just can't talk about, is a minor miracle. And that I—as a person who used to be a professional critic—had fun while watching? That's enough for me. The other things I'm working on I may have a different reaction to, who knows.

Commercially the film did not do well but it has certainly found a cult following since; is this pleasing for you?

I knew the second I saw the film at the premiere it was going to go bust at the box office and find a cult following, which is honestly not far from how the original film ended up, lol. We like to think it was ALWAYS a success. It was relatively successful, but most people really did not know about it or care, until a few champions started bulking up its reputation.

But for our film, I see it on more of a Jennifer's Body trajectory, another film that's so fun that had some extremely messy marketing by people who didn't really get what it was about. That we got a rather glowing and thoughtful essay about the artistry and subversions in our film in the print edition of the New York Times is enough for me.

The film is now available on HBO Max, do you think it will garner more new fans now it is easily available at the click of a button?

It gained a lot of new love on streaming. Also, a lot of new hate. But I'm a person who loves when something is divisive. Those are the films I championed when I was a critic. A film that was working on a level that delighted me for all its odd choices. Because I'm visible on social media, I get a lot of people tagging me in their appraisals of the film, which was awful when it was in theatres but wonderful now that it's on streaming.

A woman who ended up really loving the movie was talking on twitter about how she was told she shouldn't see it, because her boyfriend worked at the trailer house that did our trailer and they spent their Christmas party shitting on our movie and telling all their girlfriends and wives how awful it was. And then when she watched it, she didn't understand why all these guys hated it so much, and you could kind of see the wheels spinning in her discussion with her female friends.

Like, what if there are other movies I've been told not to watch that I would have liked? That's really what happened with Jennifer's Body, too. Word of mouth from people who didn't see how the film could fit into the horror pantheon, because it was so different. Also, super great that the men in charge of the marketing for your movie hate your movie. Perfect way to find your audience. Bravo.

What is your one defining memory of working on *Black Christmas* 2019?

When a handful of rape survivors started DMing me to tell me that Imogen's incredible performance and our script felt so deeply cathartic to them that they had to reach out and tell me. Sometimes you're so caught up in the fucking mayonnaise packets and how to get that damn dancing Santa from Russia that you forget why you're doing this.

And in the end, Sophia and I felt like we were telling an important story. Sure, it's told in kind of a silly way, but it was important nonetheless, and then these wonderful people remind you of what it meant to them, and you say, "Fuck the mayonnaise". You know? Fuck the mayonnaise, because this woman in Tennessee said our movie spoke to her. And then everything else falls away, because that's the only thing that matters.

Chapter 4: Beyond *Black Christmas*

xix) The Future

BLACK *Christmas* (2019) was released worldwide across the week commencing 9th December and grossed a disappointing $18.5 million worldwide. The film was heavily criticised for its uneven plot and widely shunned by fans expecting some sort of plot that related to the 1974 original and its slasher in the sorority house roots. Despite this, the film did gain an extremely vocal online community that championed the depiction of frat boy rape culture and considered it a pro-feminist horror film. Due to the low box office takings, Blumhouse has distanced itself from the film, with sources at the company informing these writers that there are no plans to revisit the universe the 2019 film created in any shape or form.

This begs the question; what is the future of the *Black Christmas* name in horror? In the closing credits of *Black Christmas* (2019) it was noted that the film was dedicated to the memory of Victor Solnicki, one of the men who helped to revive the brand back in 2005, which would result in the first remake and this version of the story. Solnicki was one of the men who held the rights to *Black Christmas* alongside his cousin Norman Griesdorf, a lawyer based in Ontario Canada. We have recently learned that Griesdorf himself passed away on 30th November 2020 just after his 87th birthday. He is survived by his wife Jeniva, his daughter Diana, son Danny and son-in-law Steve. Theoretically, Griesdorf' rights to the *Black Christmas* brand would be filtered down to his next of kin upon his passing. Original *Black Christmas* Co-Writer A. Roy Moore (who passed away during the 1980s), handed his section of the rights to friends of the family upon his passing. Only time will tell where and how these rights are reapplied to a new film.

Waxword Records' release of *Black Christmas* (1974) on Vinyl

One area that does keep the Christmas candles burning is the fans. On social media, there are numerous fansites dedicated to the film, with a discussion of the film's themes, the characters, as well as the ambiguity of Billy, are keeping the subject and film alive, passing it also onto a new generation of fans who seek out the groups/websites after seeing Clark's chiller for the first time. Merchandise wise, *Black Christmas* has never been given the treatment from cult manufacturers like Neca or Mezco (although we're guessing a Billy figure would be difficult to make since we barely saw much of him in the actual film!). But maybe a model of the house itself with Clare still stuck in the attic window could be an idea or a 3D wall model featuring Billy's eye staring intensely back at us (and our guests).

There are a handful of collectables out there, such as the aforementioned novelisation, as well as the numerous home release formats, while you can purchase a 3D *Black Christmas* poster over on sites such as eBay, which while not official, are still great fun to have, while Carl Zittrer's soundtrack had an official release on Vinyl in 2016. Perhaps if a new studio does push for a *Halloween* 2018 approach and make a direct sequel in the future, we may get more collectables, but until then, Billy remains on the shelf behind all the other Michael/Jason/Freddy figures.

xx) Billy Goes Independent

In July 2020, a crowdfunding campaign was announced for *It's Me Billy*, a fan film that would serve as a legacy sequel to the original *Black Christmas*. Set 50 years after the original film, *It's Me Billy*, follows Sam and her two best friends who are spending Christmas Eve at her grandmother's old country mansion, unaware of the danger that is hunting her. Stalked by a sinister evil that's been lurking in the shadows for nearly 50 years, Sam is about to come face-to-face with her grandmother's chilling Christmas past, the deranged psychopath known only as Billy.

Victoria Mero as Sam in *It's me, Billy - A Black Christmas* fan film

Co-Directed by Canadian filmmakers Bruce Dale and Dave McRae, the film was shot in late 2020 and early 2021 and was released online via YouTube on May 28th 2021. The film itself is from the opening scene more interesting than any of the remakes while the narrative gives us plenty of twists and turns that will make fans of Clark's film very happy.

Littered with numerous homages, as well as bringing back Billy in his original form, *It's Me Billy* successfully attempts to replicate the sinister, eerie and cold bleakness of the 1974 original, while also allowing it to break free and tell its own tale, one that really works well, and ultimately makes Billy scary again, while still an unknown persona.

Something the remakes failed to do, instead of relying more on exposition and over the top gore and violence to try to sell their unique USPs. One of the many things that this fan film proves more than anything is that there are still plenty of impressive stories here to explore within the original *Black Christmas* universe.

Rather than resetting it, or even reimagining it, McRae and company show that fans and independent filmmakers are itching to revisit the original narrative, to have a go at continuing the story, but in a way that honours as well as respects the original source material; and in an impressive and wildly imaginative way that would arguably make Clark proud.

Billy strikes in *It's Me Billy* (2021)

INTERVIEW

Dave McRae

Co-Director - *It's Me Billy: A Black Christmas Fan Film*

Tell us why you decided to do a film in the *Black Christmas* universe?

A few reasons actually. First, although Black Christmas has one of the greatest endings in all of horror and certainly doesn't need a sequel, we wanted to play in the Black Christmas sandbox and bring something special to fans who were disappointed by the two remakes. The second reason was that we saw an opportunity to showcase our filmmaking skills by producing a horror fan film with a very high level of production value. I, along with my best friend and filmmaking partner Bruce Dale, work in the film industry here in Toronto and wanted to utilize the resources and connections at our disposal. Bruce and I worked incredibly hard to bring this next chapter to life, but we couldn't have done it without our amazing cast, crew, and IndieGoGo backers. And finally, It was important for us to not just simply create our own version of the original, but advance the story in a way that felt organically connected to the original film. We thought who better to do it than Canadian filmmakers from Toronto? It just made sense to us. It felt right.

What do you think of the original *Black Christmas*?

We love it! We actually really love and appreciate that era of horror filmmaking. There is nothing creepier than a horror film that has an insidious slow burn with lots of palpable mood and atmosphere. These elements (by and large) are missing in much of modern-day horror. Black Christmas is not only a terrific example of this kind of storytelling but is one of the most influential horror films of all time. And although it's a little dated now, it's also a great example of the 'theatre of the mind' school of filmmaking. Less is usually always more in our opinion, and nothing is more truly frightening than the horror you imagine in your own mind.

With the way the film ends, were you always disappointed there wasn't a sequel?

No, I wasn't actually, and neither was Bruce. We think it's a satisfying ending. It's dark and uncertain. This was the intent from Bob Clark. Even we admit that it doesn't need a sequel. But what if there was one? How should it be one? This is where we come in.

How has the film aged nearly 50 years since its release?

Most films, not just horror films, all look dated from a certain era. We must also remember that Black Christmas (like Halloween) was a relatively low budget horror film for its time. But what makes the original Black Christmas the classic it is today, are the timeless filmmaking techniques that resonate with audiences on a psychological and subconscious level. The brilliant use of the 'theatre of the mind' approach was unnerving then, and it's unnerving now. There's this eerie false sense of security that resonates throughout the film's runtime. It's also loaded with mood and atmosphere. If you're looking for quick cuts, blood and gore and something modern, you're looking at the wrong movie. But if you're in search of an old classic horror film in the style of Hitchcock, you're in for a real treat!

What was the scariest part of *Black Christmas*?

The ambiguity of Billy. It's never revealed who Billy is, why he's doing what he's doing, or what he looks like. He's just a dark, ominous, and lurking shadow stealthily moving through the house. And those phone calls. Ohhh, those phone calls! You combine all that with a simplistic score (that is nothing more than eerie piano strikes and scrapes) with well-crafted shots that give the actors and scenes time to breathe, the cosy Christmas season turns dark rather quickly.

Bob Clark goes to great lengths not to reveal the killer in full during the original film, is this something you will carry on with for It's Me, Billy?

Yes, absolutely.

How does your story drive the *Black Christmas* narrative forward?

Well, it's a short film, not a feature, so there is only so much we can do in a limited amount of time. But the film is designed to be episodic; it's really just part of a much larger story we hope to tell in another instalment. That being said, our approach was to set the film close to 50 years after the events of the first movie.

We wanted to reveal a little more, but still, keep the mystery lurking above. We wanted to answer questions, but at the same time create new ones.

It all started with one simple question really. "If Jess survived the events of Black Christmas, what happened to her unborn baby? And did her baby have a baby at any point?" This was the beginning of penning a short script that helped move the story to the present day, and how Billy and Agnes fit into all that. Although we don't own the IP, and the film is not-for-profit, it's professional through and through and acts as a concept for a sequel.

Why did you decide to do the fan film now?

Well, the idea came to me in 2019. I turned 40 that same year, and when you turn 40, you reflect a lot on your life. I've spent over 20 years working in the entertainment industry as a professional voice actor, but I also have a background in film. I really wanted to start the process of building up my filmmaking muscles. My filmmaking partner Bruce Dale (who's also spent over 20 years in the film industry) saw it as an amazing opportunity to collaborate (like we did when we were kids) and really test ourselves as filmmakers. In the beginning, Bruce was a little hesitant about doing a sequel to Black Christmas. However, after watching the film, and talking more about it, he understood the reasons why we should do it. He loved it! We both wrote, produced, edited, and directed the film. I did all the sound design, and Bruce did storyboards and concept art. We really were a 'jack of all trades' duo.

With the 2019 film going in a different direction than the Billy motif (or so we believe), do you think there will ever be more *Black Christmas* films featuring Billy?

Good question. Yes, our film! Ha Ha!

I hope so. I think there is a lot to explore with the character while still being true to his ambiguity. The mystique of Billy must be preserved, but that doesn't mean you can't advance the narrative and keep the ambiguity intact. Maybe It's Me, Billy will be the beginning of that. We're open to taking calls ;).

As a native Canadian, does *Black Christmas* hold a special place in your heart?

Absolutely! It's arguably one of the most famous Canadian films ever made, and it helped to redefine an entire genre. It's not just a Canadian classic, it's a horror classic. And thanks to the internet and word of mouth, Black Christmas is finally getting the respect and acknowledgement it deserves from the broader horror community. We hope It's Me, Billy helps in spreading the word.

xxi) Filmmaking Influence

Black Christmas, like Halloween *and many others, has been continually cited by fans and other horror filmmakers as having a massive influence on their own careers in the industry. Below are some thoughts from a selection of celebrated creatives.*

INTERVIEW

Justin Kerswell

Producer - *Gory Graduation, Slice and Dice: The Slasher Film Forever*

Can you tell us how you first saw or heard about *Black Christmas*?

I saw it on BBC1 way back in the early to mid-1980s, when I was about 12 or 13 years old. It made an impression on me because it was so genuinely frightening and was quite unlike anything I'd seen before. This was, if memory serves me right, before I'd seen Halloween on video. It also made an impression as the BBC aired the uncut version. Presumably by mistake. I haven't heard the sentence "Let me lick your pretty pink cunt!" before or since on the channel. Especially in front of my parents.

As the pre-dates the slasher boom of the early 80s, did it feel like uncovering a hidden gem?

I was a horror obsessed child, but before seeing Black Christmas I'd had to make do with what seemed like very antiquated offerings courtesy of the BBC late night double bills. During the late 1970s and early 1980s I was well aware of the genre films that appeared with rapid succession at the cinema.

Yet, those were forbidden fruit and I had to be content with looking longingly at the salacious artworks from the bus window on the way to school and hearing breathless accounts from the older siblings of friends. So, Black Christmas – although already dated in looks – still seemed shockingly modern in its theme, violence and language.

What did you think about the decision to not fully reveal the killer?

I'm partial to ambiguity in horror films. John Carpenter's Halloween was scarier when we didn't know that Laurie Strode was Michael Myers' sister. The random nature - where anyone could be a victim (including, by extension, the viewer) fit very well into the 1970s era of paranoia and the rise of the real-life serial killer.

To paraphrase Dario Argento: real life doesn't always provide answers, so why should movies? Keeping the identity of the killer in Black Christmas ambiguous only adds to the film's permeating aura of unease – and effectiveness.

How does Billy rank for you amongst the long list of slasher killers?

He's right up there. Interestingly, for a film that provided a fertile breeding ground for the films that followed, Billy's raving psychosis – as far as cinema depictions go – seems determinedly old fashioned compared to the slow, methodical shark-like stalking of Myers and most slasher villains that followed. Billy is the archetypic raving lunatic – right down the duelling personalities on the phone. However, his sheer unpredictability remains terrifying.

Do you think without *Black Christmas* there wouldn't have been *When a Stranger Calls*?

None of these films were made inside a vacuum. Although I've never seen Fred Walton publicly acknowledge it, it seems highly likely that When a Stranger Calls was influenced by Black Christmas. Ironically, he distilled the scariest elements of Bob Clark's movie into a well-received short in 1977 and extended it into an, albeit fine film, a lesser one. Although it is often thought it was Halloween's box office success that inspired Walton to do so; he started shooting his film in October 1978 – the same month Carpenter's film started its initially limited run and before it became a cultural and box office phenomenon. Critics at the time noted the similarities between Black Christmas and When a Stranger Calls.

However, Walton's film takes its inspiration from an event that happened before Black Christmas lensed. That of an account – in a 1972 Santa Monica newspaper – of a baby-sitter who was terrorised by a mysterious phone caller, who was subsequently found to have been calling from inside the house. Of course, did that really happen? The babysitter-killer-in-the-house urban legend has been around since the 1960s at least.

It's also worth considering whether Black Christmas itself was inspired by Terrence H Winkless' little seen 14-minute student short Foster's Release (1971). Itself a rife on the same urban legend and starring Dan O'Bannon – best known for writing the screenplay for Alien (1979) and directing Return of the Living Dead (1985) – as the psycho stalking a babysitter. O'Bannon was a film school contemporary of John Carpenter and they worked together on Dark Star (1974). Incidentally, there was a 1974 film by Walter Hugo Khouri called O Anjo de Noite (which translates as The Angel of Night) about a young babysitter being menaced by a psycho calling the house. Often described as the Brazilian When a Stranger Calls it was actually released the same year as Bob Clark's Black Christmas.

Do you consider *Black Christmas* the first pure slasher?

I'd still consider Halloween as the first pure slasher. Purely because it crystallised all the elements of the proto-slashers that came before and gave us what we now consider the template for the modern slasher. However, Black Christmas was invaluable in providing inspiration to Carpenter – as were the giallo films of Dario Argento and Mario Bava. As I've already mentioned, the depiction of the raving lunatic seemed a little old fashioned. The slashers that followed also largely jettisoned the interpersonal soap opera'ish drama that was so prevalent in early 1970s cinema.

How do you think the film has aged?

The film has aged phenomenally well in terms of its structure and shock value. Of course, it looks very dated. After all, it is 45 years old. However, I imagine that modern audiences would still find it jarring. Especially the phone calls. The swearing – presumably utilised after the effect similar profanity had on audiences in The Exorcist made the year before – would still unsettle and shock audiences today.

What did you think of the 2006 remake?

Actually, I enjoyed the 2006 remake for what it was. It's a case of damned if you and damned if you don't with remakes. Black Christmas – and Halloween for that matter – are frightening partly because of their ambiguity. However, overfamiliarity means that audiences demand more – although, ironically, they want the same movie, but just more of it. Funnily enough, the concept of an escaped lunatic targeting an isolated group was considered a well-worn trope even back when Black Christmas came out in 1974. A nod and a wink and upping the gore was probably the only way they could have gone.

Are you surprised no one ever attempted a sequel given the film's slightly ambiguous ending?

Bob Clark had an idea for a sequel after the film started making money during its 1975 US theatrical run. Reportedly, he called it Halloween. With Billy having been captured and then escaping from another insane asylum on that date. Apparently, he was working with John Carpenter on an unrelated project at the time. Clark ultimately jettisoned the sequel idea when he decided he was done with horror. The rest – as they say – is history. However, Clark never bore Carpenter ill will about his film.

INTERVIEW

Adam Rockoff

Writer - *I Spit on Your Grave (2010) [as Stuart Morse], Going to Pieces: The Rise and Fall of the Slasher Film*

What's your opinion on *Black Christmas*?

I love it! Not only is it one of the greatest slasher films, but it's one of the greatest horror films, period. For the amount of money that Bob Clark had to make the film (well under a million dollars) it's astonishing what he's able to pull off. Watching Black Christmas you're really watching a director coming into his own. A director, I might add, every bit as talented as Romero, Carpenter, and Craven.

As the film predates *Halloween*, how does it rank for you compared to John Carpenter's film?

They're both wonderful films. Both classics in their own rights. Black Christmas does, however, have more of an arthouse feel. This usually isn't a term associated with the film but, watching it again, I was struck by how much of it actually feels like a giallo. What's also interesting is how stylistically different the film is from Halloween. While Carpenter favors long-shots and utilizes negative space, Clark prefers lingering close-ups. Both techniques are used brilliantly, I might add.

Do you think Billy and *Black Christmas* had franchise potential that wasn't realised?

Nah, he didn't have the marketability of a Freddy or a Jason or even a Michael. He wasn't the quintessential supernatural boogeyman, but rather a deeply disturbed ordinary young man. This isn't to say that Black Christmas couldn't have become a franchise – series have been made from far less interesting villains -- only that I don't feel that anything was squandered.

Why do you think Billy was killing the sorority girls?

Well, it could have been that the girls represented the victim from his past. The one we hear him refer to obliquely in the phone calls. Or it could be that he's just a garden variety lunatic! I lean toward the latter.

There are hints of a backstory through the phone calls, are you glad we never realise his full intentions?

Very glad. If you think about it, it's really one of the only slasher films where the killer's motivation is somewhat ambiguous. In most slashers we're treated to either a prologue or a coda where the killer's motives are clearly explained. They're still nuts, obviously. But within the confines of the story, it makes perfect sense. Clark doesn't force feed this to us in Black Christmas.

What are your thoughts on the 2006 remake?

I actually enjoyed it very much, although I realize I'm definitely in the minority. At the very least, it's way better than the remakes of Halloween, Friday the 13th, and A Nightmare on Elm Street. Having said that, there's no point in comparing it to the original. They're two totally different films. One's a bona fide classic, the other a mean little popcorn movie.

Why do you think *Black Christmas* has gained such cult status?

At risk of sounding simple, because it's an excellent film. It's also simultaneously a very dramatic film and a very funny one. The subplot of Jess's abortion, as well as the body of the girl found in the woods -- this is heavy stuff. And Clark handles it expertly. However, the comic touches are no less deftly handled. The whole "fellatio" bit is laugh out loud funny. And the characters of Barb, Mrs. Mac, and Mr. Harrison are brilliant.

Have you introduced friends to the film, and if so, how have you described it?

Honestly, most of my friends who are horror fans saw it on their own a long time ago. But if I was introducing it to some young horror fan, the first thing I would ask is if he or she likes Halloween, Friday the 13th, Prom Night, Terror Train, My Bloody Valentine, The Burning, or a million other similar films. If the answer is yes, I would just tell them, "Well, without Black Christmas, none of them would exist!"

INTERVIEW

Anthony Masi

Producer - *Still Screaming: The Ultimate Scary Movie Retrospective, The Psycho Legacy, His Name Was Jason: 30 Years of Friday the 13th, The 12 Days of 'Black Christmas', 2006, Halloween: 25 Years of Terror*

Tell us about your first experience with *Black Christmas*?

I saw Black Christmas in the mid-90s after a friend of mine suggested it to me. I remember renting the VHS from a local video store and being genuinely creeped out both while and after watching it, to the point where I had to leave the lights on in my bedroom that night, which I've never done after watching a movie before up until that point. I kept picturing Billy standing above me at the side of my bed holding a glass unicorn. I couldn't believe how much the movie got to me.

The only other movie that had that effect on me was the 2012 Maniac remake starring Elijah Wood. Both movies shared this dark, raw, style about them with unique sound-effect-driven soundtracks, which I believe had a lot to do with my lingering unnerved reaction to them.

What do you think about the character of Billy?

Much like Michael Myers in the original Halloween (1978), Billy is a cinematic assemblage, a combination of framing, lighting, sound effects, and audio. He's not just a crazy guy with an axe running around and slicing up teenagers. Instead, his menace is derived from the specific way Bob Clark directed his scenes in the movie. For example, the scene where Billy is holding the glass unicorn above Margot Kidder's character in the bed, the camera is placed from Margot's point of view looking up at him (framing), Billy is standing in silhouette with only a single wide eye looking down on us as he holds the weapon (lighting), he's murmuring something nonsensical (sound effects), with Christmas carollers singing in the background (audio).

When Billy attacks Margot, it's a terrifying experience because all of the elements of fantastic filmmaking synergistically collide in one terrifying moment. Similarly, in the scene where Clare gets attacked in front of the closet, you have the POV of Billy in the closet watching her approach (framing), standing in a lit closet (lighting), horrible yelling (audio), choking and plastic bag sounds (sound effects). Clark used the same combination of elements in the scene where Jess sees Billy in the crack of the door; the single crazed eye looking down at Jess while we hear him whispering about Agnes is probably the most simple scene in all of horror, yet is one of the most terrifying in the genre. Clark's provocative directorial decisions are why these scenes are so scary.

How do you rank the film compared to the likes of *Halloween* and *Friday the 13th*?

Black Christmas was released four years before Halloween, and in my opinion it's a far more dark and scary film that Halloween. The town of Haddonfield gets hit hard by the force called Michael Myers that's blowing through the streets, but there's still a sense of fun - like a rollercoaster - running through the movie. Gene Siskel said that Halloween, for all its tension and death, still felt "up" to him, that he was being entertained, much like an amusement park ride. Black Christmas, however, feels bleak, cold, and hopeless from start to finish, and has one of the most chilling endings ever captured on screen. For those reasons it stands alongside Halloween as one of the greatest horror films of all time. When it's over, there is a rush and you are glad you survived.

It was a bold move by Bob Clark to not show the killer during the film, did you agree with this approach?

Clark understood the time-tested filmmaking technique of 'less is more' with regards to the horror genre. Showing fleeting glimpses of Billy was far more effective than full-bodied gratuitous shots of the killer lurking around the house and killing people. When you can see a monster, your brain finds a way to be less scared of it because it uses information to answer questions which reduces fear. The questions are what create the fear.

For example, if you hear growling behind a closed door, you fear what's on the other side because you have no idea how big or small the growling monster is, if it has sharp fangs, etc., however, if you look through the key hole and see the monster - you might surmise that you can kill it easily since it's smaller than you, or that its mouth isn't big enough to take more than a small bite out of you, and the brain's rationalizing only results in a person being armed with information that reduces their fear.

Clark's decision to hide Billy in the shadows greatly increased the killer's presence and threat because audiences weren't able to get a good look at him, which caused their minds to run away with endless possibilities about his appearance and motivations. The moment a director can get the audience scaring themselves is when his/her movie is succeeding in the horror genre.

What is the scariest part of the film?

When the phone starts ringing at the end of the movie, it's being suggested that Billy has just killed Jess. The phone calls in the movie usually happen when a killing has taken place, and since Jess is left alone - and Billy is still inside the house - it has to be assumed that Billy has climbed out of the attic, killed Jess, and is making another phone call from back inside the attic. With camera lingering on the house in the final shot as the credits roll, with the cop standing outside the house on a snowy, silent night, much like the ending of Halloween where Loomis looks over the balcony to see that Myers has disappeared, Clark's small ending sends chills down the spine. When it comes to horror movies, this scene is downright scary, and all you hear is a phone ringing.

Olivia Massey's Jess isn't your typical 'Final Girl' is she?

I would absolutely classify the character of Jess (played by Olivia Hussey) as a 'final girl' because throughout the movie she is slowly isolated and ultimately left alone to fight off an assailant. She is probably the first person in horror to go deeper inside the house after learning the killer is indeed in there with her, where she ultimately confronts him and survives.

What do you think the legacy of *Black Christmas* is?

The legacy of Black Christmas resides in its minimalist direction on a low budget that results in big scares. I can only keep comparing it to Halloween because both films demonstrate that 'less is more' in the horror genre. The ending to Black Christmas literally explodes once Jess sees Billy standing behind the door, much like the ending of Halloween explodes when Laurie sees Judith's gravestone on the bed. Everything immediately kicks into high gear with no big special effects or big budget.

It's akin to the rubber band breaking, all of the tension is released and everything turns into chaos. I believe that horror filmmakers will continue to look back on Black Christmas to see what makes a truly great horror movie work. All of its techniques still resonate today, and I witnessed this with my one eyes when I attended a recent screening of the movie at a theater in Los Angeles. The person who was introducing the movie asked the audience if there were people in attendance who hadn't seen the movie before, and many hands went into the air. During the film, the uneasiness in the room was palpable, and when Jess screamed, "PLEEEAASE ANSWER ME!!", the mix of laughter and guttural groans made it obvious that Clark had his audience in the palm of his hand well over 40 years after the film's release.

What was your take on the 2006 remake?

The 2006 remake, in my opinion, was simply another way to tell the story of Billy and Agnes that in no way tried to capture the genius of the original Black Christmas. I remember seeing the movie in theaters and respecting it for going for something entirely different. Was the film necessary? No. Did it work? Yes, for what it was. Will it have an impact and be remembered? Probably not.

xxii) The Slasher Revival

With the recent slasher climate seemingly rising from the dead, more so after the success (and relaunch) of *Halloween* (2018) and which led ultimately to Blumhouse also acquiring *Black Christmas*, it seems now may be the time for Billy's return should another studio obtain the rights. The return of the Shape awoke many other long-dead properties, with other studios now looking to cash-in once again on the slasher sub-brand. Most notably, a fifth *Scream* film, simply titled *Scream, began* filming between September and November 2020 in Wilmington, North Carolina with a January 2022 release date.

Halloween Kills poster

The *Child's Play* franchise experienced its own reboot in 2019 with the release of *Child's Play*, starring Aubrey Plaza and Mark Hamill as the voice of killer doll Chucky, now powered by AI rather than a voodoo curse. With moderate box office success and mild warm critical praise, it remains to be seen whether this incarnation of the character will continue in the coming years.

Previous to this release, original writer Don Mancini announced he was filming a television series for SyFy, with returning franchise cast members Brad Dourif, Jennifer Tilly, Fiona Dourif and Alex Vincent. Filming on *Chucky* started in March 2021, with a premiere date of October 2021.

While Michael Myers' return to the big screen in *Halloween Kills* was delayed by the Coronavirus pandemic leading to the original release date of 16th October 2020 being pushed back until 15th October 2021, with a dual release in cinemas and on the Peacock streaming platform in the US.

Chucky returns in the SyFy series

One property set to switch to the small screen is *I Know What You Did Last Summer*, which is getting an 8-part adaptation for Amazon Studios. Most notable about this series is the involvement of James Wan, who will direct a number of episodes. Production began in Hawaii on the series, with a release on Amazon Video set for October 2021. In February 2020, Bloody Disgusting broke the news that Screen Gems were working on a modernised reboot of Jamie Blanks' 1998 meta-slasher *Urban Legend*. The project would be directed by Colin Minihan, an independent filmmaker best known for *What Keeps You Alive* and *It Stains the Sands Red*. Although, since this announcement, this project has been shelved indefinitely.

While readers may be familiar with some of those titles, they may be less familiar with the 80s slasher *Sorority House Massacre*. This Roger Corman production from 1986, is also set for a modernised treatment, Norman Reedus (*The Walking Dead*) is noted by Deadline as one of the producers.

Another icon of horror cinema is also expecting to make a return again in a new *Texas Chainsaw Massacre* film, which is (again!) a sequel to the original featuring 'old man' Leatherface. Despite a creepy looking poster, at the time of writing, initial test screenings for the film have reported audiences giving it a very poor reception as well as feedback. The film is being touted for Netflix.

Since the death of Wes Craven in August 2015 the *Nightmare on Elm Street* series has remained completely dormant. The last venture for Freddy Krueger was a hollow 2010 remake starring Jackie Earle Haley, which didn't have the involvement of any of the original cast and crew. CBR.com reported in September 2019 that the Craven estate had acquired the rights to the *A Nightmare on Elm Street* name and the character of Freddy Krueger. Writers are able to reclaim their work after 35 years and with Craven's passing four years previous the rights were transferred to his estate. A few months later in November 2019, it was reported on Bloody Disgusting that the Craven family were now accepting pitches for a new *Nightmare on Elm Street* film. The pitches were said to be for feature films plus any potential HBO max series adaptations.

In October 2021, it was revealed that Victor Miller had won the domestic rights to the Friday the 13th series, with a case having been going on since 2018. This would require Miller to agree on a deal with Sean Cunningham to see a new Friday the 13th film or TV/streaming series becoming a reality in the near future.

While all of this activity within the horror genre is great news for fans, as well as filmmakers within the genre continually praising Clark's film, it does beg the question will it lead to more *Black Christmas* movies? The answer is... it's hard to say. Hardcore slasher fans who know the original *Black Christmas* inside out and would love to see a modernised update or flash-forward sequel (ala *Halloween* 2018) to Clark's original, but the big question remains - will it make money?

A question more so highlighted over the less than stellar response to the 2019 film, which fans have argued has tainted the brand name. A lot of Hollywood productions are made by committee (the most notable recent example being the debacle behind *Star Wars: The Rise of Skywalker*) and while we may all want to believe that the story is paramount, it is ultimately the films appeal to the masses that will get it shot and in cinemas and streaming services. After almost 50 years, do *Black Christmas* and Billy still have the ability to send chills down spines? Only time will tell.

Chapter 5: Conclusions

DESPITE the ever-polarising remakes, imaginative and professional spin-offs and other media, the power of the series always comes from and pulsates from Clark's original 1974 chiller every time. Without it, we wouldn't have the remakes (be that a good or bad thing in a reader's eyes), we wouldn't have the initial prototype for the slasher films that followed, and we wouldn't have the film that inspired John Carpenter to create *Halloween*. There's a lot to love and both thank *Black Christmas* for it seems.

But it is the unworldly power the film ignites and wields that fans, as well as the cast and crew, as well as the cast and crew remember and speak of continuously, some having remembered it for over the past near enough five decades now even if not being able to precisely put their fingers on why the film has endured. "It is still lauded as one of the best of the genre" comments Lynne Griffin, continuing that "it makes me very proud and Humbled at its continued notoriety and success!" John Saxon always believed that the film's subtle approach was something that made it stand out both back in the 1970s and even today with horror fans who are discovering it for the first time. It is devoid of over-the-top special effects and Saxon maintained that this was one of its selling points speaking back in the 2000s; "Seeing it 27 years later, experiencing the pieces put together better like a spectator, in that sense it jumps out at me now as I hope it will for all spectators", he comments. "Maybe horror films have always had a central figure, like Dracula or the Mummy or something like that. Some kind of mysterious or malevolent entity you know".

"This film has it, but on a very naturalistic basis", he continues. "This is not anything supernatural but some kind of expression of humanity that is tormented and capable of horrific things. The scenes of violence, while a few of them are graphic, it wasn't something that was pandered or sold in of itself. It was probably something of the time that people still winched at, I mean I winched watching it just now. But afterwards, almost at a distance, special fx took over and stories diminished. *Black Christmas* was still from a time where story mattered and story led into some violence, but the violence wasn't pandered. I just sensed the dynamics of tension and twists. Unexpected turns, being something that worked. It could hold interest and deliver something more"

Jess sleeps after her night of chaos in *Black Christmas* (1974)

Olivia Hussey agrees with Saxon's opinions too it would seem, especially with the ambiguity around the film's conclusion and the presentation of Billy himself;

273

"even at the end, I believe you never really know who it is. I think today they show too much in films, you know. I think a lot of times, like Hitchcock, you don't really see anything, but you have the idea that you've seen, other than the bodies once in a while, the thought of some man standing behind a door, peering at you, [that] is a lot more frightening than watching somebody - you know, you see the bodies once it's happened, but you don't actually see it happening. And to me that's a lot more terrifying, the thought of something [rather] than the reality of watching somebody hacking somebody you know".

Hussey has been continually surprised over the decades at the fascination people have with the film, even noting how it is one of comedian Steve Martin's favourite films; "I met him when he was doing *Roxanne* and he said you know you were in one of my favourite films and I said *Romeo and Juliet*, he said no, *Black Christmas*! I saw it 23 times, I loved it! It's in his collection so that was flattering. It did very very well in Europe, you know. It's one of those little cult films".

She continues how "once a year or something, every Christmas, they show it at these movie theatres and people go to watch *Black Christmas* and then some other Christmas movie and I didn't know that. I went there, I think, last Christmas for the first time and I was shocked at how many people love this film, you know". Surprisingly "I didn't see the film for years after finishing it, because scary films scare me but then when I finally saw it, I was really proud of it. It was just a beautiful little film and I think Bob Clark is a genius of a director. I wish he did more films like that in fact and it is a classic in its genre. It's as much a classic as *Romeo and Juliet* or Jesus *of Nazareth* in its own way. It has a huge fan base; I get a lot of emails and messages on *Black Christmas*".

She also compliments the fans further, especially for keeping the film alive for so long and continue to do so it seems; "they are amazing you know…all these people come [to screenings], with their popcorn and their black eye makeup and it has got a cult following and they genuinely love the film - they know every bit of dialogue you know - they know the characters, it's really a compliment - very nice".

"I think the fact that it's a classic and that I'm still getting emails today about it, means that the film is holding up. I mean yes, now you can have a lot more special effects, a lot of gorier films, but I think that is a really terrifying film because it is so simple and it's so basic. It's somebody that's terrified; it's a madman that's living in a sorority house. I mean the whole idea of it is terrifying and it's all more the idea than the actual slash and gore, you know it's the idea of being murdered that's more terrifying".

Before her sad death, Kidder would always speak very fondly too about the film, as well as why it was still being discussed today; "It was one of those things that crept up on you gradually. You'd made this obscure Canadian horror movie and didn't think anything of it and moved on to the next thing and then five or ten years later, some guy will stop you on the street and go "Oh God I loved you in *Black Christmas!*" And you think, oh that's interesting and then if it happens enough times, you get the point; a lot of people watched it, loved it and kept their memorabilia".

"I still have tons of people coming up and asking for autographs for *Black Christmas* stuff. It's just amazing to me! This was a long time ago, this was what we made almost 30 years ago. It's sort of fascinating, the way it turns out that something that you didn't put the same weight to as you might have other things, turns out to have this kind of extraordinary longevity. And look at the cast, look at all the cast who went on to do well! It's a classic", she mused warmly.

The crew themselves look back on the film with fond memories, noting the different reasons they believe the film has continued to be a firm horror classic; "We were making a picture that was different and progressive of its time. We understood that", remarks Production Designer Karen Bromley, while Co-Producer Gerry Arbeid reflected that "none of us, except maybe Bob, thought it was going to be a gangbuster film". Thinking back on the film himself, Clark was always upbeat about the project, never shying away from discussing it as much as possible. On the Tartan DVD documentary, *Black Christmas Revisited*, Clark expressed how "I thought it was a good scary, classic horror story, and it does have a way of surviving. And I hoped to break new ground by the attitude and treatment of the actors, the reality of their world. And employing some new and certainly reworked and rethought cinematic ideas. It's an interesting film, a hit film on one level and a cult film on another. I hoped!" concluded Clark with a twinkle in his eye.

It does seem that the longevity of *Black Christmas* won't be slowing down anytime soon. Despite poor reception to the brand through the remakes, the original film is still continually discussed, written about and is always high up in various top ten lists of both horror films, and in particular, Christmas horror film lists on numerous websites. Additionally, the fandom as well continues to keep the film in the public eye, while distributors such as Scream Factory and 101 Films certainly see financial merit in the film with the release of their Collector Editions, wherein fans have been treated to painstakingly cleaned up 2k prints of the film as well as remastered sound and bonus features from surviving cast and crew. While the ending of the original *Black Christmas* was left open and ambiguous, its legacy, its influence as well as critical response will continue to build in appreciation. Something we can all be sure Clark himself would have been thrilled and honoured with.

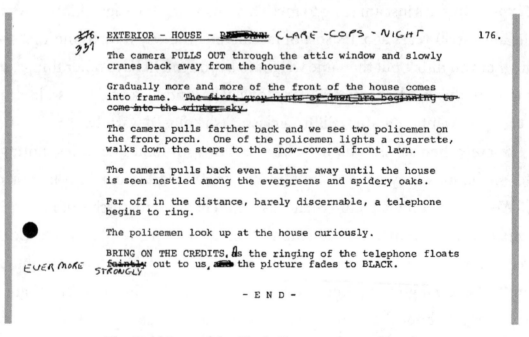

The Final Page of the *Black Christmas* script (1974)

Other Christmas Horrors

While *Black Christmas* is often heralded as the first 'slasher' by many horror fans, it wasn't actually the first one to surface in the decade or so following Alfred Hitchcock's *Psycho*. Here are some other horrifically festive additions for your home cinema collection you may want to seek out from 1972 right up until the modern-day.

Silent Night, Bloody Night (1972)

The first was *Silent Night, Bloody Night*, a low budget stab at a psycho killer feature where a killer wielding an axe stalks a lawyer and his girlfriend in a house that used to be an asylum. A slasher fan site, said this of *Silent Night, Bloody Night* -

"This movie has it all--it's ambitious, gothic, disturbing, atmospheric, scary, twisty, a whole lot of fun to watch--oh, and well-acted, written, and directed...If *Night of the Living Dead* set the standard for zombie flicks to come, *Silent Night, Bloody Night* set the standard for approximately every slasher flick that followed".

Home for the Holidays (1972)

The made-for-television movie *Home for the Holidays* premiered on ABC in November 1972 and told the story of four daughters returning home to their dying father, who they believe was being poisoned by his second wife. From here the women begin to fall prey to a killer in a yellow rain slicker.

While it feels more like a soap opera at times, *Home for the Holidays* does feature some commendable performances, including Jessica Walters (*Arrested Development*) and Sally Field (*The Amazing Spiderman*) as two of the Morgan sister clan.

Home for the Holidays probably leans heavier onto the Giallo sub-genre with its whodunnit element, rather than straight-up slashers that would dominate the 1980s.

To All a Goodnight (1980)

While *Black Christmas* wasn't a fully commercial success, it would take Hollywood another six years to revisit the Christmas motif in the wake of the breakout hit *Halloween* with an exploitation slasher predating *Friday the 13th*.

On 30th January 1980, David Hess' *To All a Goodnight* was released. The cast includes the film debut of Jennifer Runyon (*Ghostbusters*) plus adult film star Harry Reems (*Deep Throat*).

To All, A Goodnight was the first horror film to introduce a 'Killer Santa' as a group of teenagers are stalked across campus by a maniacal killer. While not the most technically proficient slasher ever released, the film was made on a paltry budget and does contain a great twist where it turns out there are two killers on the prowl.

Christmas Evil (1980)

While *Christmas Evil* (aka *You Better Watch Out*) is often lumped in with the slew of 80s slasher films, this feels more like a psychological exploration into the mind of a madman. We follow the plight of Harry Stadling, a toy factory worker who was scarred as a child upon learning that Santa Claus isn't real. After he suffers a nervous breakdown and is bullied at work he finally snaps and embarks on a killing spree.

Christmas Evil is certainly not levels above its slasher counterparts, but it does try to do something different with the developing motifs and is certainly grimier and nastier than a lot of its brethren. Much like *To All a Goodnight* it also has an ace up its sleeve with a polarising final sequence, which will either make you laugh or frown with irritation.

Blood Beat (1983)

Blood Beat leans more into the supernatural as we follow a woman based near a deer-hunting country in rural Wisconsin who is taken over by the spirit of a

Japanese Samurai Warrior (seriously). The happenstance of Christmas is simply a plot point here, as a young couple who become our protagonists are attending a seasonal family gathering when they run afoul of our supernatural villain. *Blood Beat* could be a microcosm of the 80s slasher with its bonkers plot, random characters and cheesy dialogue in abundance.

Don't Open Till Christmas (1984)

Finally, in 1984 the Brits got in on the slasher boom with the by-the-numbers slasher schlockfest *Don't Open Till Christmas.*

This slasher had the dubious honour of having three directorial teams involved across a two year period to get the film to the big screen. Original Director Edmund Purdom quit before being replaced by Derek Ford, who lasted just two days on-set before the distributors hired Ray Selfe to complete filming with the help of Alan Birkinshaw.

The killer in *Don't Open Till Christmas* also dons a Santa Claus outfit before going on a killing spree across London whilst being pursued by Scotland Yard's finest. The most notable name in the cast list is Caroline Munro (*Maniac* and *Slaughter High*), who plays herself in a bizarre and meta scene.

Silent Night, Deadly Night (1984)

Whenever you quiz horror fans about Christmas slasher films, one of the first suggestions is Charles E. Sellier Jr's *Silent Night, Deadly Night.* Despite its slasher stripes, *Silent Night...* does attempt to do something different with its antagonist Billy who witnesses his parents get killed as a child by a man dressed as Santa Claus on a deserted highway. From here, he and his younger brother are shipped to a Catholic orphanage where they are abused by the staff. This leads to Billy finally snapping and going on a killing spree dressed in a Santa Claus costume, punishing anyone he feels has been naughty.

Of all the Christmas slashers, *Silent Night, Deadly Night* is the most controversial as it was pulled from release just a week into its theatrical run because of protests about its depiction of a killer Santa Claus. Since its re-release on DVD by Arrow Video in 2009, it has gone on to gain cult status amongst slasher fans. This can be considered one of the only Christmas slasher franchises (outside of *Black Christmas*), as it spawned four sequels, with the first two featuring characters from the original whereas the fourth and fifth films chose to take the series in a different direction. Also, in 2021 another remake of *Silent Night, Deadly Night* was announced.

Jack Frost (1997)

Owing more to the success of Freddy Krueger and the Chucky film series, *Jack Frost* features a serial killer who is turned into a murderous snowman. This is not to be confused with the Michael Keaton feature released a year later; with Director Michael Cooney's feature played more for ludicrous laughs and outrageous set pieces than scares.

Mortal *Jack Frost* kind of needs to be seen to be believed; and less said of its sequel *Jack Frost: The Revenge of the Killer Snowman*, the better.

Santa's Slay (2005)

Once the *Scream* series revitalised the slasher as a viable commodity for Hollywood studios, a slew of imitators would flood theatres over the next 10 years, all trying to grab a slice of that box office cash. While Dwayne Johnson has become one of the largest stars in Hollywood, former wrestlers didn't always equal box office gold.

Santa's Slay features WCW star Bill Goldberg as a demon who loses a bet with an angel and has to spread joy and happiness as punishment. Once the bet is over, the demon Santa goes on a bloody killing spree.

Silent Night (2012)

By 2012 the horror remake trend of Hollywood was in full swing, with Steven C. Miller's loose remake of *Silent Night, Deadly Night* one of the best of the bunch.

Starring Malcolm McDowell (*A Clockwork Orange*) and Donal Logue (*Gotham*), we follow a killer dressed as Santa who is preying on a small town and offing their victims in bloody and creative ways. Owing as much to the slasher as the *Saw* franchise, *Silent Night* is a gore-filled ride with a series of impressive kills (including one involving a wood chipper) and an interesting twist finale. This film was partially inspired by the real-life Covina Holiday Massacre which took place on Christmas Eve 2008.

Dismembering Christmas (2015)

This low budget slasher was shot across 12 days in Wisconsin and follows a group of twenty-somethings who spend a winter vacation at a lake house and are subsequently hunted by a madman. Despite its constraints, *Dismembering Christmas* harks back to the 80s heyday of the slashers with the use of practical gore effects and a masked killer that recalls the villain from 1983's *Curtains*. Interestingly the idea for this film is allegedly a spec script for a *Friday the 13th* sequel and was produced by the aptly titled Slasher Studios following a crowdfunding campaign.

Good Tidings (2016)

Another British entry to the Christmas slasher ensemble is the independent production *Good Tidings* from Stuart W. Bedford.

Here we follow a homeless war veteran who is sleeping rough in an abandoned courthouse in Liverpool with other homeless people who are terrorised by three escaped mental patients dressed as Santa Claus. Despite its budgetary limitations, *Good Tidings* is a good stab at a Christmas slasher with some creative kills, three silent and imposing killers plus an excellent synth-based soundtrack.

Christmas Blood (2017)

Christmas Blood (aka *Juleblod)* is a Norwegian stab at the Christmas slasher, following a previously incarcerated killer continuing his original massacre in a small northern Norwegian town dressed as good old Saint Nick. This is essentially

Director Reinert Kiil's yuletide version of John Carpenter's *Halloween*, with his killer profiled as 'pure evil' plus he is seemingly unkillable to boot. While nowhere near Carpenter's stalk and slash classic, *Christmas Blood* is an admirable modern slasher clone.

Mrs Claus (2018)

The second directorial effort of independent American Filmmaker Troy Escamilla owes a debt to the low budget 80s slashers such as *To All a Good Night*.

Despite generating production costs through crowdfunding, Escamilla assembles a decent cast which includes 80s scream queens Brinke Stevens (*The Slumber Party Massacre*) and Helene Udy (*My Bloody Valentine*). *Mrs Claus* follows a group of college students who are hunted across their sorority house during a Christmas party.

Escamilla clearly is a fan of the golden era of practical gore effects from the likes of Tom Savini and chooses to let the corn syrup flow without resorting to CGI blood which is sadly becoming more prevalent in horror of all budgets.

Acknowledgements

Most of our research has been taken from treatments, screenplays and filmmaker interviews which we conducted throughout 2020-21. However, it is important to acknowledge that we also turned to outside sources for some of the insights provided within this book, to help present as in-depth a commentary we could about the making of these films in the *Black Christmas* franchise. We must therefore recognise and send out a warm thank you to those who have produced special features for numerous commercial home video releases of *Black Christmas* 1974, 2006 and 2019. The audio commentaries, bonus features, archive interviews as well as press and websites have all helped us deliver insights from those who are sadly no longer with us, but who are still as pivotal to this book as well as those thankfully still with us. We are forever grateful and hope you enjoy this book too.

Huge thanks to Dan Duffin, who has not only supported this book from the start but has provided us with a wealth of private imagery to use in this book. Forever thankful.

Additional thanks to Kaush Patel for all the time scanning and digitising various press kits and home video covers.

Author Bios

PAUL DOWNEY is a freelance writer working primarily on horror and genre cinema for his own website *Bloody-Flicks.co.uk* as well as contributing to *Scream Magazine*. He is also the director of the independent horror film festival, Bloody Flicks Awards, which takes place on an annual basis, celebrating the very best in independent short horror cinema. From watching John Carpenter's *Halloween* from a young age, Paul became obsessed with the genre from there on, becoming a regular reader of Fangoria, Shivers and Starburst Magazine. He has multiple awarded qualifications in Film and Media Studies plus a journalism degree. He works full-time in marketing and enjoys writing about and watching films.

Twitter - @BloodyFlicks

Website – Bloody-Flicks.co.uk

DAVE HASTINGS is an award-winning filmmaker with movies across a wide range of genres under his belt. He has directed, co-produced as well as co-written numerous feature films such as *Checking In, The House of Screaming Death, Sustain* and *You Are My Sunshine*, while his short films have found equal success at film festivals worldwide, tackling all kinds of narrative and characters. He grew up on films from a very early age, especially horror (notably Hammer films, the *Halloween* series, *Friday the 13th, Black Christmas* 1974 and *Godzilla* movies), and always credits his love for the movies to his parents, Sue and Ken who got him interested in watching them initially. He has an MA in Film & Screen Studies, while he also currently lectures in film and media part-time at a local college. When not lecturing in film, he spends the remainder of his time working on new projects announced for the screen in future under his production company banner Lightbeam Productions, while he is currently prepping for his PhD in Canadian Horror Cinema.

Twitter: @the_doctor1310

Website: www.LightbeamProductions.co.uk

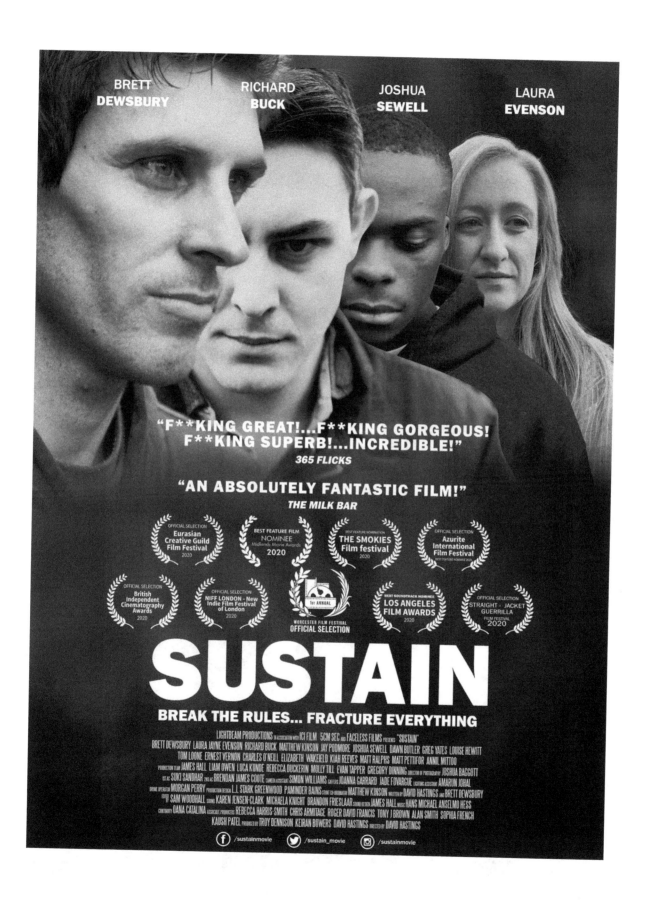

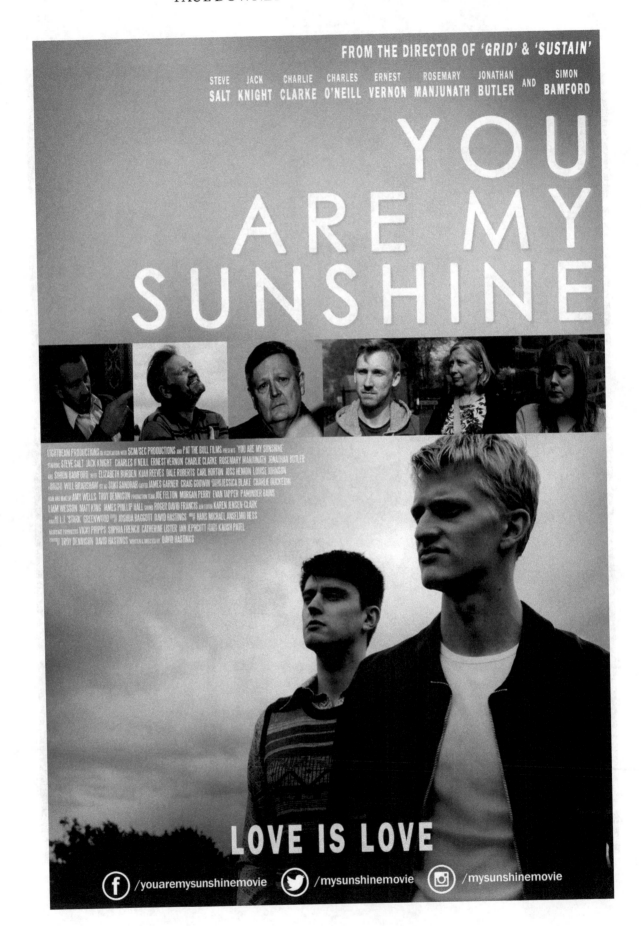

Copyright © 2022 by Bear Manor Media

https://bearmanor-digital.myshopify.com

All rights reserved. No part of this publication may be reproduced, distributed, or transmitted in any form or by any means, including photocopying, recording or other electronic or
mechanical methods, without prior written permission of the publisher, except in the case of
brief quotations embodied in critical reviews and certain other non-commercial uses permitted
by copyright law.

Any unauthorised duplication, copying, distribution, exhibition or any other use of any kind
may result in civil liability and/or criminal prosecution.

Index

CPSIA information can be obtained
at www.ICGtesting.com
Printed in the USA
LVHW052322190123
737484LV00010B/693

9 781629 338705